J. Blanton Belk

J. BLANTON BELK

It's an unfinished world,
and it's still in the making…

PEDIMENT

Battle Ground, Washington
Pediment Publishing
2020

Pediment Publishing, a division of The Pediment Group, Inc., Battle Ground, Washington 98604
pediment.com
© 2020 J. Blanton Belk Jr.
All rights reserved. Published 2020.
Printed in Canada.

Library of Congress Control Number: 2020907826

ISBN: 978-1-59725-912-5

Permission for lyric in subtitle
"Unfinished World" music by Herbert Allen and Pat Murphy, lyrics by Paul Colwell and Pat
Murphy. ©1987 by Up with People. Used by permission.

Photo credits
Dust jacket photos:
Front cover: Photo by Chris Mooney, Chris Mooney Photography ©2020.
Inside front flap: Betty and Blanton Belk at the 2016 Albuquerque International Balloon Fiesta
hosted by Linda Weil and Up with People, Cast 76E. Photo courtesy Up with People, Cast 76E.
Back cover: Photo by Ajay Gupta.

Dedication (opposite):
Top: Photo courtesy of Chameli and Surina Belk-Gupta.
Bottom: Photo courtesy of Belk-Arenas family.

This book is dedicated to our four grandchildren,
Chameli Elizabeth and Surina Katherine Belk-Gupta and
Thomas Blanton and Mateo Alfonso Belk-Arenas.
The world will be a better place because of you.

CONTENTS

Photos follow page 278

FOREWORD

"He would like to bring Up with People to México," is the message I received from Wes Christopherson, Chairman and CEO of the Jewel Companies. Jewel was a business partner in our innovative "all under one roof self-service stores" in México in the early 1970s.

Wes and I shared a belief in the power of active citizen participation to contribute to a better world, which led him to introduce me to Blanton Belk. After a short conversation, it became immediately clear that Blanton was a passionate and tireless promoter of these ideals with an ongoing project of international dimension. It was called Up with People.

That is why I accepted to serve on his Board of Directors and later, the International Advisory Board of Up with People for more than two decades. During that time I came to know and appreciate the many qualities that made Blanton such a charismatic leader. From the early days of the organization, he proclaimed that casts would travel to many countries, even those with closed borders such as China, Russia, and Cuba. Over the years he made good on that promise and in October of 2014, I had the privilege to join him and the cast in Havana. He was closing in on his 90th birthday with no decline in his contagious enthusiasm and energy.

I am grateful and honored to have met Blanton and through him, many world leaders. I will never forget standing next to astronaut Gene Cernan as he shook hands with Pope John Paul II who expressed his admiration at meeting someone who had landed on the Moon.

Tenacious, charming, curious, joyful, loyal, and down to earth are just a few of the words that come to mind to describe Blanton. I believe you will see them reflected in these pages that recount a life well-lived with purpose and generosity. Incredible experiences will give the reader a glimpse into the impact he has had on thousands of young people from across the globe, sparking a multiplying effect for generations to come.

I am proud to be Blanton's friend, along with the inseparable Betty, his life companion and guiding light of a close and exemplary family.

Manuel Arango A.
Founder
Mexican Center for Philanthropy

PREFACE

I find myself writing this book with one foot in the past and the other pointed firmly toward the future, looking forward through the lens of lessons well learned. I was born and brought up in the provincial South, and I grew up with an ever-expanding global vision. I realize there are many reasons for that as I look back over the first 95 years of my life. I have worked around the world for more than 70 of those years, trying to help convert a vision of global peace and understanding into an international reality.

As a boy growing up in Florida, Virginia, and South Carolina, I fished and hunted with my dad, a Presbyterian minister who encouraged me to think for myself and whose ideas spawned controversy. I spent idyllic summer vacations with my Wannamaker grandparents in South Carolina. I shared college days with my Belk cousins, some of whom later headed the Belk's Department Stores throughout the South. During my college years, I went through the Naval V-12 Program, which trained and supplied officers to the US Navy during the war years. I served as an officer on active duty on a PCC boat in the Philippines just after the end of World War II.

After concluding my time with the Navy, following my father's example, I set out to see what one man could do to make a positive difference in the world. This led me to participate in the leadership of Moral Re-Armament (MRA). MRA was founded in 1938 as an international movement for moral and spiritual renewal. It was active in bringing the nations of the world together into peaceful dialogue and establishing programs that helped rebuild war-ravaged Europe and Asia.

Living in other cultures awoke in me a vision and brought me in touch with the lives, hopes, and struggles of millions worldwide. During this time, I met and fell in love with Betty Wilkes, a Yankee girl who has been my wife, partner, and best friend for over 65 years.

During the turbulent decade of the 1960s, colleges and universities became the battleground for students demonstrating what they were against and what they wanted to change. I was one of a small group who said, "We know what students are *against*. Let's find out what they are *for* and give them a voice." This turned out to be a tipping point and led to the creation of first Sing-Out, then Up with People, a unique nonprofit global educational organization and leadership program. It brought young people from around the world together to present a dynamic musical demonstration of their hopes for the future.

There were important, deep relationships along the way that guided my efforts. President Dwight D. "Ike" Eisenhower, Chancellor Konrad Adenauer of Germany, the great Olympic athlete Jesse Owens, and DeWitt Wallace, founder of *Reader's Digest*, were among those who guided me as we incorporated Up with People in 1968. Our goal was to equip young people with the leadership qualities of global perspective, integrity, and motivation to serve others. Over 22,000 students from more than 138 countries have participated, 800,000 families worldwide have opened their homes to these dedicated young people, and 1.1 billion have seen a performance or been touched by their message.

When the Bamboo Curtain came down, Up with People was the first international group of students to be invited to travel and perform in the People's Republic of China. When the Iron Curtain began to crumble, we again led the way in bringing our casts to the Soviet Union, traveling, interacting with, and performing for the Soviet people. Earlier, at the Munich Olympics in 1972, Up with People lifted the spirits of the athletes in the Olympic Village following the tragic assassination of members of the Israeli team. I've received thousands of letters from men and women who shared these Up with People experiences and are now making a difference in their communities around the world.

Although I am no longer involved in the day-to-day operations as Chairman of the Board and President of Up with People, I remain as its founder and chairman emeritus, and I've stepped up whenever the organization has called on me. Betty and I are also deeply involved with land conservation, protection of our environment, and the preservation of wildlife in our beloved American Southwest.

So this is our story, a compilation of memories. In writing these recollections we honor the many who have been part of a movement that swept the world and have helped Betty and me navigate the twists and turns of the long road.

In a complex society with overwhelming issues, one person's memories are by definition an incomplete historical record. They are personal waves in a sea of emotion and data. I do not pretend that this is the definitive, complete story of Up with People. I hope the stories here will add toward that more lofty exercise, which I leave to others. This is simply the journey as Betty and I have traveled and remember it.

As with any memoir, these are my best recollections and as accurate as possible. But given the vagaries of memory and the decades that have passed since many of these events occurred, some people may remember things differently.

PROLOGUE

My Grandfather's Funeral

"What Color is God's Skin?"
Everyone's the same in the good Lord's sight.

I was in the middle of my senior year as a cadet in the Naval Reserve Officer Training Corps (NROTC) program at the University of North Carolina in Chapel Hill. The country was mired in the final months of World War II and America had been on a war footing since the bombing of Pearl Harbor in 1941. One day in July 1944, I received an urgent call from my father. Naturally, I was nervous when I picked up the phone on the desk of the officer of the day. My father knew of my love and affection for my grandfather, J. Skottowe Wannamaker, who we grandchildren called "Papoo." So my father broke the news of Papoo's death in his most caring voice, assuring me that my grandfather had died peacefully in his sleep. After a moment my father said, "I hope you can get leave and meet us for the funeral in St. Matthews." I was given leave papers, packed my duffel bag with a clean uniform, and removed all the leaves concealing my Ford '56 coupe with the rumble seat—naturally, cadets were forbidden to have cars!

St. Matthews is a small town in the Piedmont area of South Carolina. Just the name conjures up so many memories. My mother took me there as a baby, and I then spent every summer in St. Matthews at the Great House owned by my maternal grandparents until I was 18 and joined the Navy. Their home was always filled with grandchildren, aunts, and uncles. I can shut my eyes and be whisked back to those idyllic summers and the smell of rain on ripe honeysuckle, the large white scuppernong grapes, the fig tree in the yard with the tire waiting to swing. The roosters that awoke us, a bevy of grandchildren lined up sleeping on the screened porch on the second floor. The freight train that came through every midnight unleashed horns and whistles, and with a roar flushed out all the bats hidden in the rafters. The smell of oil on leather in the gun room, anticipating quail hunting with my uncles' pointers on the two great plantations. Memories, memories!

My grandfather was an amazing man. His father, my great-grandfather, had been murdered by carpetbaggers. His mother had died early. So being the oldest boy, he was left to raise and educate his two younger brothers. One was sent to Duke University, where he eventually became a dean, serving for more than 40 years. The other brother became a missionary in China. Papoo was an entrepreneur, banker, and public servant in Calhoun County in South Carolina. He was elected president of the American Cotton Association and later of the American Bankers Association.

I was jerked back to reality when my car rolled into St. Matthews on an asphalt road. I was shocked. What had happened to those wonderful sandy roads where my friend Hence and I had prided ourselves on walking barefoot all summer to town without a whimper? I had come home again, but now everything was different, and we were in the midst of World War II.

The extended family was gathered in the lovely white-framed Presbyterian church, and my father conducted the service. When it was over, we got into our cars and drove to the nearby cemetery. As we got out of our cars and walked to the entrance, all of us were struck with the sight of 40 or 50 Black people standing against the picket fence. They could not come into the cemetery itself. How had they gotten there? None of them had cars. And none of their houses were equipped with telephones. There were some buggies with mules and horses tethered, and a few bikes leaning against the oak trees. Many had walked from Papoo's plantation south of town and Uncle Frank's from the north. And also from farms far and wide in Calhoun County. Word had gone out from person to person and farm to farm that the patriarch and founder of Calhoun County had died. They all respected "Mr. Skottowe" and had cobbled together or borrowed dark suits and dresses, and they had come. Women and men had hats, and the men were holding them over their hearts. My eyes quickly ran down the line, and I caught a glimpse of my friend James. Long ago, my grandfather had chosen him to accompany me on my hunting and fishing trips. His baseball cap was also over his heart and his eyes were on the ground. James had been my friend in so many wonderful outings. We had bonded together. I especially remembered him as a smart, athletic boy. There was no recognition today.

I'm embarrassed to say so, but this was the first time that segregation with all of its evil hit me in the face. I had lived with it. We took it for granted. But it never felt the way it did on that homecoming for my grandfather. Maybe it was Papoo's last message to me: Do something about it. Do something about this evil in our land. It was as if the words of "Amazing Grace" had spoken to me: "I was blind, but now I see."[1]

There was a certain nobility and grace without bitterness emanating from the Black people on the other side of the fence. They were determined to be there and share in our sorrow and be part of it. They certainly reached *me*. It was not an epiphany, but a seed was planted and the will was set to find a way to do something about it in the future. This experience led me some years later to Dr. Martin Luther King Jr. When my grandfather was lowered into the ground, I thought, a generation is over. It would never be the same again. And it wasn't.

We returned to the Great House and had our own memorial service. Each child had an anecdote or a story, and we said goodbye to Papoo on a high note. Since I had to leave shortly for Chapel Hill, I had a goodbye moment with my father and mother and my three sisters, Lillian, Jane, and Barbara. They knew I was to be commissioned and would probably end up in the Pacific Theater. My mother was in tears. As I drove away, I felt I was leaving behind my childhood, but I also thought what a lucky young man I was to have been so blessed with such an extended family.

1

The Preacher's Son

"The Old Man and the Boy"
It made a man of the boy, and it kept the boy in the man.

I was born on February 4, 1925, in Orlando, Florida, to a mother who knew how to make the best of things and a father who did not believe in giving up. Preaching was in the blood of our branch of the Belk family. My father, also John Blanton Belk, was a Presbyterian minister and the son of a Presbyterian minister who was also a poet with a passion for education. My paternal grandfather, George Washington Belk, was a descendant of the Belks who had immigrated to North Carolina in 1760 from England, and my paternal grandmother was Mary Thornton Blanton Belk, born in Cumberland, Virginia.

My father was born in Chatham, Virginia, on July 3, 1893, the eldest of eight children—four boys and four girls. At that time in the South, the eldest son was expected to become either a minister or a doctor. My father complied by becoming a minister. My Belk grandparents never had a lot of money, but that was not their main concern. They made do with hand-me-downs, and my grandmother made good, simple meals out of the wild game my grandfather hunted, the vegetables they raised, the cornbread she baked, and, especially, her biscuits and milk gravy.

My grandfather often traveled around the South on horseback filling the pulpits of ministers who were either ill or away and holding revival services. He was a handsome, stately man with a debonair mustache. He was a published poet as well as a preacher. When the writer Joel Chandler Harris died, my grandfather, a friend of Harris's, wrote this poem entitled

"The Passing of Uncle Remus." It went like this:

The Rabbit will hide as he always did,
And the sly Fox will do as he always did.
But no one can tell what they think and say
Since Uncle Remus has passed away.[1]

My grandfather's other poems were like love letters to my grandmother, whom he idolized, as many Southern men seemed to idolize their ladies. He is a strong figure in my mind, as is Grandmother Belk. I knew her longer because my grandfather died when I was a small boy, and after his death she lived with us when we settled in Richmond, Virginia. My grandparents were very proud of my father.

After spending 18 months in France during World War I, my father came home to the North Carolina mountains that he loved. For a time he taught school at Mills River, a small town just on the edge of the beautiful Pisgah National Forest. He had tramped all over those majestic mountains when they were still part of the vast Biltmore Estate, developed by George Vanderbilt near the turn of the 20th century.[2] Dad had fished for brook trout up and down the cold, rocky rivers, and had tracked deer in the snow-laden foothills of Mount Pisgah. He was a fine wing shot and a dedicated dry fly fisherman, deeply at home in the mountains and aware of their bounty as well as their occasional dangers. One year he left his deer camp and walked across the mountains in the moonlight to be home with his parents for Christmas Eve. Early in the predawn hours, he sensed that he was being followed. Every time he stopped to look back, something would slink into the shadows. He became more and more apprehensive, and as he neared his parents' farmhouse, he broke loose and ran. His mother had an uncanny ability to feel fear when her children were in danger. That cold night, she grabbed her husband's double-barreled shotgun, flung open the back door, and fired a shot in the air. My father ran breathlessly into the safety of the house. When daylight broke, they found the tracks of a panther that had stalked my father all the way across the mountains.

It was Grandfather Belk who in a sense arranged the marriage of my parents. He was holding a revival service at the Presbyterian church in St. Matthews, South Carolina. He met Mr. and Mrs. Skottowe Wannamaker, a leading family in that church, and their lovely daughter Jennie. "You must meet my son," Grandfather Belk said. The man who would become my father was at that time a lieutenant and eventually became a captain in the Anti-Aircraft Artillery Service in France during World War I. Later, when he returned from the war, he accompanied my grandfather to another revival service in St. Matthews. My father had a beautiful tenor voice, and he went with his father to do some singing. Grandfather Belk saw to it that my father met Jennie Wannamaker, who was then engaged to a banker. My father used all his charm and wooed Jennie away from the banker. Their marriage delighted both the Belk and Wannamaker families.

For their honeymoon, the newlyweds went to Cashier's Valley in the North Carolina mountains. They stayed in a small cabin way back in the mountains where there was good trout fishing. My mother, who came from a patrician family in the Lowcountry of South Carolina, had never before been in such a wild place. She made the best of it, however, as she did throughout her life. There is an old, yellowed photograph of the two of them, she wearing boots and knickers and Dad holding a fresh-caught speckled trout. His smile is much bigger than Mother's.

My father was the greatest influence on my life. Not only did I learn from him, but I had a deep love for him as a father certainly, but also as a confidant, comrade, and friend. I never once doubted his love for me. He was a renaissance man, bold and courageous, always trying new things. Never satisfied with the way things were, he was constantly looking for ways to make them better. He was handsome, fit, and charming, a true Southern gentleman. He became an eloquent minister, authored two books, *Our Fighting Faith* and *A Faith to Move Nations*, and many articles. He loved classical music and opera, and he kept trying to master the violin. He played golf and tennis and was such a good carpenter that he would later build a roller coaster for my sisters and me in our backyard.

When Grandfather Belk was dying, the family gathered at his bedside.

They would later tell the story of the moment when he asked them to sing "When They Ring Those Golden Bells."[3] Even though my grandfather was not singing with them, they all felt they heard a high tenor voice—his voice—join in the song. Just before he slipped away, Grandfather Belk took my father's hand and said to him, "Blanton, you look after the family now—and be sure that Sam and Frank [his younger brothers] get an education." My father, the loyal, responsible eldest son, was totally faithful to my grandfather's deathbed wish.

My father became a minister, like his father before him. From the University of South Carolina, where he completed his undergraduate studies, he went to Union Theological Seminary in Richmond and then on to the Columbia Theological Seminary in New York City. After Dad earned his Doctor of Divinity degree, he became a minister and was an astute teacher of the Bible, making the stories come vividly alive and connecting them to our everyday existence. Dad taught me lessons that have stayed with me to this day, imbuing me with his love of life, his love of people, his love of the natural world.

When I was growing up, Dad didn't lay down a lot of rules. He encouraged responsibility, yet he never broke my spirit. He let me make my own mistakes. He didn't talk to me a lot about values, but I learned by seeing the way he treated the family and the way he treated his friends and other people—everybody he ran into. I learned my father's values from the way he lived his life. There are useful books on values, of course, but the most important way to transmit them is to live yourself the way you hope your sons and daughters will live. My parents gave me that gift.

I can remember my father taking me to Daytona Beach, Florida, to watch the car races, which were held on the beach. I saw Sir Malcolm Campbell race his Bluebird and break all the speed records of the day. I remember picnicking on the sand dunes overlooking the enormous white stretch of beach that reached to the rolling Atlantic and seeing my first airplane, with its brightly colored wings, come down the beach, very low. Some 35 years later I would stand on another Florida beach watching astronaut Captain Gene Cernan as he departed Cape Canaveral for his journey to the Moon on Apollo 17.

My father was a strong, forceful man, yet very genteel and considerate. He was a walking encyclopedia on the Civil War.

I often reflect on what I absorbed by standing on the ground where history happened and hearing my father talk about it. That experience influenced me later in life when we developed Up with People. I knew from my boyhood experience that the whole concept of education carried much more meaning if students could travel to the places in the world where history had happened and contemporary events were taking place. That history and those events would live with young people because they had been there.

When I was seven, Dad gave me a fishing rod—a fly rod, casting rod, and reel. He gave me a single-barrel .410 shotgun when I was eight. He taught me to use the rod and the gun, and he taught me stringently. Once on a quail covey rise, my youthful excitement got the best of me and I shot too close to my father. He told me sternly that the powder would leave a lasting impression on his hunting coat. That was a hard, frightening lesson to learn, and it left me in tears. I never forgot it, and I never shot close to anyone after that. Since he and his family had hunted game for sustenance, my father instilled in me the principle that you do not ever shoot or catch anything you do not plan to eat. Never, never shoot a covey of quail down to less than five, he taught me. Never leave your footprints when you don't have to. Always bury your campfires. Always ask permission before entering someone's land. Always close and lock gates that are closed and locked.

Dad loved the forests, the Milky Way, and the full Moon, and he taught me to love them too. He could read the forest floor like a map. He studied the tracks left by animals who lived there. "This is a raccoon," he would say. "That's a possum that just went up the persimmon tree. There is a buck deer following a doe—and, yes, those are truly turkey tracks. The circle you see over there in the sand is where a covey of quail dusted their wings. Yes, that's a large oak tree, and this is holly. Over there is cedar, and that's a pine. The pine will burn quicker, but the oak will burn longer. If you can find an old cedar post and chip off bits, you've got the best fire-starting mechanism in the world. This is a turnip field. Now if you pull one out, take your knife and cut that turnip on a frosty morning, it will taste great!" I tried it, but it never did.

He was a Christian, but in his view, God does not belong to one church. He taught us that the Almighty belongs to all peoples of the earth, just as planet Earth, the heavens, and the universe belong to God. He believed that because God is also Nature, Nature is sacred. My father thought that people could commune with God when and wherever they pleased, and if one did not believe in God, one could still become more human by communing with nature.

Dad was also an excellent gardener and farmer. He had bought extra vacant lots next to our home, and he tilled, fertilized, plowed, and planted them. He also had the occasional use of an old mule named Molasses. Dad and Molasses worked our garden with tender loving care, producing a bumper crop of wonderful tomatoes, corn, asparagus, okra, and beans. I personally drew the line, however, when it came to eating the kale, mustard, and collard greens.

My father was a great man, and a profound, shaping influence in my life, but he was, thank goodness, not a saint. He was wonderfully human. His shooting was constantly getting him in trouble. We were living in Florida when it was time for my sister Jane to be born. My mother thought the baby would come any day, but Jane's advent had an unfortunate timing, as it coincided with the opening of the deer and turkey hunting season. Dad just had to go hunting—and he did. Of course, later that very morning my mother went into labor. The state police were dispatched to find my father. Dad was at Tosohatchee Game Preserve where he had spent a thrilling morning flushing a large wild turkey—a gobbler—which he killed with one barrel. When the turkey fell, a buck deer had jumped up. My father killed the deer with the second barrel. The state policeman found Dad and brought him back to Orlando, sirens blaring. Dad proceeded up the stairs of our house on his hands and knees to make peace with his wife and greet his new daughter.

From Florida we moved to Huntington, West Virginia, and then to

Richmond, Virginia, but we traveled back to Florida when we could. I especially remember a trip we made from Richmond to Fort Myers Beach, Florida, when I was 10. A friend had loaned our family her cottage on Fort Myers Beach. On the way there we stopped in Daytona Beach, where our Uncle Frank Belk lived. He was our father's youngest brother and my folk hero. He was tall and thin, played the guitar and sang, and smoked a pipe. At that time, he was selling Havana cigars all over Florida and in adjoining states. He loaned us his outboard motor, and we drove on to Fort Myers, where Dad paid $25 for an old boat with a pair of oars. I had the time of my life running the outboard motor in this boat.

We shared a dock with a man who, it turned out, was a religious fanatic. He announced to us one day that the world would come to an end on the following Friday, and that he and his followers would gather on the beach, dressed in white wraps. They would be ready for the Rapture and because of their religion, they would be taken straight up into Heaven. The rest of us would go to Purgatory. My sisters and I were simultaneously scared and delighted with this scenario. We were up at daylight on the designated Friday because this marvelous event was supposed to take place at sunrise. Sure enough, there in the shallows stood our neighbor with 25 or 30 other people, all clad in white, praying and looking up to the heavens. We stood on the screened porch of our cottage, fascinated. Suddenly I thought, "Gosh, if this actually happens, how will we go through the porch ceiling if we get lifted up to Heaven?" Our neighbor and his companions stood singing and shouting "hallelujah" as the sun rose. Then, much to their dismay, the sun kept rising, and rising, but they didn't. Just in case God's timing was off, they waited for an hour or more as the sun grew hotter and hotter still. Eventually, they slowly disbanded. Disappointed to miss the spectacle, yet relieved that the world was going on, we ate breakfast and then went swimming.

Those were special summer days in Florida, but the most idyllic summer days were spent with my Wannamaker relatives, my mother's people, in St. Matthews. Every summer day there was an adventure. Grandfather Wannamaker, "Papoo," was the heart of our big family.

Papoo was terrific on the typewriter, a skill he had learned along with using Morse code back in the days when he worked as a telegraph operator for the railroad. For years he worked on a book about our family history—a big book, which can be found today in their local historical society. But as a boy I knew none of this about Papoo. I just knew that he was a spellbinder of a storyteller and a grandfather who loved to tease and even spoil his grandchildren. Papoo was also a great psychologist. He knew how to get his grandchildren to behave and cooperate when nobody else could. When my mother's sister Aunt Punch was getting married, I was chosen to be the ring bearer. I was five or six, and I did not want to be a ring bearer, especially when I found out I had to wear a coral-colored silk suit. I thought it was a ridiculous outfit. I did not want to wear it, and I did not want to walk down the aisle in the church carrying a pillow with a ring sewn into the top of it. Finally, Papoo took me aside and said, "I caught a big toad, and if you do this, I'll give you the toad." I couldn't resist that toad, so I wore the suit, and I walked into the church, and I carried the pillow—and as soon as that was done, I ran out of the church. I figured I had done enough to earn that toad.

My Wannamaker grandparents lived in a big, white two-story house next to the railroad tracks in St. Matthews. My mother, her two sisters, and her brother were born there, and they grew up in that spacious home near the cotton fields. They called it the Great House. Many rooms. Some I've never been in. In summer, when all the shades were down, it was cool inside. A peaceful place, even when full of grandchildren. Sometimes I would stand alone and listen to the hum of the fans. A wide veranda with a red marble floor circled the front porch, where there was a swing. Uncle Lambert, Aunt Tugar's husband, was always sitting there smoking his cigar. The driveway ran under the portico, and I often left my bicycle there. A wrought-iron fence defined the boundaries of the yard, and in typical Lowcountry fashion, a second-story screened-in porch, often called the sleeping porch, surrounded the house. With its dark, cool interior, the house was a haven to enter after a morning of fishing or swimming or just walking barefoot on the sandy road. The Great House held us all together.

It enveloped us with love and laughter. There was always room for everyone. We were a swarm of kids, all doing our own thing. My closest cousin was Henry Zimmerman, called "Hence" for short, while everybody called me "Brother." We had lots of hours free to do what we wanted, but meals were the gathering times. We all had to come to meals and be seated at the large table on time. Papoo sat at the head of the table, and Grandmother, "Mamoo," sat at the other end when she wasn't going back and forth to the kitchen to get a new dish.

My father once asked Mum Sue, the cook, "What is the secret of your delicious scrambled eggs?" Mum Sue answered in her mesmerizing Southern drawl, "Well, Reverend, it just depends on where the perspiration drips!"

I still dream about the abundance of delicious food in St. Matthews—Southern food, savory and tasty and fresh from either the garden, the fields, or the woods. The midday meal in the South was called dinner, and it was something to experience. The large, oblong table was packed with family members, with Papoo and Mamoo at each end, and Uncle Frank and his wife, Aunt Laurie, across from each other in the middle. There was always fried chicken or roast beef or pork. I loved the small civet beans over rice, spiced with chopped chilies. There were a few kinds of corn—Country Gentleman, which had two rows and then a blank row, Golden Bantam, or white corn. There were bowls of squash and okra and string beans, and large sliced tomatoes so delicious that the Good Lord doesn't make them anymore. All these vegetables were grown in the garden behind the house along with juicy watermelons. There were Mamoo's pickles and homemade bread and country butter. For dessert there was a light cake, or figs off the family fig tree, or big, striped watermelons, called rattlesnake melons for the stripes.

Between meals, we had enormous freedom to embark on our own activities, but we had to pay any consequences. Our elders believed that it takes a village to raise a child—especially a swarm of children in the summertime. All unknown to us, a "spy" network of aunts, uncles, neighbors, friends, and cousins regularly reported to headquarters on our activities, For instance, someone said, "Did you know that after the heavy rains,

Brother and Hence were trying to go through the flooded pipes under the railroad tracks?" That came to a screeching halt!

There was a great fig tree with a big black tire affixed to a branch, and we loved to swing back and forth on it. For bigger adventures there was the barn behind the house with a tin roof where Hence and I experimented in being early astronauts. One day I stood on the barn roof holding a large black umbrella as my cousins urged me to slide down the roof, launch myself off into space, and float gently to Earth, using the umbrella as my parachute. It didn't work out that way. Mission Control had planned it all wrong. As I was on the way down the roof, an exposed nail tore through my short pants and my butt, and on takeoff, my concentration was focused on that and not on opening the "parachute." At least my fall was partly cushioned by straw and cow manure.

We went swimming most mornings in the St. Matthews swimming pool. I was already a good swimmer, but Hence taught me to do a back-flip from the diving board. We swam and played tag until exhaustion and hunger set in, and then we'd walk home barefoot to Mamoo and dinner. Hence's feet were already toughened up when I arrived for the summer, but walking barefoot was a matter of male pride, no matter how hot or rough the pathway home might be. My city feet suffered as I conditioned them over the hot gravel and sand, but by the end of the summer, I could walk on hot stones, dirt, tar, and any other peril and never miss a beat.

If there was anything we loved more than swimming, it was fishing. On some summer days Uncle Frank took charge of Hence and me. Sometimes his pickup truck would suddenly stop up above the swimming pool. Uncle Frank would call out, "Do you boys want to go fishing or do you want to keep swimming?" Stupid question, we thought, as we quickly gathered up our clothing and ran to the truck.

When it was bedtime, we stretched out on our assigned beds or cots upstairs on the screened-in sleeping porch. During the summer all manner of grandchildren and cousins slept on that porch during the sultry nights, when heat, humidity, the thrumming of June bugs darting about like little helicopters, and the flights of mosquitoes could make sleeping a challenge.

Occasionally on moonlit nights you could see bats flitting around. I acquired a great fear of bats after Hence's mother, my Aunt Frazile, told us that a bat had actually flown into her hair, and her maid took so long to cut the bat out of her hair that it turned white overnight. Hence and I were transfixed by this story and never for a moment doubted its accuracy. The night trains also made it hard to sleep. The train came whistling and roaring down the tracks, belching smoke and passing just 200 yards in front of the house. It was enough to make us dive under our sheets and stay there until daylight.

I practiced a private ritual soon after my arrival in St. Matthews each summer. I would slip off by myself to check certain places in Papoo and Mamoo's house, just to be sure nothing had changed since the summer before. There was the back porch lined with baskets of fresh vegetables, freshly picked from the home garden. Under the tables the rows of rattlesnake watermelons just pulled from the watermelon patches. I always had to open Uncle Frank's gun closet, and even today the smell of oiled leather and gun oil takes me back. Soon I was satisfied by my secret survey that nothing had changed. Then I knew I was home.

2

Youthful (Mis)Adventures

"It Takes a Whole Village"
When you go down by the river watch out for those crocodiles.

My best friend in those idyllic days in St. Matthews was my cousin Hence, the son of my grandmother's cousin. He lived across the railroad tracks in a great white house on a hill. One day, Uncle Frank Wannamaker had taken us fishing, and here we were in the beautiful, slow-moving river in South Carolina called the Combahee. It had been a lovely lazy afternoon fishing and paddling on the river. We had also gone through several tropical showers with some lightning, but the lightning had been so far away that Hence and I stripped off our clothes and let the cool rain wash our sweaty bodies. Then, the sun would come out and we would dry out, put our shorts and T-shirts back on, and continue fishing.

Hence and I were both excellent paddlers, and we were taking turns paddling and fishing. We had entered a lovely backwater, more like a canal off the main river. The storm had flooded the rice fields, and the runoff was pouring into our stream. It was stirring up lots of nutrients, and the fish were feeding. I was in the bow tossing a popping bug with my fly rod, and if you got it to roll out just right, it would go under the moss hanging from the trees and you'd almost instantly have a strike. I had just gotten a big one and fought a lovely bass, called a trout in South Carolina. Suddenly, Hence said to me in a whisper, "Don't move but there's a big alligator just under the dike coming out of the rice field." As I looked, this huge alligator slid off the bank and headed our way, its intense eyes fixed on us from just under the surface. Hence said in another whisper, "Brother, get down on the bottom of the boat and don't move and don't breathe! These monsters can flip their tail and turn us over." We were two frightened little boys, toe to toe, scared out of our wits. We could just see over the gunnel of the boat, and the alligator was fast approaching—there was nothing left to do but pray. Just as the gator got to the boat, it slipped beneath the water, its back scraping the bottom. Both of us were sure we were going to be flipped over and devoured. Then the scraping stopped. We were terrorized, wondering what next, but we stayed still and flat in the boat. Slowly, very slowly, it moved along and popped up with those scary eyes still fixed on us. Finally, with a mighty flip of its tail, it turned and headed for the far bank. We suddenly remembered to breathe again but continued to lie on the bottom of the boat, fearful that the creature might return. When we told Uncle Frank our harrowing experience, he said quite calmly, "Don't you know alligators don't eat people? Only crocodiles do that." Hence and I were not convinced.

Fishing with Uncle Frank was a frequent occurrence. We would scramble out of the pool, change into our shorts, run up to his Chevrolet, and hop in. Sometimes it was a car and sometimes it was a pickup, but it was always a Chevy because he ran the local Chevrolet dealership. We'd take off to the beautiful, clear Edisto River that ran through the South Carolina Lowcountry, or the Santee Cooper River, or once the Ashepoo. We would usually paddle down the river, fishing with fly rods and casting rods for big red-breasted bream or bass.

Once we were paddling up a small creek under overhanging bushes. You had to watch closely for the cottonmouth snakes that would sometimes drop down into your boat from the overhang. You had to be skillful with your paddles to get those snakes overboard quickly. But up this particular small creek, an alligator surfaced right in front of us. We paddled over it and its angry swirl shook the boat.

My father was a beautiful fisherman. He was fishing in the backwaters of the Edisto River one day when he too saw the eyes of an alligator surface among the lily pads. Dad was adept with a fishing lure called a Zaragoza. It was said to be named after the notorious dancing girls in Pensacola, Florida, because that plug would dance around on the top of the water. Dad threw it in, just for fun. The alligator had other ideas, however. He opened his jaws and clamped down tight on the plug. Dad fought that alligator for more than half an hour and finally pulled it into the boat, to the dismay of the man who had been paddling the boat. He shouted, "Parson, if you bring that alligator in the boat, I'm going out of the boat!"

They managed to subdue the alligator with a chain and loaded it into the trunk of Dad's old Plymouth. They gave the alligator a ride back to the Millwood Pond in St. Matthews, and wrestled that alligator into the pond, which is still home to its offspring. Needless to say, nobody swims in that pond anymore, except for the bass and bream.

The local press at the time picked up the story that Parson Belk had caught this alligator and fought it for 35 minutes. Months later, some friends in California sent Dad a newspaper article reporting that the Presbyterian minister Dr. J. Blanton Belk Sr., had been fishing in South Carolina and wrestled a giant alligator for four hours before landing it. According to this news report, the alligator was 10 and a half feet long. So the story had grown as it traveled to the West Coast.

Hence and I were always working on projects, so much so that later on, looking back, I thought, "Move aside, Tom Sawyer! Here comes Henry Zimmerman!" One summer Hence and I decided to build a boat, and Papoo asked one of his hired help to work with us because he understood boat building. All that summer we worked in one of Zimmerman's big barns. It had a dirt floor, and our boat-building guide drew the outline of a rowboat on the floor. He showed us how to lay out big pine planks within the outline. We drove small stakes into the ground, and then the pine planks were bent on a curve to resemble the side of the boat. Next, we nailed on ends and we nailed on sterns and we learned how to insert the floorboards. Working hard off and on through most of July and all of August, we had almost finished the boat. Then we noticed great cracks between the boards, which we filled with melted tar. This closed the cracks but increased the weight of the boat about four times. Finally, we made large paddles out of pine.

We finished our boat about the time that a large new reservoir in St. Matthews was completed. Our boat was transported to the reservoir in a horse-drawn wagon, and the whole family came to the reservoir to see us launch that boat. Nobody could have been prouder or more excited than Hence and I were. Off we went into the lake. Our boat floated. Pleased and proud, we paddled and drifted. Then we looked down to the end of the lake where a large speedboat was circling, pulling somebody on an aquaplane, the forerunner of water skis. Suddenly Hence said, "Good grief, Brother, that big speedboat is coming toward us!"

Sure enough, that boat was headed right at us. At first we thought they were going to swerve away, but when they got about 15 feet from us, we realized they weren't changing course. There was going to be a collision for sure. Hence jumped over the bow of our new boat, and I went over the stern. I sank to the bottom of the lake, grabbing onto weeds and holding on for dear life. I could hear the roar of the speedboat's outboard and finally, after what seemed like an eternity, I surfaced. Our new boat had been completely demolished. What was left of it floated around in pieces with bits of tar. Hence and I hung on to the big boards, both crying. Such a great victory one moment—and then total defeat the next. This may have been the shortest lifespan of a boat in history.

The speedboat came back around, and the people were full of apologies. They had planned to come at us and scare us and then swerve away, but one of the ropes on the wheel of the outboard motor had broken. When the man at the wheel tried to swing right, the wheel no longer controlled the motors, and they came right over the top of us. We finally paddled ashore, unhurt but completely broken over this experience. In his typical fashion, Papoo said, "Don't worry, boys. We'll build a bigger boat, and it will be even better!"

Back home in Richmond, a few years later, I had another misadventure with a friend and a boat. The first sign of trouble, for my poor mother at least, came just after daylight. The phone rang in our home in Richmond, and my mother answered. An agitated woman's voice was saying, "Did you have a son paddling a canoe in the James River early this morning?" My mother froze, thinking the worst when the voice continued, "He and his friend are now in my house in the bathroom trying to stop shaking. They rang my doorbell, and when I looked out, I saw two ghost-like figures in stocking feet covered in icicles."

The day before, Clark "Little" Tinsley, my neighbor and close friend, had decided that since below-freezing weather was coming through, ducks would be on the James River. We could sneak in a shoot and still get back home in time to change for school. We were both attending St. Christopher's School at the time. We had informed our parents, and I had borrowed hip boots from a friend and my father's 12-gauge automatic shotgun. We parked my jalopy next to the river, unloaded the canoe from the roof, and broke ice until we got to running water. It was dark, before daylight. Clark was in the bow and I in the stern as we paddled upstream.

Just at daylight we put the paddles in the boat, loaded our guns, and drifted back. Shortly we saw two wood ducks flying directly toward us about 30 yards up. As they veered off to our left, both of us fired at the same moment without thinking. The canoe shot out from under us, and we were instantly immersed in frozen water. I came up, grabbed the overturned canoe, and helped Clark. But my hip boots were filled with water and starting to drag me under. I handed my gun to Clark, and going under, I got the hip boots off. One of them sank to the bottom and the other I threw up on the overturned canoe. By this time we were becoming numb, and our wet hair had frozen.

Clark was saying, "I can't hold these guns any longer, my hands are freezing on the metal barrels." One was my father's, and I replied, "Don't you dare turn loose of those guns!" We were in great danger of hypothermia, and time was running out. But I seemed to have no fear, just an overwhelming desire to get the boat ashore and save my father's gun. Our paddles had been swept downstream, but after kicking and pushing the boat from the stern, we finally hit bottom. Another problem was that we were on the wrong side of the river. We turned the canoe over, dumped out the water, grabbed two large branches from a fallen tree, and took off for the other side. We pulled and paddled, gasping for breath with hoar frost streaming out of us as if we were smoking.

We thought we were cold in the water, but now as the wind blew through our frozen clothes, we knew we were freezing. I said with chattering teeth, "Little, if we can only make it to the shore, we can start the car and turn on the heater." We just barely made it through the heaving current in the middle and then hit ice along the shore. By that time I had no feeling in my hands, as both of us crashed our tree limbs through the ice to break a path to shore. I fought off hallucinating. We made it, jumped out, pulled the canoe on solid ground, raced in stocking feet on gravel, feeling nothing, and headed for the car. I found the keys hidden under the back wheel and started the engine. It fired then died. Out of gas. Clark and I were shaking uncontrollably. I yelled, "There is a house up on the hill." I don't know to this day how we did it, but we made it up the hill and rang the doorbell. A "Florence Nightingale" answered the door and took us in, water, ice, and all. We tried to take hot showers, but even the cold water felt as if we were being scalded.

What happened after that is a blur. I know our host wrapped us in blankets. My father and mother arrived with fresh clothing, and after many thank yous, we were taken home. Somehow, my Dad brought gas and got the jalopy running and home with the guns. He never mentioned it. Both Clark and I came down with roaring colds and were out of school for some days. Thank God, no pneumonia. I think it was the second night home, I awoke with a chill and pure unrelenting fear of my near-death experience. Clark reported a similar occurrence.

During the crisis, I had no fear and learned something about myself in critical situations. All my father said to me after several days was, "I'm proud you pulled through. I trust you learned a lot from that experience." And I did. Never go in a canoe or boat without life vests or floating cushions. Tell people exactly where you are going. Don't borrow other people's hip boots. Never try to get in a duck hunt before school. And never, never have two people shoot at the same time, on the same side of a canoe. The great thing was that my father still had complete trust and belief in me. So often in the future knowing that carried me through.

Not all of my misadventures involved boats—or were as life-threatening. One came thanks to my eldest sister, Lil, and my beloved 1934 Ford coupe. Lil was an extraordinary woman, and if it had not been for an alcoholic husband, she would have made a bigger mark on the world. In my dreams, I see her still, herding my other sisters, Jane and Barbara, into my Ford coupe with the rumble seat, saying "please be on time." With the car parked on the downward slope in front of our house, they'd pile in, books, lunches, and all, release the brakes, and let the car roll downhill until there was enough speed to engage the clutch and pray the engine would start. Then in a cloud of blue smoke from the exhaust they would disappear around the corner.

Lil would drop the girls off at high school and then head for Westhampton, the women's college attached to the University of Richmond. In March 1944, she had been elected president of the student council and was a terror on the field hockey team. She had originally attended Hollins College but transferred to Westhampton during the war to save the family money. I can picture her at Hollins in the Shenandoah Valley of Virginia, where she was president of the sophomore class. She kindly invited her little brother to attend a school social and escort one of her closest friends, Kit. I drove up in my Ford coupe, somewhat apprehensive as to what this friend would look like. At the same time, as a senior in prep school, I was flattered to be attending a college dance. This was another time and place in history. There were very strict rules, and my sister strongly briefed me on the culture at Hollins: "You'll meet your date at the social before the dance, along with all the other young men who've been invited. You must not, at any time, break away from the dance and be alone."

So I met my date. To my surprise, she was a little coy with a lovely face and a knock-me-dead figure. I am sure I stuttered when Lil introduced us. I know I experienced butterflies in my stomach when she gently shook my hand and said, "I've heard so much about you. You're better looking than your picture." I was smitten. We danced well together, sat at a table with Lil and her date, and drank gallons of un-spiked punch.

It was a hot spring night, and without any air-conditioning, the ballroom with all those bodies was adding to the heat. Without thinking, I said, "Let's get some air." Kit replied, "What a good idea." So hand in hand we slipped out of the side door and found a bench, under a large oak tree. We sat close together and cooled off and heated up. Suddenly reality hit, and she exclaimed, "Oh my goodness, this is against the rules!" and jumped up. We slipped back into the side door. But the Gestapo of Hollins saw us, and Kit was turned in. Her name must have been written down for censure, but nothing happened immediately. We danced some more, drank more punch, and talked about the war and what lay ahead for all of us.

When Kit mentioned that their semester would soon end, and she would be returning to Buffalo, New York, for the summer with her parents, I said, "Why don't you return via Richmond and we could meet again." It was an impulsive remark. I learned later, to my embarrassment, that she took it as a more formal invitation. With a hug and a goodnight kiss we parted with a "see you soon." I returned to Richmond.

Our school year ended, and my friend and classmate "Buzz" Doer invited me to accompany him to spend a few days at his home on the Eastern Shore of Maryland with its great beaches, boats, and fishing. So there I was, enjoying life without a worry in the world, when the phone call came through from my father and Lil: "Kit is here, where are you?" The frost in their voices could freeze a phone line. My God, I had forgotten all about my invitation. It is no easy trip from the Eastern Shore, across the Chesapeake Bay Bridge, back to Richmond. And I had no car, since Buzz had driven me. So with a midnight-to-dawn bus ride to Norfolk and a long wait in the bus station for the bus to Richmond, I only arrived in time to take Kit to the train station. The blossoming relationship came to an abrupt end. All my humble and sincere apologies had no effect.

There wasn't even a chance to talk with Kit privately since Dad and Lil had formed a protective shield around us and drove with us to the train station. We did exchange a letter or two, but it was too late. On top of this, Lil poured more salt on my wounded pride by underlining that my bench sitting at the dance with Kit had cost her dearly. She kept saying, "Kit could handle the grounding at campus because she knew you cared for her and would see you at summer break."

It was humiliating, but I found some solace in my friendship with the Tinsley boys. Clark kept saying, "She should have written you that she was coming, and if she didn't, Lil should have." But time heals and life moves on. Even Dad and Lil spoke to me again by the following month.

3

Growing Up in the South

"Home Foundation"
Maybe good times maybe bad
Maybe happy maybe sad
We are made of what we had in the family

We moved often, as preacher's families usually did. My parents had started out in Piedmont, South Carolina, where Lil was born. Next they moved to Orlando, Florida, where my other sisters, Jane and Barbara, and I were all born. Two of my sisters made dramatic entrances into the world: as I've already said, Jane was born on the day the deer hunting season opened. Barbara was born during the epic Okeechobee Hurricane in September 1928, in which over 2,500 people in Florida died. She was the only one of us to be born in a hospital. Dad actually assisted in the delivery room, holding a candle while the surgeon turned baby Barbara in the birth canal because she was a breech. I have the clear memory at age three of being sent outside the house in my rubber boots, kicking the leaves left by the hurricane, and feeling a little peeved at all the attention being given to this new baby.

We lived in Orlando for nearly 10 years, our longest sojourn so far in one church. Then Dad was called to a church in Huntington, West Virginia, and from there to be the minister of Grace Covenant Presbyterian Church in Richmond, Virginia, in 1933.

We settled into the church manse on Seminary Avenue—Dad, Mother, my three sisters and me, our cook and housekeeper, Fanny Tate, and Aunt Lila, of course. Aunt Lila was a sister of Mamoo, and she came to help my mother when Jane was born and never left, to the dismay of my father. Our family never had much money, but we children never knew it. There was so much love and affection that we never thought of ourselves as poor. As my sister Barbara recalls, our father was always taking care of people, so it seemed like odds and ends of people were always living with us. We were surrounded with people all the time—some of them staying with us temporarily, and some of them coming for food or other help during the years of the Depression. There might be old men sitting on the steps of the manse, waiting for a meal Fanny would prepare for them. Once when Dad was visiting patients in the hospital, he brought an elderly mountain woman home to stay with us for a few days. Her son was a patient in the hospital, and she didn't have any place to go.

I had a paper route during the Richmond days, getting up at 4:30 in the morning and riding my bike through the dark streets to the market where the newspapers waited, all bundled up for the paper boys. We would gather our papers, roll them up, stuff them in the baskets on our bicycle handlebars, and take off. As we rode through our assigned neighborhoods, we tossed the papers onto the porches. The newspapers were delivered for 15 cents a week, and each Friday I had to collect that money from each of my customers. I kept delivering papers all through high school. There was always that one cantankerous woman on my route who refused to pay the 15 cents every week, but I left her a paper anyway.

From the time we arrived in Richmond, my father was thinking about how he could best serve his new church, and how the church could best serve the people of the city. As he set out on his pastorate in Richmond, he said, "I prayed that I might find a theme around which I could build up my life and ministry in this city."[1] Dad loved politics—not church politics, but the politics of local, state, and national government. He was a serious student of what was going on in the world. I wonder if secretly he would have liked being a senator or governor. I know he would have made a good one. Sometimes he took friends—such as US Senator Willis Robertson of Virginia—duck and quail hunting. When the senator came down from Washington to visit, he always stayed at our house and loved

Fanny's cooking. He and Dad enjoyed some great hunts together, and as a boy I liked to listen to the senator talk and to learn more about the workings of government.

For many years Dad greatly enjoyed being the chaplain of the Virginia General Assembly. As he thought about the challenges facing the nation and the world, he came to what he called "a revolutionary conception of what a church is meant to be and a determination to fight for that."[2] Part of his thinking was reinforced by what he was learning about the philosophy of Dr. Frank Buchman, a Lutheran pastor. Dad first encountered Dr. Buchman in England during one of his conferences. At this particular conference in London, Dad met Bill and Kay Wilkes, Betty's parents.

They were drawn to Dr. Buchman's belief that if individuals, with God's help, could change themselves for the better, they could then work together for a better world. The organization was very much a part of the evangelical movement at the end of the 1920s and into the 1930s, and was accepted at the beginning as a great revival. By the mid-1930s, my father began to speak openly about his convictions that, "The Church must be the doctor to bring healing to our nation's ills"[3] and to the problems confronting the world.

In 1937, there was growing tension and conflict in Richmond and Grace Covenant Presbyterian Church over the ideas and vision my father was expressing. Some people found him innovative and inspiring; others thought him radical and even threatening to conventional beliefs. My father was a lightning rod for the growing discontent. That year, he was dismissed from his pastorate at Grace Covenant. Seven hundred members left in support.

I was 12 then, and I didn't begin to understand all the issues and conflicts in the adult world in Richmond and beyond. I only knew that our secure life in Richmond had changed dramatically. The morning newspapers I delivered now carried the story of my father's dismissal, along with his picture. I heard enough thoughtless words at school and in the community to make me embarrassed, even ashamed. We moved out of the manse that had been home into temporary quarters at a friend's farm on the outskirts of Richmond, where we lived for about a year and a half. Later we moved to the edge of the city, to Edmonstone Avenue in Westhampton, into a house in a new neighborhood. This is where I made some of the best friends of my life, and where my sister Barbara met Jim Tinsley, the boy she would eventually marry. We bonded with the Tinsley family, who lived two houses down on our street. They had three sons. Another boy, Gene "Snuggy" Summers, and his family lived across the street. We were a close-knit neighborhood. My sisters and I were not taken out of our old schools but driven to school every day. I attended Chandler Junior High School and then Westhampton Junior High. Eventually, Dad was able to arrange a scholarship for me to attend St. Christopher's School, a prep school for boys in Richmond.

Dad and Mother did their best to keep our home life on an even keel, but children in a family—especially a close family—feel the stress and tension, even if they don't know or fully understand the causes. That was the time in my life I developed acne, a sign of the stress and distress I was feeling and an additional source of embarrassment for me.

My father's idealistic passion meant that some doors were closed to him forever. But new, unexpected ones opened. Numerous members of the Grace Covenant congregation had decided to leave with my father and urged him to organize a new church. He sat down with a few friends and supporters. After many meetings and much prayerful thought, they concluded together the kind of church they wanted to build and asked my father to be the minister. The spirit of these meetings is best described in this passage from a history of their new church, named St. Giles' Presbyterian Church: "The warmth of fellowship, the genuineness of love, the happiness of every heart, the spirit of adventure, the willingness to sacrifice, the unanimity of purpose, all combined to convince the leaders, who had arranged this first meeting, that God's Holy Spirit was surely guiding and blessing them in their efforts."[4]

One of his friends gave him a check for $5,000, the first significant gift made to the new church. When the church buildings had finally been finished, the friend told my father that the day he had handed over the check, he said to a neighbor about the gift, "Unfortunately there is not the slightest possibility of success but at least I wanted to encourage them."[5] Happily, Dad and his supporters proved the man wrong.

Frank Buchman's organization began to be called Moral Re-Armament (MRA) in 1938.

In 1942, with the encouragement of Clara Jane Ford, wife of Henry Ford, who told Dr. Buchman about the clean air and cool, invigorating summer breezes of Mackinac Island, Michigan, MRA held the first of several international conferences there. It drew people of all backgrounds from more than 100 countries. My whole family attended one of the first of these conferences in the summer of 1942 on Mackinac Island, as did the Wilkes family.

4

Navy Days

"Mabuhay Pilipinas!"
Long live the Philippines

In those early days, when few Americans had any access to television, radio provided entertainment and news for most US households, including ours. On December 7, 1941, a day I will never forget, our family gathered around the radio in the living room of our house on Edmonstone Avenue in Richmond. I was 16, sprawled on the floor, listening intently and trying to understand what President Franklin Roosevelt was telling the nation. The Japanese had bombed Pearl Harbor. We were shocked and spellbound. While we couldn't yet comprehend what it all meant, we knew our world was changing, perhaps forever.

Sad to say, I had to ask my father, "Where is Pearl Harbor?" This is how parochially we lived as a family. Dad produced a map and gave us a geography lesson, made necessary by this stunning tragedy.

For a while, despite all of this, life went on as normal for my family and our neighbors. In the fall of 1942, I was a senior at St. Christopher's School, when my father told me I needed to make an important decision. I could be drafted into the Army when I was 18. "You've got to decide," he said, "what you are going to do, son. Do you want to go into the Army or the Navy? If you want to go into the Navy, you'll have to enlist." He was going to leave the decision to me, and it would be the first major decision I had made in my life. Dad had the wisdom to let me make the decision on my own. The consequences—success or failure or something in between—would be my responsibility. If it didn't go well, there was nobody I could blame but myself.

The war was coming much closer to home. My boyhood friends were joining the Army, Navy, or Army Air Forces. My close friend Clark joined the 101st Airborne, and as a paratrooper later would be dropped behind enemy lines in Normandy in preparation for D-Day. His older brother Jim, who later married my sister Barbara, became an Army Air Forces lieutenant and as a pilot later flew the "Hump" (the Himalayan Mountains) from Dumdum Airport in India into Hangzhou in China. One of my other future brothers-in-law, Rice M. "Mac" Youell, joined the Marines and would fight throughout the Pacific.

It seems a terrible thing to say, but by late 1942 all of us approaching the military draft age were excited—longing to get out of the structures of formal education or routine jobs into life in the world, even the world at war. We wanted to test our potential, very much as young people in the 1960s did—and perhaps as young people in every other decade do. We were too young and untested to even imagine what lay ahead for us in wartime. We didn't think in any detail about being wounded or killed in battle, or about coming home with emotional scars that would never heal. One of our neighbors came home after the war and committed suicide. Others carried traumatic memories for years, buried inside.

I was nearly 18 and ready to go to war. I signed up to join the Navy. I had orders from the Navy to get into a college. I graduated from St. Christopher's and enrolled at Davidson College in Davidson, North Carolina, in January 1943, a month before my 18th birthday. I went to Davidson with great expectations of a reunion with my first cousins, Tommy and George Peters, who I idolized. They had already been at Davidson for two years and were big men on campus, leaders in sports and fraternity life. They weren't nearly as glad to see me as I had expected, though, and had very little time for a college freshman. Still, George got me going. My St. Christopher's classmate Eugene Desportes had also joined the Navy and enrolled at Davidson, and we were roommates. I signed up for NROTC courses but did not yet have orders to report for active duty.

Davidson was near Charlotte, home of my Belk cousins, and John, the oldest, was a star on the college basketball team, along with Tommy and George. John's father, Henry Belk, was known as the "Merchant of the South" because of his success with the Belk's Department Stores. The spacious Belk home in Charlotte was often the weekend destination for Davidson boys. Mary Belk would walk around and check the rooms to see how many students had come home with the Belk boys. Davidson was a school with high academic standards and probably would have been my school of choice even if the war and the Navy had not intervened. Once I stepped on that campus, I was no longer the preacher's kid or the adored only brother or the popular young cousin, Brother Belk. I was just a college student, to be judged on my own with all the other students. I couldn't depend on the Peters brothers or the Belk cousins or anyone else. I had to look to myself to make things work in my life. It wasn't easy, but it was essential to my growth and maturity.

In the summer of 1943, I was ordered by the Navy to report for duty at the University of North Carolina at Chapel Hill. The university had become a large staging area for the war effort. I was enrolled in a new program called V-12, designed to train college men for leadership roles in the Navy to meet the need for personnel in World War II. The nation was building more ships and other sea craft and needed to train more officers to command them. I read later that the program was also designed to train future leadership for the country. Also, making it possible for them to get a college education and a military commission at the same time. I had been transferred to the NROTC program so that I could stay on the University of North Carolina campus and work toward my degree as well as my Navy commission.

Students had come from all over the country, and this military culture was brand new for me. Boy, did I learn from it! During our senior year a number of veterans began to return from the war, among them 21-year-old men who had commanded B-25 flights over Europe. They were older in every way and brought a maturity and motivation with them that made a difference on campus. Some of these students were called Mustangs because they had already served in the Navy and were more mature than those of us who had just come out of high school.

For the first time in my life, I was part of a Southern minority because the majority of students came from other parts of the country, especially the Northeast. I greatly enjoyed meeting all these people from different cultures and different places, and I enjoyed the sense of discipline, purpose, and camaraderie of the whole military regime. Tough, seasoned chief petty officers were assigned to train us, and they would line us up in the morning, order us to stand at attention, and keep us standing there a long time—until one or two men would inevitably pass out. They would just let the men fall flat, forward or backward, and once it started it was as contagious as a yawn.

The training regime was rigorous and competitive, and you knew if you didn't make it you were going to be out of the V-12 program and assigned to be a seaman, and that was that. Frankly, I loved the competition. I excelled in intramural sports, where I won the diving championship. It was a completely new life for me—a break from Richmond, a break from the problems my father had with his former church, and a break from the snobbery at St. Christopher's. It was a chance to develop on my own and discover my own potential.

The commandant of the Navy operation at Chapel Hill was Captain Swede Haslett, and incidentally, a contemporary and close friend of General Dwight Eisenhower. Captain Haslett and his wife befriended me. I became a company commander, which allowed me to wear two silver bars and a star on the other side of my collar, meaning I was a cadet officer. I was often saluted by Army and Navy undergraduates. When you are 19, that does a lot for your ego. I felt I was part of an enormous cause in the world, one in which every red-blooded young American at that point in history wished to be engaged. This was a period of great patriotism and great conviction that there was evil afoot in the world, because of Hitler of Germany and Tojo of Japan, and that we must do all we could to see that freedom was preserved for future generations.

I found that I responded to the challenges of leadership. I wanted it. I liked it and reveled in it. It just seemed natural to take on a leadership role. From my father I inherited the ability to read people. I could very easily read the officers who supervised our training, some of whom I liked and some of whom I judged differently. I could determine what they really wanted from me and then make my decision about what to do. Those navy days certainly gave me a chance to try my wings and test my own potential. When we were commissioned on October 27, 1945, I was one of the few men in our class to receive a letter of commendation from the Secretary of the Navy.[1]

In April 1945, my father made a special trip to Chapel Hill to bring me very sad news. Tommy Peters, my first cousin and close boyhood friend, had been killed while leading his platoon as a second lieutenant in the Battle of Nuremberg, Germany. Several days before his death he had been awarded the Silver Star for heroism. His platoon had been trapped, and being the athlete he was, he told them all to run through the split trenches and get out of the sniper fire. He stood there alone, with the platoon's whole supply of hand grenades, and threw them like baseballs—he had a tremendous throwing arm. He held off the German attack so that all of his platoon escaped unscathed. Three days later he stood up and did something all officers were warned not to do: to point. This revealed to the snipers he was in command, and as Tommy pointed to give directions, he was machine-gunned down.

The news of his death was a terrible blow. I was raised in a family with three sisters and no brothers, and Tommy was as close to being a brother as anyone outside the family could possibly be. It was typical of my father to understand the depth of feeling I would have over this awful news and to make a special trip to tell me in person, to grieve with me, and to console me. Even today when I hear of people who are trying to find their fathers or connect with them, it's a mystery to me. My father was there with me and for me from the day I was born until the day he died.

My first orders for sea duty came in late 1945 and to report to the Brooklyn Navy Yard for small-craft training in preparation for joining my boat in the Pacific. Two days later, I was aboard a train to San Francisco on December 17.

I'd never been west of the Mississippi River before, and the trip to California was awe-inspiring. The grandeur and sheer size of the United

States came home to me as I spent five days with my face glued to the train window. Those who fly coast to coast miss the wonder of it all. I'll never forget passing through Colorado at dawn, raising the window shade and seeing a beautiful five-point mule deer standing close by on a hillside.

On December 22, I checked into the bachelors officer quarters at the San Francisco Naval Yard, where I was delighted to find an old school friend, big John Moore, from Boone, North Carolina. He had graduated a year earlier from University of North Carolina and was returning to his boat in the Philippines. Ten days later on January 2, 1946, we embarked together on a 15-day trip across the Pacific aboard a troop transport ship. I had plenty of time on the long journey to enjoy the tall tales from the weathered sailors on board who'd been involved in many battles across the Pacific.

On January 21, we landed in Samar in the eastern Philippines. It was pouring rain our first night. Big John and I lined up in the officer's mess for chow, but when we were given a few pieces of bread, we noticed it was covered with black specks. The cook assured us they were sesame seeds, but they turned out to be weevils. Good protein, I'm sure, but I took a pass!

Big John and I were notified that our boats were located some distance northwest in Manila Harbor, but local transportation was not available. We gathered our duffel bags, headed for the airport, and talked our way onto a military plane that was going to Clark Field, just outside of Manila.

My first look at the shockingly widespread destruction of war came during that flight. We flew over Corregidor, from which PT boats had evacuated General Douglas MacArthur and taken him to Australia in 1942. The pilot took us low over the Bataan Peninsula, site of the horrible Bataan Death March, where so many men were left to die on the side of the road or packed into boxcars headed to Japanese prison camps. Finally, on January 26, we saw the destruction of Manila itself; all civilian housing was destroyed. It was comparable to the destruction of Warsaw, Poland.[2] We flew low over Manila Bay, where more than 750 sunken ships and barges cluttered the harbor.[3] We saw the famous Dewey Boulevard, where royal palms had been cut down by the Japanese to make a landing strip for their fighter planes. The city was utterly destroyed. Suddenly we were face to face with the horrific reality of war and its aftermath.

Big John and I parted company at Clark Field. After a weekend in Manila, I hopped on the landing craft that took me to my boat, USS PCC-1178. When I arrived on the January 28, I saluted the quarterdeck and asked the officer of the deck for permission to come aboard. "Permission granted, sir," he replied.

A patrol craft control boat (PCC) is larger than the famous PT boat of John F. Kennedy and PT 109 fame. It can be likened to a junior destroyer: 173 feet long, with a cruising speed of 21 knots with a crew of four officers and 50 men. Its mission was anti-submarine warfare, convoy escort duty, and coastal patrol. There were 50 depth charges on its stern, and the main offensive armaments were anti-submarine rockets called mousetraps and hedgehogs. There were 20-, 40-, and 50-mm machine guns mounted primarily for defense against attacking aircraft, and one big 3-inch gun mounted on the bow.

I reported to Captain Doug Roberts, who'd been aboard for some time and had received orders to return to the States. The boat had been through a typhoon so strong that it sunk a cruiser. PCC-1178 had ended up on the beach, but everyone was safe. The captain had declared an emergency, which the men later told me they commemorated by breaking out a case of Haig & Haig Scotch whiskey.

When I arrived at the boat in January 1946, the oldest man aboard was the boatswain's mate, who was 25. I had my 21st birthday aboard the boat on February 4, 1946. As a newly minted naval ensign joining a crew that had been in the Pacific for almost two years, I was considered an outsider and had to prove myself. I enjoyed the challenge. I consciously tried to do more than was expected of me. I was particularly conscientious because I had heard the old rumors that ensigns were sometimes pushed overboard when they were disliked, and I was determined that wasn't going to happen to me!

Following the end of hostilities in 1945, this boat had continued serving the occupation forces in Okinawa and the Philippines. My first assignment was gunnery officer, and later navigator. We sailed all over the islands, from Guiuan on Samar in the far southeast to Subic Bay and Luzon in the Lingayen Gulf and Zamboanga, where the monkeys have no tails. We kept a careful watch as boats had been lost on patrols. Once we spotted a mine, the gunner's mate would detonate it with rifle fire. It was a challenge to the marksman's expertise.

One day, the boatswain's mate took several crew members and went ashore in Subic Bay. They commandeered an old army truck and drove far back into the bush until they located an abandoned Japanese tank. They stripped it of its 36-inch spotlight and two small leather seats, brought them back aboard, and welded them on each side of the flying bridge. They became great places to sit when you were sailing hours on end.

On March 1, 1946, we received orders to escort two other PCC boats on their return to the States, so by April 9, we were finally on our way home. The Pacific Ocean is one hell of a big lake. Some days the sea looks like glass with not a ripple as far as the eye can see, almost as peaceful as a mill pond in Virginia. Other days it's like a gigantic Niagara Falls, with green water breaking over our bow, sweeping down the decks and over the stern. On those days no one dared to step out, and every hatch was battened down tightly. On calmer occasions we cut the engines and drifted, letting everyone swim in the warm water, though the gunners always made sure someone sat in the crow's nest with a submachine gun, watching for sharks.

We had fuel to last only 12 days so our trip took us island-hopping from the Marshalls to the Marianas to Johnson Island and Hawaii. We pulled into Enewetak in the Marshall Islands expecting to take on supplies only to find that an atomic bomb test was scheduled close by and all the other ships had left port except an ice cream ship. Where in the world it came from I will never know, but we certainly ate our fill of delicious, cold ice cream.

One day I got bored and went into the emergency supplies to pull out a long coil of fishing line. With the help of the boatswain's mate, we tied the line to a Japanese feather, a heavy fishing lure, and fastened the end of the line to one of the depth charges, then let it drift back some 100 or more yards. I had been a fisherman all my life, and I didn't expect a fish to actually take anything on a lure at 25 knots but what the hell, I was fishing!

I had the early morning watch so I was sitting on one of our new seats courtesy of the Japanese and watching the day dawn. Suddenly I was shaken out of my day-dreaming with yelling coming from the stern. I couldn't make out what they were shouting until the seamen arrived on the flying bridge, saying, "Mr. Belk, you've got a fish on your line." I did something then that was spontaneous but not totally legal as an officer on watch—I left my watch and tore toward the stern where I was surrounded by four or five seamen urging me on. At that point I could see splashing way back in the wake, and it certainly looked like a fish. One of the seamen handed me a pair of gloves, and hand over hand I was bringing my fish aboard. I was so totally focused on this that I didn't notice the seamen had all disappeared down the hatch, and the hatch had been closed. I expected to hear cheering when I brought my catch aboard but I had been abandoned. By this time it was predawn, and one could see quite well, so when I hoisted my catch aboard I could almost see the fish flopping on the deck. On closer inspection, it was not a fish at all but a soaked pair of dungarees stitched at the bottoms with the Japanese feather attached to several of the belt buckles. I had been taken! Silence descended on PCC-1178.

Our navigational systems were antiquated compared to modern technology. Once, to make matters worse, our gyro compass failed and I had to use a sextant at sundown to record the position of four stars north, south, east, and west as quickly as possible. It was a tricky business when the seas were rough. Then I hurried into the map room, hoping my calculations would give us at least a 10-mile estimate of our position. Hope springs eternal.

Somewhere in the mighty Pacific we ran into a strong storm that lasted the better part of five days. No one dared to go on deck. It was impossible to get a navigational fix from the stars, sun, or Moon. It was pelting rain with heavy cloud cover. At one point we actually made a half circle and were sailing back toward the Philippines! Fortunately, the storm abated, the sun came out, and we were able to establish our position when we stumbled on an atoll with a single palm tree identified as Johnson Island. The crew let out a cheer and applauded our navigational dexterity. Little did they know, nor did we ever let on, that we had relied primarily on dumb luck.

We finally reached the Hawaiian Islands and Pearl Harbor in May 1946.

We could still see the remains of the USS *Arizona* and other destruction from the Japanese attack on the harbor. It was a haunting evidence that made me recall that morning in late 1941 listening with my family to President Roosevelt on the radio.

Before we left Pearl Harbor I had a surprise visit from a friend and classmate from my prep-school days, Tom "Tubby" Towers, who was also an ensign in the Navy. He was stationed in Hawaii, and we reminisced and compared notes. Tubby wanted to know if I planned to make the Navy my career. I told him that while I wouldn't exchange my naval experience for anything, I was moving on.

Our orders after Hawaii were to sail through the Panama Canal and on to Norfolk, Virginia. I was delighted to be returning to my home state. While in Pearl Harbor, however, our orders were changed, which is typical of the military. We were to proceed instead to Swan Island in Portland, Oregon.

I learned an invaluable lesson on this final leg of our journey that has lived with me ever since. I was on early morning watch when suddenly I heard a loud explosion from the stern of the boat. The boatswain's mate ran to investigate and came rushing back with a frightened look on his face shouting, "It looks like two men are dead." I notified the captain, and he went to investigate. It turned out that several of the old navy hands had been celebrating, waiting for their first glimpse of the US shoreline. They had taken the fulminate of mercury, an extremely powerful explosive, out of a depth charge and poured it out onto the deck. The gunner's mate told the chief mechanic it would make a great welcoming flame upon returning to the States if he lit a match to it. It was windy, so when he leaned over with his cigarette lighter to put the flame to the fulminate of mercury, the explosion knocked them both unconscious.

Fortunately it was a dispersed blast, and though there were serious injuries, everyone survived. The right side of the chief mechanic's face was lacerated and both his eyes were a mess. By this time, we were close to shore, so we radioed Astoria Naval Station, urging them to send a helicopter with a doctor to pick up the injured. They radioed back that since we had no medic to confirm the injuries, they couldn't send a helicopter.

Furious at this denial, we opened our engines to full throttle and headed for the mouth of the Columbia River, radioing for a pilot to be ready to take us through the sandbars. A dory met us in the rolling open seas, and a seaman, standing along the railing as his big rowboat went up and down, literally snatched the pilot aboard. It's fair to say he landed running, straight up to the flying bridge, to instruct our helmsman on how to navigate the sandbars straight into Astoria, where an ambulance was waiting at the dock. The chief mechanic did lose sight in his right eye, but the Navy doctors did such a fine job that even though his face was badly injured, there was little disfigurement or scar tissue.

It was June 26, 1946, and we weren't allowed to leave the boat because we had to go through an investigation into the incident by the Naval Board of Inquiry. I was scheduled to fly home to be at my older sister Lil's wedding. When I told my father what had happened, he immediately wanted to call our senator to have me cleared to travel. I begged him not to, feeling that would be a mistake. Naval law requires that if anything happens on your watch, whether in the bilge or in the furthermost corner of the boat, you are held totally responsible. I could not abdicate that responsibility.

Once the Board of Inquiry finished its review of the accident we were free to go. The boatswain's mate and gunner's mate helped me ashore. As I thanked them, the boatswain's mate said, "Sir, would you mind if we took a photograph together, since you are our idea of what a naval officer should be?" I was quite moved and felt that this was about the highest praise I could possibly receive. We shook hands and wished each other "anchors aweigh" and good sailing.

I stood for a few more moments looking at PCC-1178. I had come to view the boat with great affection, especially because it brought us safely approximately 6,500 miles across the mighty Pacific Ocean. I always had a love and respect for boats and the water, which had been greatly enhanced by this experience. It continues to this day.

A few weeks later my promotion to lieutenant (j.g.) came through. I was mustered out of the Navy in Washington, DC, and rode the train back home to Richmond. I took a taxi from the train station but asked the driver to drop me off a few blocks away from home. As I walked past Monument Avenue to Register Boulevard and Edmonstone Avenue and approached our house, my two bird dogs came running out from the yard to greet me. I had a wonderful reunion with my family, although my mother was greatly concerned at how darkly suntanned I was from the Pacific sun.

Years later, when my dermatologist found a small skin cancer on my face, he attributed it directly to those days on my PCC boat and the broiling Pacific sun. During that time, we sat bareheaded and unprotected, before the advent of sunscreen and with no knowledge of what the after-effects might be. In fact, it was often so hot on the steel-plated deck that our cook claimed he could fry eggs on it.

The war was over. I was home again, and I faced overwhelming uncertainty as to my future. Millions of veterans around the world must have felt the same way. My sister Lil urged me to go back to college and finish the two or three courses I needed for my degree, but I had no interest in doing that just yet. That could wait until later. For now, I needed something more.

I thought back to the nights when I was on early watch in the middle of the Pacific Ocean, anticipating the unknown. I had preferred the morning watch, from four to eight, when I could sit alone on the flying bridge and marvel at the vastness of the sea and sky. I would look out over the endless ocean and spot Polaris, the trusty North Star, to be sure we were heading on our proper course—north by northeast.

We are but a tiny speck in the universe, and the rhythm of nature overwhelms us. It is always on time. The sun, the Moon, the stars, the seas all interact as one. Thus it has been for trillions of years. What power put this all in place? Will this ever be taken away? Will the North Star always be there? Will the sun always come up in the eastern sky?

It has often been said that there are no atheists in foxholes during wartime, and I can attest to the fact that the same is true in the middle of the black, immense Pacific. Many nights I sat alone in the dark wondering if God would guide me as I decided what to do next with my life.

5

Falling in Love

"We'll Be There"
And when we make it, let me say,
The thing that I would really like to do
When the band begins to play
I want to have the first dance with you.

Without realizing it, I fell in love with Betty Wilkes the first time I met her. My father had urged me to come to Richmond for a weekend from Chapel Hill in 1944, to meet friends of his from New Jersey who were on their way to Florida. I didn't have a clue as to what this was all about, but there was a certain command in my father's voice, so I went. I dressed in my full naval cadet uniform. I had just turned 19 and wasn't prepared for the cute, enthusiastic 14-year-old who was being introduced to me by my father. In retrospect, it seems quite a miracle for a 19-year-old to say that he was smitten by a young girl of 14—but I was. Years later, both Betty and I were convinced that our families had planned the meeting. We can only thank them!

Betty stood smiling at me with her blonde hair, blue eyes, long sweater, and saddle shoes, a typical teenager. She was 14 going on 15, and most importantly, she was laughing at all my jokes. There was something about her that made me feel completely at home. I was so enjoying myself that at the end of the evening, I approached her father and asked if it would be alright if I drove Betty back to the Jefferson Hotel in downtown Richmond where they were staying. Bill Wilkes didn't answer but walked over to my father, and I could overhear my father saying, "I think it's fine. Blanton is a gentleman, and he'll certainly get her there before 10:00." I did just that.

It was in a sense a small moment, but Betty lingered in my mind. When I had returned home from the Pacific two years later, one of the first things I did was borrow my father's car and drive to Summit, New Jersey, to visit the Wilkes family in 1946. Since they were such good friends of my mother and father, I just called to say I was going to be in the area and I'd like to say hello. They invited me to dinner. I wanted to make a good impression, so I found a dry cleaners to have my only civilian suit cleaned and pressed. That was the first time I'd ever sat in a barrel in my underwear while that was taking place—it was also the last time!

Bill and Kay Wilkes welcomed me at the door and immediately wanted to know how my mother and father were. Betty was there with them—now a beautiful young woman. We said hi, and she introduced me to Peg and Ann, her two sisters, and then to Tom and Bill, her two young brothers, who carefully checked me out during the whole meal. Bill and Kay Wilkes went to Sarasota, Florida, every winter for his health and would take the boys with them. They had a chance to watch games and even meet some of the Boston Red Sox players at Payne Park. I think I made quite a few points when I told them the story of our University of North Carolina baseball team playing the Navy preflight team in Chapel Hill. They could hardly believe that the stars of the preflight team were the famous Ted Williams, Buddy Hassett, and Johnny Pesky of the Red Sox. They were all training to be fighter pilots. I said that every time Ted Williams came to bat, he hit a long drive into center field and walked to first base, where he pulled his hat down over his head and refused to go to second until there was a clean hit. The same was true of third base and home plate. I covered all of this and never mentioned that when the game was called for darkness, they were leading 17–1.

It was a good evening, and I had a growing feeling of affection for the family. I don't know if Bill or Kay knew my motives for dropping by. I hoped that every time Betty spoke to me directly or asked a question, they didn't recognize the flutter in my heart and the slight reddening of my face. There was definitely something there between us, but I wasn't ready to pursue that. At the moment, I had some mission to perform, but I was sure at the right time something more and something important was going to develop with this young woman.

When I said my goodbyes, Bill Wilkes said, "You know Blanton, we have a guest room and you're welcome to stay with us." Before I left Richmond, my father had advised me to get a room in a motel in Summit and not stay with the Wilkes family if they offered. Parents are so damned perceptive! I did telephone the next morning to thank Bill and Kay for a delightful dinner party; luckily, Betty answered the phone. I had a chance to tell her how much I had appreciated getting to know her family and that she was turning into a most beautiful young woman. She replied, "Thank you. Are you and your family going to be at Mackinac Island this summer for the conference? Perhaps we'll see each other again there." It was still just a friendship, but stay tuned.

6

Peacetime

"There's Gonna Be Another Day"
When we come to a river that's too wide,
We'll build a bridge to the other shore.
When we come to a wall that's too high
We'll build a door, yeah, we'll build a door.

My father always said to me, "Do what you can about the world, son. Service to people is the essence of life. It is an effective and satisfying way to live." He urged me to "search for ways to make the biggest possible contribution with your life in the world." I was developing my own personal conviction as to what would capture my complete attention and energy. It must be exciting as well as challenging. Architect and city planner Daniel H. Burnham's words really spoke to me: "Make no little plans. They have no magic to stir men's blood and probably themselves will not be realized. Make big plans. Aim high in hope and work."[1] I wanted to find the work that would stir my blood, and I wondered if the key to finding myself was to reach beyond myself.

As I tried to figure out what to do in my postwar life, the thought came to me: Why not go have a look at MRA when they have one of their big conferences on Mackinac Island? If my father, the inspiration of my life, felt that MRA had an exciting international program, perhaps I might find something for myself there.

I traveled to Mackinac with my family in August 1946, and I was excited by what I found. From Mackinac our family went on to Canada for a holiday, enjoying some wonderful canoeing and trout fishing, and a very happy time altogether. We headed home to Richmond, but by the time we reached Buffalo, I had the strong feeling that I wanted to return to Mackinac to take a more serious look at what was happening there. My father seemed sad that I was leaving the family again so soon after returning from the Navy, but he never put pressure on me—he was 100 percent supportive. The decision to go back to Mackinac would shape the rest of my life.

Most of all, I was impressed with the World War II veterans who were gathered there that summer: Bob Amen, who had been a major on Patton's Red Ball Highway; Alex Drysdale, who had flown P-38s in the Aleutians; Leland Holland, a decorated Army infantry man who fought through Germany; Jimmy Newton, who had come back from the Philippines as a major; and my future brother-in-law Bob Hogan, who had gone through Germany into Berlin with the Army. There were also some fascinating veterans from other parts of the world: Major Vernon Erickson, a tank commander from Canada, whose tank was the first through the Falaise Gap in France, a feat for which he was highly decorated; Wing Commander Ed Howell of the British Royal Air Force; and Dick and Dave Channer, brothers raised in India and both British Army captains, who became great friends of mine.

Like me, these veterans had participated in the military and now wanted to contribute in peacetime. They felt that MRA might offer a framework through which significant contributions could be made in rebuilding international relationships. There was a sense of mission akin to what we veterans had felt throughout our military experience. Now that the war was over, people were deeply concerned about how to build and sustain a lasting peace in the world.

So here we were, veterans who a year or so before had been fighting against fascism in Europe and imperialism in Japan, banding together with others to go back into these conquered lands. Not gloating about a victory but sincerely looking for a way to help Germany and Japan come back into the family of nations. For all it would be a wrenching experience, for they had lost close friends and family. I carried my own heartbreak over the death of my cousin and close friend Lieutenant Tommy Peters.

Great decisions had to be made. World War II was over but not the war of ideas, which if anything was intensifying. There was communism and capitalism. The Soviet Union and the United States both had atomic capabilities. Would the Western powers—especially the United States—throw their might and heart into rebuilding enemy lands or forever desert these countries?

Sadly, few people seem to remember today that the United States, a country made up of all races and nationalities, resolved to rebuild the countries it had helped to destroy during the war. Many people around the world have forgotten what our country did during those postwar years, when it could have gone a far different way. There were forces hard at work toward a different outcome. Providentially, there were leaders then who were compassionate visionaries and who looked beyond the hatred, cruelty, pain, and divisions of the war to a different future.

There was General Douglas MacArthur in the Pacific. He may have had his egotistical, arrogant side, but he made a full, painstaking effort to put Japan back on its feet and establish democratic principles in that country. There was a visionary, General George Marshall, who as US secretary of state after the war, conceived the Marshall Plan for the economic recovery of devastated Europe. Imagine where we would be today had President Harry Truman and Congress not rallied fully behind that plan. It was a shining moment in American history, when a conquering nation could conceive and implement such a strategy, devised to rebuild what we and our allies had destroyed. It was America at its best—a compassionate, nonjudgmental, forgiving country offering help wherever there was a need in the world.

I was excited by the challenge. In the early 1950s, I visited General Matthew Ridgway, who had been in charge of the 82nd Infantry Division and its transition to the 82nd Airborne Division during the war. He said to me, "War is not the answer. This war had to be fought, but for the future, we must find an alternative." I think many veterans came out of World War II feeling that way.

In the United States in 1947, MRA staff members wrote and produced a musical show called *The Good Road*. You might call it a musical tribute to the principles of democracy.

At the end of the North American tour the cast regrouped back at Mackinac, where a group of young Europeans from all over the continent arrived to join them. In October 1948, a decision was made to take *The Good Road* to West Germany. Before you could travel through postwar Germany, however, you had to get permission from the countries that now controlled the four sectors—the United States, of course, Britain, France, and the Soviet Union. General Lucius Clay was the military governor of occupied Germany. After visits by a task force in Germany, the general gave his endorsement and permission, which opened the door into Germany for this whole mission.

Along with a group of my fellow veterans and 100 young people representing 30 countries, I joined *The Good Road* mission to Europe with my sisters, Jane and Barbara in the fall of 1948. We traveled to Europe, spending six days at sea on the USS *Aquitania*, which had been a troop transport ship during the war. Also aboard that ship were beautiful Betty Wilkes and her sister Ann. Our paths had crossed in Richmond and at Mackinac, and now they were crossing again—not yet merging, although we were getting closer. Betty wrote to her parents that we stood side by side as we departed. Stay tuned!

So few people today experience the Atlantic crossing by ship. It is definitely the way to go, as your time clock, your stomach, and your body rhythms can slowly adjust to another continent. We landed in Cherbourg on the coast of France, where some of the young Americans just had to stretch their legs on land and toss a football around, much to the amusement of the French railroad conductors. Little did we know then how popular American football would become across Europe in the future. In Cherbourg we boarded the train for Switzerland, where we would go to Caux for a staging area at the MRA conference center there.

Performing the show in Europe was a step toward goodwill and reconciliation. It was a colorful, attractive, and dynamic production featuring 100 young people in national costumes, and it proclaimed dramatically the basic ideas of freedom and the necessary conditions of a sound society.

On the morning of October 9, 1948, a cavalcade of buses, vans, and private cars left Zurich for Munich. I was one of 260 mostly young people and veterans from 30 countries who traveled from Caux to Germany— the largest civilian "invasion" to enter Germany in the years just after the war. What a contrast we experienced, going to war-worn Germany from neutral, battle-free Switzerland where food was plentiful, coffee was rich and real; light, warmth, and peace was abundant. We were going from a country lush with prosperity to Germany, a battered and shattered nation with a broken population. The German youth had known nothing but Hitler and fascism their whole life.

When we left Zurich I took a window seat on the bus taking us to Germany. As we wove our way through the roads in the Alps and then through the Gotthard Pass, I spotted the concrete military "pill boxes" on the ridges guarding the entrance to Switzerland. They were still fully staffed with Swiss soldiers.

I had seen war-torn Manila and the Philippines, but nothing there had prepared me for the sight of devastated Germany. It was smashed, demolished. On our way to Munich we stopped in the ancient city of Ulm. Almost all of it lay in ruins—twisted steel and mountains of rubble. We stood in what was left of the historic cathedral there, surrounded by what remained of the city, where a mass of people lived in the ruins of houses. We were silent as we gazed up at the blue sky through the gaping hole in the cathedral's dome, where a 500-pound incendiary bomb had come crashing through during an Allied air raid. The bomb had not exploded or the beautiful stained glass windows would have shattered forever. Some of the people called it the Miracle of Ulm.

All of us were as apprehensive about this meeting of cultures as the Germans were, but the women of Ulm tried to make us feel welcome. Here was our first experience meeting with the German people. They had come cautiously to welcome this international group. You could see it in their body language. Young and old stood together in the center of the bombed-out cathedral. There was no eye-contact—they were almost hiding behind one another. They were broken and defeated.

How were we to break the ice with the German people? We hoped that music might help us solve that problem. Our group sang a song written in German especially for this mission. All of us were in the chorus, and we had learned to sing this song—how well I won't comment on, but we tried. We dedicated the song to the women of Ulm as a thank-you for serving us tea and homemade cookies and pastries. We could only imagine how many housewives had contributed their month's ration of sugar and flour to make this possible. They seemed to be touched by the fact that we were singing the song in German and letting them know that we had come to offer a hand of friendship in the rebuilding of their country.

Music did not break the ice, but it caused a fault line down the middle. This was the first time in ages that an international group had sung a song in German that wasn't propaganda. The people of Ulm seemed deeply moved. We were moved as well to see a glimmer of hope for the future appear on so many faces.

Music can certainly create an atmosphere and open a door, but it was those of us in *The Good Road* who had to prove to the cautious Germans that our motives were not suspect. Hitler had used music to advance his propaganda, so as the people listened to us that October day, they were carefully studying those of us who were singing, wondering: What motivates them to do this? Why are they here? They had been fooled too often not to be wary and cautious. It was our visible spirit and bright hope for the future that reached out and touched the German people. Against the bleak backdrop of ruined towns and cities in Germany, *The Good Road* was bright and colorful and spirited, with our young people bursting on the scene. It was light and joyful and hopeful. The performances electrified the German audiences.

There was a yearning in the hearts of the German people to connect and make friends with the outside world. We felt it first when we arrived in Ulm and then throughout Germany. Crowds stayed on after our performances. They were starved to talk and full of questions: Who are you? Where are you from? What is your city like? What do you do? What motivates you to do this? How did the war affect you? Do you think Germany will survive as a country?

The conversations in Ulm finally had to end because we were due in Munich before nightfall. Almost half of the houses in Munich had been destroyed during the war. Nevertheless, many of the members of our group were housed in private homes. There were hardly any hotels and very few extra bedrooms left anywhere in Germany. I remember vividly walking down a darkened Munich street—no street lights—kicking piles of leaves, trying to avoid the potholes in the road. I was cautiously looking for the house where I had been offered hospitality while we were in Munich. Luckily, I was billeted with a young Swiss man from Zurich who spoke German. He also, as a good Swiss, had a flashlight attached to his pocket knife. We found the house, and an elderly woman took us in. Her small, coal-burning stove was emitting warmth and brightness. I'm sure she was using her month's quota of coal to welcome us.

Our hostess did not speak English, but there are other ways to communicate. When we offered her packets of coffee, flour, and sugar she was utterly taken aback. She stood quite still, as if mentally devouring these gifts. Tears came to her eyes as she gave both of us a motherly embrace. We sat together quietly and watched the fire glow. She fed us cabbage soup and hard bread. I don't recall much of the conversation, but my Swiss friend did his best to interpret what she said. She had survived by living in her basement, making coffee from acorns, and scrounging for food. She stayed there night after night as the bombers came over the city. She never mentioned what had happened to her husband and family, and we did not ask.

She did ask why I, as a Navy veteran, had brought myself halfway around the world to visit a former enemy. Our new friend could hardly believe that there were so many American and Allied veterans who were committed to building peace now that the war was over.

The next morning we found her sitting in her tiny kitchen with a blanket around her shoulders, cupping her hands around a mug of coffee. She pointed to both of us and said, "Yours. *Danke schön.*" It was her first cup of real coffee in years.

The Good Road was a phenomenon. We performed to overflow crowds in Munich, Stuttgart, Frankfurt, Dusseldorf, and Essen. Our audiences were moved not just by the message of the music but by the bright, hopeful young participants from around the world who expressed faith in the future. Looking back, I don't think any of us—especially the war veterans in the group—were so naive as to think that music and song alone could heal the ancient hatred and divisions in Germany and the rest of Europe. It was the gesture, the effort of people from various countries reaching out in friendship with no hidden agenda, that might make some difference.

The trip certainly made an enormous difference to all of us who were part of it. The effort also brought home to us that we and the Allies might have won the war, but we certainly had not won the peace yet, though we were taking a step forward. "You have opened a new window on the world to us," some of the Germans said. "You have reached out a hand and welcomed us back into the international community. Your coming with such a group shows us that we are again accepted."

Our experience in Germany was intense, with 15 performances in 16 days. We had been able to move about the country with relative ease because of the *autobahns*, which were for the most part still intact. Hitler and the German government had done everything they could to protect these roads during the war so that their troops could move swiftly. General Eisenhower's positive impressions of the *autobahn* system led later to his concept for the interstate highway system in the United States.

We talked one night with a group of students, some of whom had been Hitler Youth (Hitler-Jugend). They wanted to know the difference between patriotism and nationalism. I can't recall exactly how we answered—something along the lines that patriotism means you love your country and are devoted to it, but you still respect other countries. Nationalism means you believe that your country and your culture are superior to all others, and that only you and your country and culture are right. If you believe your way is the only way, your perspective becomes exclusive and divisive.

Everywhere we went in Germany we lived with German families who had room to take in a foreign stranger or two. Families were bold to allow us to stay in what was left of their homes, yet nervous and frightened as to what the rest of the world might think of them. There were still no lights on the German streets, no bus service, very little heat, and hardly any telephone service. It was a blackened and fractured world. There was no way to measure the war's toll of human suffering and loss. This had a profound and lasting impact on me. "There has got to be some alternative to war," I thought. I was deeply, emotionally moved, not just by what I saw with my eyes but even more by what I learned through halting conversations with German families.

Here we were in a Germany that had been completely destroyed, and there was a very divided Eastern and Western Europe.

In the fall, the German countryside was beautiful. That Thanksgiving some of our group were invited by the US military to have dinner with the troops at their military base in Frankfurt. I met a colonel who invited a few of us to have the honor to fly on one of the planes into Berlin with the airlift which was part of the Marshall Plan. It was scary to be flying into the heart of Berlin, in the Soviet Zone, at that time, but we went anyway and delivered a load of food and returned the same night. Then we moved on to the Ruhr, where concerned Dutch citizens had floated a boat down the Rhine so we could have a place to live and sleep, take hot showers, and eat hot meals.

As I traveled with my colleagues through Germany, for the first time in my life, at the age of 23, I witnessed the potential power of a large group of people who were united in a common goal and mission. They grabbed attention and effectively used that power. Power can be used for good or for evil, depending on the goal, and our goal was to build a lasting peace. I realized that it is not so much what you say that moves people but rather who you are and what you stand for. Your inward passion communicates regardless of language. I also learned that because each country is unique, and each citizen of each nation is unique, comparisons are odious. As we sang and talked and traveled our way through Germany, we hoped that we were helping to establish a "good road" step by step, person by person.

7

Citizens' Diplomacy in India

"Room For Everyone"
Sometime soon the time must come
When there'll be room for ev'ryone

How does a Southern boy with a Christian background and a Protestant upbringing learn to communicate in a Hindu/Muslim world? I was about to find out. In 1952, I had the opportunity to explore a part of the world I had never seen before. Frank Buchman invited me and a large and diverse international group of people to accompany him to Ceylon and India.

Traveling with us was a group of young British men, including Vere James, Hugh Nowell, and Dick and Dave Channer, whose father had commanded a Gurkha regiment on the frontier of India. The journalist Peter Howard, formerly a political columnist for Lord Beaverbrook's newspaper the London *Daily Express*, was also part of this group. He was becoming Dr. Buchman's right-hand man. I traveled to London to help in preparations for this trip. Some of us were housed with an Anglican minister and his wife in the Soho area of London. It was bitter cold and foggy, and we gratefully warmed our hands on the omnipresent steaming hot cups of tea we were served. We also received the required immunizations for travel in India. By mistake, the doctor injected a double dose of yellow fever vaccine in my arm, which made me violently ill for several days.

I had recovered by the time we flew from London to Beirut to Karachi, Pakistan, and then to Ceylon. In Ceylon, I was housed with an Anglican bishop in a large rectory situated along a lazily flowing canal brimming with strange creatures. My ground-floor room with its barred windows overlooked the canal, and tired as I was, the strange sounds emanating from the canal kept me awake. I was in South Asia, in the land of tigers and crocodiles. I lay there fitfully, imagining what creatures might slither out of that canal, creep through the bars, and descend on my bed, despite the mosquito netting. In the middle of the night a firefly flickered across my room, but suddenly a rush of wings, which had to be a bat, grabbed the firefly right out of the air. Hot as I was, I pulled the sheets up over my head, recalling the terror of the bats nested in my Aunt Frazile's hair in South Carolina so many years ago!

We took one musical production called *Jotham Valley* and a drama called *The Forgotten Factor* to South Asia. It was a huge job to transport and house all the people, scenery, equipment, and props needed to produce these shows, and some of the sets were to be built once we arrived in India. Many of the people were housed with local host families. I was most involved with the country western musical called *Jotham Valley*. It tells the story of two brothers in the American West in conflict over water rights, a subject that would resonate with India. Throngs of people lined up to see the show. Sometimes we had to put on extra performances because so many people wanted to attend.

From the small island country of Ceylon, we went by boat to Bombay, India (now Mumbai)—an almost shocking transition from a small country to a land of more than 375 million people.

The Indians seemed eager to have us, constantly going out of their way to make us feel part of their families. After Bombay, we traveled to New Delhi.

Dr. Buchman met Pandit Jawaharlal Nehru in 1926. In 1947, he became the first prime minister of independent India. Pandit Nehru, as well as other political and social leaders, extended the official invitation to MRA to travel in India. Nehru loaned Dr. Buchman Jaipur House, the former residence of the Maharaja of Jaipur in New Delhi, as a central meeting place during the trip.

One of the memorable occasions was when Prime Minister Nehru came for tea with Dr. Buchman. Vere and I were flattered to be asked to meet him outside and open the doors of his official limousine. We welcomed Prime Minister Nehru and ushered him inside. Dr. Buchman could not walk easily so he received him in the drawing room along with a party of 20 guests. Nehru was impressive. He was dressed in his starched *achkan* with a red rose in the lapel. He was slight, of medium height but radiated power. Dr. Buchman had met him years before when Mahatma Gandhi and Nehru were working together on India's independence. Before he left, Buchman introduced him to each of those present, and Nehru went around the circle of friends, speaking to each. When Vere and I were introduced we told him how much we appreciated the hospitality of the Indian people. He seemed to be most interested.

In New Delhi, Vere and I were housed in a large flat with a member of Parliament, Shri N. Keshava, known to us as Keshavaiengar, his wife, and their teenage son. The winds that came out of Siberia and whistled through New Delhi at night were bone-chilling, and to counter this, Vere and I padded the springs on our beds with the *Hindustan Times* and the *Times of India*. Never had the Indian newspapers performed a more important function! I shall always remember and pay tribute to what those papers did to provide warmth. Our hostess made terrific curries, including some that were red hot. Vere, who had a weak stomach, miraculously produced some color-coded pills with no medicinal value whatsoever. He placed these on the table whenever curry was served, saying how sorry he was but that his doctor had prescribed antibiotics and he was not allowed to eat spicy food. He pulled off this complete fabrication very well, so extra-large servings of curry appeared on my plate.

The stay with our host family was a two-way street in intercultural communication and understanding: they studied and observed us as carefully as we did them. We were their first foreign guests. The man of the house was definitely the head of the family, the boss, but the shy wife was the strength of the family. As she warmed up to us, she asked about our families and about life in the United States and England. We shared pictures and answered and asked many questions about families, schooling, politics, and cultural life.

Vere and I were awakened on our first morning by strange noises emanating from the next room. After several days of this, we learned that a group of members of Parliament met there each morning for yoga. We were invited to join, which we did, much to the amazement and amusement of all the MPs. Since they spoke fluent English, there was much give and take and the opportunity to get to know these men, who represented districts throughout India.

One morning at breakfast, our host asked us if we would like to meet Dr. Rajendra Prasad, the first president of the Republic of India. We were excited and honored and went straight away to tell Frank Buchman and Peter Howard about the invitation. A few days later, Vere and I joined them on a visit to the presidential palace in New Delhi. Our host launched right in, telling the president that we were the young American and young Englishman who were living with his family. Dr. Buchman spoke to the president about his association with Mahatma Gandhi and Prime Minister Nehru. Peter Howard directed Vere and me to be sure that members of the Parliament received tickets to see *Jotham Valley* if they wished. The show was free, but a ticket was required for admission. Our host, Keshavaiengar, provided a room for us in the House of the People, or Lok Sabha as it was called, to distribute the tickets. Immediately, we had lines of people outside the doors and down the hall. Later we learned that quite a few were selling the tickets to friends and others.

During the Christmas season in New Delhi, there were several large dinner parties at Jaipur House for our hosts and friends that we had met. We thought of our own homes so far away. On reflection, perhaps the palm trees and the desert character of India were more reminiscent of the first Christmas than our distant snow and mistletoe.

At one of the parties I met a charming English couple who, when they found out I liked shooting, invited me for a hunt. They offered to pick me up and provide a gun for my use. When I mentioned that I had no proper shooting clothes, my host said, "Wear that western outfit we saw you wear in *Jotham Valley*." So several days later, at six in the morning, there I stood on a street corner in New Delhi in my cowboy outfit and Stetson hat, waiting for my new friends. As we sped through the countryside, I could see large cultivated fields of sugarcane, corn, wheat, and barley. The Indian gamekeeper at our destination was a small, sinewy man with a toothless grin and twinkling eyes. He was quite taken with my cowboy gear and tried on my Stetson, which came down over his ears. He handed me a side-by-side English double-barrel gun and a handful of 12-gauge cartridges.

As we circled a sugarcane field, the gamekeeper carried on an animated conversation in Hindi. Translated, he was warning us that a tiger had been spotted by villagers nearby, and we needed to keep a keen lookout. I expected to see a Bengal tiger burst out of the sugarcane headed directly toward me. I had no idea what I was supposed to do with a tiger and a shotgun loaded with bird shot but decided it was just one of the hazards you lived with in India. We encountered no tigers that day, only gray partridges that would be delicacies for the table.

The Indian government provided our group with a special train for our journey through the vast country. Captains Dick and Dave Channer were in charge of this expedition. While each compartment of the train opened to the tracks, there was no passageway from compartment to compartment. There were four to six people in each compartment in our part of the train, and we slept on hard bunks, one above the other. Everyone was given a meal ticket. There were three sittings for dinner, and the train stopped briefly for each one. Those in the dining car would disembark and head back to their compartments, while the next sitting clambered aboard the dining car. The Channers and I had been reading James Corbett's *Man-Eaters of Kumaon*, and we quietly passed the word that we were in tiger country so beware! As I recall, this was a complete fabrication, but it did accelerate the pace of people getting on and off the dining car—especially late in the evening when we were stopping in forests or fields.

There was a bath in the first-class carriages but no showers or baths on our part of the train. After days in this grungy state, we stopped in Hyderabad, where I befriended a colonel in the Indian Army and reported our predicament. He immediately offered the military barracks for our use. It was a comical sight late the next morning to see the men and women of our group lined up gratefully on the train station platform waiting for the military trucks. It was noon, the Indian sun was blazing down, and there stood Betty Wilkes just aside from a group. She was wearing a cotton dress and a large straw hat. The sun shining through the straw illuminated her face. Our eyes met as I walked by, and I simply stopped in my tracks. For the moment, we were the only two people in the world. My heart was pounding, and I felt my face flush with an electric current. It was at that moment that I decided I would ask Betty to marry me. There was a strange voice somewhere in the distance yelling in my ear, "Hey mate, where the hell are you? You're in charge of this group." It was Vere, and he was shaking me back to reality. Then, all the men and women were loaded onto the military trucks for their showers, the women going one direction and the men going the other. Refreshed, we boarded the train again and headed south through the countryside.

In the great southern city of Madras (now Chennai), the home of the Indian movie industry, I was given a car and driver to deliver show tickets to people in a residential neighborhood. At one stop a woman in a beautiful sari greeted me cordially in Indian fashion, as if I were expected. I showed her my envelope of tickets and tried to find out where I was, but she did not speak English. She immediately ushered me over to a dignified gentleman who took me in tow and escorted me into the wedding of his niece. He did not seem to be disturbed that I had come into the wrong place. Instead, he seemed delighted that a young American had stumbled onto the scene of the festivities. Soon I was garlanded with flowers and given the traditional Indian *tikka* on my forehead. My host turned out to be a movie producer, and this turned out to be the first day of a three-day wedding celebration. I felt it would be rude to hurry away, so despite the driver and the car waiting for me, I spent several delightful hours meeting various and sundry personalities. It was a swirl of magnificent saris and elegantly dressed men, being feted with delicious hors d'oeuvres.

Finally, when there was a pause in the celebration, I expressed my thanks and told my newfound friend that I must leave. He agreed only after I gave my assurance that I would return the next day at an appointed hour, which

I did. When my host read in the Madras newspaper about the visit of our international group and learned that homes were still needed for some of us, he invited me to come and bring a friend to stay in his guesthouse. In fact, he insisted. The next day, I moved into the beautiful guesthouse with Brian Boobyer from England, a famous Oxford University rugby player of his day. The guesthouse had many servants, and we were quartered on the second floor.

Our host apparently thought it would please Western guests if he installed a Western-style toilet, which he did. Perhaps since the toilet had a seat, he felt it should have a view of the beautiful garden. Therefore, he had his plumber place it on the big balcony overlooking the garden and the street. Brian seemed to relish using it and waving to passersby below. I made the excuse that it would be rude if one of us didn't use the traditional Indian bathroom, which I proceeded to do.

Brian and I were treated as royal guests. Each evening we had a bath, donned the freshly laundered cotton *kurta pajama* the maids had prepared, and joined our host for dinner. A Madrasi curry is something to dream about. The further south in India you go, the hotter the curry. We ate on banana leaves in the traditional Indian way. After each course the leaves were replaced with fresh ones, and we washed our hands in the wash basins in the corner of the room, preparing for the next course of the feast. Very quickly you become part of the Indian culture. We were literally taken into the heart of our host family's home.

From Madras we went north to Calcutta (now Kolkata). In the great train station in Calcutta we came face to face with the immense poverty in the land. There must have been 10,000 people sleeping in the train station, with little or no sanitation, little or no water, each family sharing four square feet of floor space and cooking over small charcoal fires. It was in this setting with these people that the saintly Mother Teresa moved and toiled.

After nearly seven months spent traveling the length and breadth of India, living on a vegetarian diet (I never felt better), moving in all kinds of conditions, and enduring the heat and confusion of the land, Frank Buchman decided to take a break in Kashmir. Vere and I had befriended a young Indian businessman, Brij Thapar. When he heard that we were going to Kashmir, he offered us his family's summer house in Srinagar.

It was an exciting drive from Lucknow, in the state of Uttar Pradesh, over the Banihal Pass into the Vale of Kashmir. The drive up and over the pass was both spectacular and hair-raising. At one point our Sikh driver came to an abrupt stop as we rounded a narrow bend. As we looked ahead, it seemed as if the road had disappeared. A recent landslide from the mountain had covered the road and dropped it into an 8,000-foot abyss. We all got out of the van thinking that the driver was not going to pass this dangerous part of the road.

Our driver herded us back into the van. We thought he might be turning around, but with a screech of tires on the gravel road, we hurtled forward at full speed over the landslide, sometimes at a precarious 30-degree angle. Miraculously, we landed on the other side. Just as the sun was setting and we were nearing the summit, he swerved again as a large Russian bear ambled across the road. Finally, we drove through the pass and down the winding switchback into the Vale of Kashmir. Even at dusk we could see the valley floor below, with endless miles of flowering fruit trees, truck gardens, lakes, and rushing mountain streams. Betty says that it was one of the most gorgeous memories of her life. It was indeed a paradise after the dust, poverty, and heat of urban India. It was still—and remains—a disputed land between the Muslims of Pakistan and the Hindus of India.

The guesthouse turned out to be beautiful, located on a mountainside overlooking the valley. The weather was wonderful, and we had free days to rest, bike, and play golf. I even went on a fishing trip. A large contingent of United Nations observers were billeted in Kashmir not far from where we were staying, and I went over and introduced myself. A Canadian major and I struck up a friendship with mutual interests, and one day he invited me to join him for some trout fishing. He furnished a fly rod and tackle, and we set off into the backcountry with his driver in a UN jeep. In about an hour we reached a magnificent fast-flowing stream, cascading on long runs, and ending in beautiful large pools. Years earlier, during colonial times, the British had arranged to transport rainbow trout by pack animals over the rugged mountain passes and planted them in the rivers and lakes of Kashmir. The fish adapted beautifully in the new environment and grew to great size.

As I fly-fished down the river, my thoughts were on nothing more than the next trout in the next pool. I was completely at home in my own world and having good luck fishing. Suddenly the major hurried my way with a message that his headquarters had just called him on his portable radio to say they needed me as soon as possible back in Srinagar. Sheik Muhammad Abdullah, the "Lion of Kashmir," would be attending a special performance that afternoon of *Jotham Valley*. The UN driver rushed me back just in time for me to put on my Western outfit for the performance.

One day a letter reached me from my mother—it had been following me around for the past two weeks, and the news was not good. My father was unwell, and my mother was wondering whether I would consider coming home to be with him. She even said, "I can't think of anything that would give him a bigger boost than for you to walk in the room!" When I told Dr. Buchman about it he immediately replied, "You must go, and you can go by way of London and take some of my wardrobe and my walking cane for the coronation. Tell Oliver I want him to accompany you as far as London." Oliver Corderoy was a delightful personality, a World War II veteran and one of the people who was committed to helping Dr. Buchman operate with his limited energy following a series of health problems.

It was bittersweet to say goodbye to everyone, not knowing when we would meet again. We had traveled together through the length and breadth of Ceylon and India. We had not only survived but come out better people. Our international group had made permanent friendships that might encourage India in the future to reach out and be part of the global village. Whatever effect we may have had on India, India had had a tremendous and lasting effect on all of us.

I found myself transplanted to an immense, totally different culture. Looking back on the seven months I spent in India, my most vivid recollections are of my host families who opened their homes to me and the new friends I made throughout our travels there. These memories stand out even after 67 years. For me, India will always be the people. In the end, it is the people, not the places, that remain forever in your memory.

In London, I bade farewell to Oliver and flew across the Atlantic to New York and then Richmond on May 4, 1953. My three sisters knew of my decision to return but neither my mother nor my father were aware. It was late afternoon when I opened the front door and walked into the sitting room where my father was reclining in a chair. When I said, "Hi Dad," he looked startled and shaking his head, he got to his feet. With tears in his eyes said, "Welcome home, son I can't believe it's you." We were both a bit overcome and before our bear hugs were over, my mother appeared at the door. I turned around and gave her a big hug and a kiss. She said, "It's really you and you've come all the way from India and my prayers have been answered. Your sisters assured me you would come."

Some years later, I heard that President John F. Kennedy asked Prime Minister Jawaharlal Nehru what his thoughts were about the Peace Corps. Prime Minister Nehru implied that the Peace Corps recruits would learn a lot from their time in India. We certainly had!

How little did I realize at the time what a great part India would play in our lives. That encounter eventually led to my marriage to Betty. Years later, our older daughter, Jenny, married Ajay Gupta, a young engineer from India. Ajay and Jenny and their two daughters, Chameli (jasmine in Hindi) and Surina (goddess in Sanskrit), connect us forever to that great land.

8

Our Marriage

"Tomorrow's A Picture"
I want to keep painting with you.

It was September 29, 1954, and the MRA conference being held at Mackinac Island's Grand Hotel was just ending. I made arrangements with friends to tell Betty that I wanted to have a short chat with her in the living room of one of the hotel's suites. I went early to prepare myself.

My friend Eric Millar found Betty and asked her to come meet me in the living room. She later told me that she was a little nervous but hopeful that this might be a proposal. I was alone. I stood up when Betty came in and suggested she sit on the couch. I thought I'd better get right to it before I lost my nerve.

"Betty, I have been in love with you for years. And I'm asking you to marry me." There was dead silence. She appeared nervous, and I was getting more so.

She nodded slightly. "Blanton, you know I'm not an outdoor girl. I know nothing about hunting and fishing," she said.

"That's not what I asked you! Will you marry me?!"

"Oh, that! Yes!" she said nodding her head firmly.

I was greatly relieved and had an instant premonition that my life had just been made whole. I had no doubt this was the beginning of a tremendous adventure for both of us.

I pinned a beautiful corsage on her, and hand-in-hand we walked downstairs to find her parents to give them the great news.

Betty knocked on their door, and her mother answered. "Guess what,

Mom!" she said, "We've just gotten engaged!"

Her mother had no doubt about Betty's feelings for me, so a smile spread quickly across her face and her happiness was evident. In the back bedroom, Betty's father had heard us and came out to congratulate us and quickly went back into the room to take a nitroglycerin pill for his heart. We told Betty's parents that we wanted to be married in December at their church in Summit, New Jersey. Having just two months to organize a formal wedding was a daunting task, but they agreed. Betty said that she would go home with them right away to start the preparations.

Betty and I together called my parents in Richmond to tell them. They were delighted, and when I asked Dad if he would marry us, he of course agreed. We learned later that when my mother informed my three sisters, the word came back, "Thank God, he's finally asked her. It's about time!"

The next morning, Frank Buchman took it upon himself to introduce us at the general assembly meeting. He said, "Blanton finally found the courage to ask Betty to marry him!" That brought forth a standing ovation as we made our way to the podium. Afterward, many of our friends came forward with congratulations. Vere James was one of the first who said, "We never thought you would get around to it—my congratulations, mate!" That was a universal feeling, but it made no difference to us since we were now engaged and on our way. Charles "Charlie" P. Howard—a civil rights activist I had recently met in Chicago and who would become a big influence on my life—gave Betty a big hug and said, "What a beautiful pair you make." He added, "Somebody needs to look after Blanton. I'm most happy it's you Betty!"

We had two days of bliss before Betty left with her parents to prepare for the wedding in Summit. Frank Buchman had said to me after the morning session, "Now just disappear and enjoy yourselves." And we did just that.

An island like Mackinac is not an easy place in which to disappear. Being a woodsman, however, I found places along the lake and in the forest where we could talk and share our dreams for the future. We were at complete peace and filled with shared happiness. Those two days whizzed by all too quickly, and there I was standing on the dock waving goodbye to Betty and her parents as they sailed away for the mainland. My heart went with them!

Then reality hit. Betty was on her way to Summit for the next two months, the conference was ending, and my new friend Charlie Howard was preparing to return to Chicago—what in the world would I do next? I was soon to find out! I found Charlie waiting for me in the dining room where we had talked so much during the last weeks. It almost seemed like a second home. Charlie started right in by saying, "I've been thinking about your desire to get involved in the civil rights struggle. Why don't we have a go at it together? You've been saying that character is as important as color. Perhaps two such characters as you and me moving together as friends might be the only message we need." He turned to me with a grin and asked, "What do you think?" I replied, "That turns my crank, I fully agree—let's give it a go." Charlie then added, "It could be payback time for both of us." I left Mackinac with Charlie by car, and we went on to Chicago and continued to New York City, beginning what would be several years of traveling together, talking about and working on civil rights.

The whirlwind of preparations for the wedding proceeded, and it all came together. Betty invited my three sisters, Lillian, Jane, and Barbara, to be three of her bridesmaids. Betty's older sister, Ann, was her maid of honor. However, Betty's younger sister, Peg, had to miss the occasion because she and her husband, Maury Clark, were living in Japan where he was on duty with the US Navy.

The wedding day, December 11, approached, and plans seemed to be going well. Betty's father had driven her and her mother into New York City to Best and Company, a department store, and said, "Betty, you have exactly 90 minutes to find a dress." And she did.

Two hundred guests were invited. The Central Presbyterian Church in Summit never looked more beautiful. We had invited the international MRA chorus to provide the music, and their rendition of the Hallelujah Chorus from Handel's *Messiah* was a great finale for our wedding ceremony. My father conducted the service and did so with spirit and grace.

At one point during the wedding ceremony, Betty said to me, "Stop sighing!" I was just doing some breathing, which in itself was making me dizzy. But I got through it all without fainting.

The entire wedding service, I am told, was beautiful, but to Betty and me it was all a blur. Before we knew it, we were Mr. and Mrs. Blanton Belk Jr. and headed to the reception, which was in the Short Hills Country Club in a nearby town.

Unfortunately, there was a small blip on the screen. It started to snow and there was a long line on the sidewalk waiting to get into the receiving line to greet the wedding couple. Brian Boobyer, one of my ushers, took it upon himself to clap his hands to get everyone's attention. He announced that the whole line was to follow him through a back door to the dining hall. There, they were seated and missed completely the opportunity to see Betty and myself. Years afterward different relatives commented, "Who was the Englishman that kept us from congratulating you on your wedding day?"

Betty and I were seated at the head table, flanked by Dr. Buchman and Prince Richard of Hesse-Kassel, who had become a close personal friend. There were a number of speeches by the guests. Charlie Howard asked if he could say a word. In his commanding voice he said, "Blanton and I have been traveling together, and he's become a close friend. In fact, I want to say he is the first white Southern man I've ever met who is not a chauvinist."

I spoke at the end of the reception but for me, it was one of the very few times in my life that I had no idea what I said. After the reception, we went upstairs to change into our travel clothes. We came down the stairs to the usual rain of rice and jumped into the back seat of our new car. Our friends all snickered as we sat there for a few seconds before we realized one of us had to get in the front seat and drive to the Princeton Inn.

Betty insisted she wanted a beach honeymoon, but it was December and we couldn't afford Hawaii. My Aunt Punch offered her house in Myrtle Beach, South Carolina, so off we went. I had been telling Betty since the day we were engaged that the Belks owned the South. It was confirmed when we crossed the Mason-Dixon Line into Virginia and to her amazement the first sign we saw said "Belk's." Of course, it was referring to the Belk's Department Stores (owned by some of my cousins), which were spread across the South, but Betty was impressed.

Hurricane Hazel had hit two months before, and unfortunately the house next door had been split in half by the storm. The moisture from the storm had filled Aunt Punch's house with mold, which set off Betty's allergies. So we moved to a motel near the beach with a great view of the Atlantic Ocean. We could watch its mighty waves curling and breaking on the beach and swirling back again when the tide went out. There was a wonderful seafood restaurant next door. The oysters on the half-shell followed by red snapper or grouper fillets were worth writing home about, and of course Betty loved the periwinkle soup with fresh Florida key lime. When the manager learned that we were on our honeymoon, he gave us a private corner table with orders to his waiters not to bother us unless we called. We didn't talk a lot but often sat together completely enjoying each other's company. Sometimes we laughed a lot reliving the first moment we met in Richmond. Both of us felt that it was the magical moment when we fell in love without realizing it at the time. Clearly, the lightning strike that had stopped me in my tracks on the station platform in Hyderabad was a wakeup call. I decided at that moment that I would ask Betty to marry me while we were in Kashmir. Unfortunately, that had to be put aside when I had to leave India suddenly. Now here we were, Mr. and Mrs. Belk, so we drank a toast to the wisdom of our parents who first brought us together!

Sharing our deepest thoughts, we both felt working with Charlie might fulfill the promise I had made to myself after my grandfather's funeral. Here was the opportunity, and I would give it our best.

These possibilities excited us as we drove north to spend a few more days with Dad and Mother and my sisters for Christmas and New Year's in Richmond. We had promised to join Charlie early in the new year in Nashville, Tennessee.

9

Charles Preston Howard

"We Shall Overcome"
Oh deep in my heart I do believe, we shall overcome some day.[1]

In the mid-1950s, with the civil rights struggle exploding across America, my grandfather's message was ringing in my ears: "Do something about the evil in our land." In early spring 1954, a friend had invited me to meet Charles P. Howard in Chicago. It was as if we were meant to meet at this time. Charlie was a journalist and had been a first lieutenant in the US Army in World War I. He was born in South Carolina and currently was living in New York City. He had received his law degree from Drake University in Iowa, and in 1925 he cofounded the National Negro Bar Association. By 1954, he had already paid his dues in the civil rights struggle.

We hit it off and talked long into the afternoon, sitting in a restaurant beneath the "L" train in Chicago on a spring day. He shared with me how, as a newly commissioned officer he took his bride, Maude, on a honeymoon train trip in October 1917. They went from Des Moines, Iowa, to Columbia, South Carolina. There he stood in his full military uniform yet they were prevented from entering the dining car. The conductor said to him, "Blacks are not allowed." He was furious but stood his ground, saying, "I'm an officer in the US Army. I just married my childhood sweetheart, and I'm being blocked from our honeymoon dinner together." They called for the military police and had him and Maude escorted back to their seats without any food. All I could say was how sorry I was to hear about such treatment.

Charlie turned to me, wanting to know what had prompted me as a white Southerner to want to get involved in the civil rights struggle. I told him about the epiphany I had experienced at my grandfather's funeral. He listened intently, nodding and saying at the end, "I understand, I understand!"

At this point I told Charlie I was on my way to an MRA conference at Mackinac Island, Michigan. I asked, "Why don't you join us there and have a look?" Several weeks later I had word from Charlie that he would accept my invitation and to please send him the facts and dates. In late September he came and was impressed with the international gathering. He kept saying to me, "There's something special here, everyone seems to be getting along and enjoying each other."

We had long lunches together and the more we talked, the more we seemed to have a lot in common. Charlie spoke often about his three sons who had all graduated from college and were active in the civil rights struggle. He shared with me his frustration with the snail's pace of civil rights legislation, which had eventually driven him to move for a time to the Soviet Union. That had been disappointing to him because he found there the same prejudices he lived with in America. Charlie had also delivered the keynote address at the Progressive Party convention when Henry Wallace ran for president in 1948.

Since Charlie had been born in South Carolina, he was curious about the time I had spent on my grandfather's cotton plantations in St. Matthews and my long friendship with James, with whom I went hunting and fishing. Charlie was impressed that my Presbyterian minister father, after a considerable battle, had led the way for the Richmond Ministerial Association to invite the first Black ministers to join and it became a friendly, workable association.

After seeing Betty off to prepare for the wedding, I needed to make my plans. Charlie and I latched on to the idea of traveling together, two Southerners, two former military officers, one white, one Black, spreading our message that character mattered more than color. His first thought was that we should begin our adventure in Chicago. He said to me as we drove south from Michigan, "You've been introducing me to your friends mostly in the white world. Now, I want you to meet my friends in the Black world.

Because if you want to improve the racial situation, it's important that you understand our world, and I'll do my best to introduce you."

In Chicago, he took me to meet the great Jesse Owens, a man who had won four Olympic gold medals in front of Adolf Hitler in the 1936 Olympics in Berlin. When Charlie introduced me as his new friend from Virginia, I could feel my knuckles crack from Jesse's handshake. Jesse remarked, "Charlie, I think it's the first time I've seen you moving around with a white Southerner." Charlie paid great tribute to what Jesse had done as a role model for youth everywhere. Jesse said to me when we parted, "I know that you are involved in race relations but if you ever get involved with young people, let me know. That's where my heart is." I never forgot that, and when we started Up with People I remembered his offer.

Next, we drove to Dellwood, an MRA center in Mount Kisco, a suburb of New York City. Charlie and I were each given a room and welcomed to come to meals when we were there. Two of the other guests were delegates from the conference at Mackinac, both from South Africa, one Black, one white. When they heard we were there, we had an invitation to dine with them that evening. Of course, Charlie invited them to accompany us on a tour of Harlem the next day. That was an experience. We had breakfast together and took off in my car guided by Charlie. He was in his element as we walked the streets of Harlem, stopping in stores, saying hello, and introducing us to people he knew.

Charlie was full of life showing us the sites when suddenly he said, pointing across the street, "Good Lord, there's my old friend Paul Robeson. I thought he was out of the country. Come on, I want you to meet him." Robeson, the famous singer, actor, and activist, had a group around him but when he spotted Charlie, he broke free and came right over. They gave each other hugs. Then Paul said to Charlie with quite a twinkle in his eye, "Do these guys know what you are up to, Charlie?" That led to a humorous introduction focusing first on me as a white Southerner. Charlie said, "Blanton here comes from an old Southern family." Paul said, "I have just got to believe you, Charlie, but who are these other men?" Charlie introduced the two South Africans: Dr. William Nkomo, who was well known as a pioneer in the anti-apartheid movement, and George Daneel, an Afrikaner who had been captain of the famous South African Union rugby team called the Springboks. Paul jumped on that saying, "My God, we have something in common. I played a little football myself at Rutgers University. I must pay tribute to you." Paul had graduated from Rutgers Phi Beta Kappa and valedictorian of his class. He was one of the first Blacks selected as an All-American football player and also graduated from Columbia Law School. Right away he started singing on the street corner as all of Harlem seemed to go quiet, his bass baritone echoing between the buildings: "There's the Amsterdam Dutch and the Rotterdam Dutch, / The other dam Dutch and the goddamn Dutch!"[2] and all the other verses of that old drinking song. George loved it. When we said our goodbyes, Paul said to Charlie, "You two men keep this going—there's far too little of it in our country today."

That evening, we had a delightful dinner party together with much laughter as we relived our day in Harlem. Except for Charlie it was a first for all of us, and we thanked him for taking us. He looked around the table with a big smile and said, "It was worth all the effort just to see the look on George's face when Paul started singing the drinking song! It was great fun to be with you today. I've been thinking to myself, here we are white and Black from the USA and the Republic of South Africa enjoying each other, let's hope it's a good omen for the future."

Two nights later Charlie acquired tickets for me and a friend, a young newspaper man from Australia who had represented his newspaper at the recent conference at Mackinac. We attended a Cab Calloway show at the Cotton Club in Harlem. Charlie was whisked away by some of his friends but not before he escorted us into the club and properly seated us at a table. My friend said to me on the way home, "There were definitely two shows there tonight. The first was certainly the artistry of entertainer Cab Calloway but the other was the enthusiastic response of the audience. The whole audience was caught up and for a minute, I thought I was going to be jerked up to join the dancing. I hope I've caught both in the article I'm dispatching to my paper in Melbourne."

Charlie announced the next morning at breakfast that he'd been working on dates for us in Philadelphia, Pennsylvania, and Washington, DC, and we should drive south the next morning. We had use of Jack and Connie Ely's home at 2419 Massachusetts Avenue in Washington, affectionately known as "2419," and we would be welcomed there. We could easily make our noonday speaking engagement at the Pyramid Club in Philadelphia and then go on to Washington. I was nervous when we arrived in Philadelphia since I was the only white man in an exclusive Black club. For a few minutes I realized what Black people felt like living in a predominantly white society. However, quickly I felt completely at home with the warmth and welcome I received, due in no small part to the way Charlie introduced me. The folks there went completely silent when I shared my epiphany story about my grandfather's funeral. Charlie then spoke, underlining his commitment to civil rights, adding how impressed he was with Martin Luther King Jr.'s effort to bring it about through nonviolence. Originally Charlie had been very cautious about this approach until he had seen it at work and became convinced it was the right way to go. When the president of the club thanked us, he said, "It's not just what you two men said, it is what you two men represent in friendship and trust that speaks to us louder than your words! We thank you for coming and assure you that we are with you in this mission." Charlie said to me as we drove away, "You are the first white Southerner, Blanton, that I've wanted to introduce to my world."

Our goal over the next several months was to reach out and see if we could make an impact in the historically Black colleges and universities since Charlie knew many of their presidents. With this in mind, after our wedding and honeymoon, Betty and I made a date to meet Charlie in Nashville to begin. We started our visits with Fisk University and Tennessee A&I University. We were speaking and meeting students and exchanging ideas on the relationship between the races. We continued on to Morris Brown College, Morehouse College, the women's college Spelman in Atlanta, and finally went to Tuskegee Institute in Alabama from which Charlie had graduated.

He was so excited to take us there and spoke with such respect of his friend and mentor who had been president when Charlie attended, Dr. Booker T. Washington. We were enthusiastically received, and they certainly went out of their way to welcome Charlie. We were put up in a very nice guest residence. The next morning the president of the university gathered students and faculty for us to speak to them informally. We had a very spirited back-and-forth discussion, and it was obvious that the professors and students were studying us as well as what we were saying. At one point, one of the students said to Charlie, "I like your concepts but how would I ever go about meeting a white student my age and try to make a friend?" Charlie answered carefully, saying in effect that he totally understood how tough that would be but he firmly believed that young people with their creativity would find a way if they wanted to make it happen. When we left, one of the professors said to Charlie how much all of them had appreciated the conversation. He then added that as far as he was concerned, it was the friendship and humor between the two of us that had spoken loudest to him. As we drove away Charlie said, "I can't come here without remembering the saying that Booker T. Washington told me: "I will allow no man to drag me down so low as to make me hate him.""[3]

When we arrived back at the home of our friends, the Woolfords in Atlanta, a message awaited us with news that Mary McLeod Bethune, the founder of Bethune-Cookman College, had died on May 18, 1955. We were asked to represent MRA at her funeral to be held on the college campus in Daytona Beach, Florida. I had met her first in Caux, Switzerland, at an MRA conference. After Charlie and I put Betty on a plane for Summit, we drove to Daytona Beach. Charlie immediately ran into an old friend, John Sengstak, publisher of the *Chicago Defender*, a Black newspaper. Much of the Black leadership of America was present for the funeral service on May 23. President of Bethune-Cookman College, Dr. Richard V. Moore invited Charlie and me to say a few words. We also participated in the dedication of a marker on Bethune's grave site with her chosen words: "Moral Re-Armament—To be a part of this great uniting force is the crowning experience of my life."[4]

10

The Statesman's Mission

"Common Beat II"
A symphony with many parts.
A human melody deep in my memory
A common beat of our hearts.

In June 1955, Peter Howard invited Charlie, Betty, and me to be part of what was called the "Statesman's Mission." Charlie and I joked around as to whether we fit the category of statesmen. We agreed they had invited us to represent white and Black coming together during America's civil rights struggle. We were happy to participate. Peter Howard had written a script for a powerful musical play called *The Vanishing Island*. This depicted the worlds of totalitarianism and democracy, pointed up the weaknesses of both, and ended with a solution. Naturally Howard, a newspaper columnist, had written a section of the musical about the press. Charlie represented the publisher of a Black newspaper in America. His performance was both lively and sometimes humorous, especially when he would forget his lines and ad lib instead. Peter often felt that Charlie's ad libs were better than the original lines! Betty and I were not involved in the show but were sent ahead instead to the Philippines and Burma (now Myanmar) via Japan to work with the sponsors. It was a challenging experience, and we enjoyed all of it. All of this was going on while Charlie was polishing his thespian skills.

We took the occasion of being in Japan to visit Betty's younger sister, Peg, and her husband, Maury, who was an ensign at the naval base in Iwakuni, Yamaguchi Prefecture. We had hardly settled in when an urgent message arrived from Peter Howard saying, "Please fly immediately; your presence is needed in Manila in the Philippines." Without knowing more, my brother-in-law arranged for us to catch the next military cargo plane from Iwakuni to the Philippines, talking his way through a lot of red tape. We ended up on a cargo flight to Okinawa with a message to the military to please get us on the next flight to Manila. We were crammed into side-facing bucket seats sucking oxygen from a small tube. There was a full load of cargo strapped down in front of us in the middle of the airplane. We arrived at the Naha Naval Station but there was no connection to Manila until daylight the next morning. The mess hall had shut down so we stopped in the commissary and bought a soda and cornflakes, and that was our dinner.

Gordon Wise, a friend and former Australian military veteran whose father was prime minister of Western Australia, met us at the airport in Manila when we arrived from Okinawa. He immediately briefed us on the so-called crisis. We needed to get official permission for the four Japanese members of the Diet (Japan's bicameral legislature) who were part of our mission to enter the Philippines. At this point no Japanese had been allowed to set foot on Philippine soil since the end of World War II. The wounds and memory of the horrible atrocities inflicted on the Philippine people were still too raw. Gordon had requested an appointment with President Ramon Magsaysay, hoping that his word would clear the way. Fortunately, President Magsaysay's secretary had been in touch that afternoon confirming an appointment for the following morning. We were relieved but still under a lot of pressure from Peter Howard. The four Japanese were waiting to know whether they should get on the plane for Manila or stay in Tokyo. Gordon kept saying, "I wonder if the people on our mission in Okinawa understand the hurdle that we are putting in front of the president."

Knowing that we were far from securing permission and to offer a small relief from this situation, I suggested we take a taxi and tour the city and especially Dewey Boulevard, which borders Manila Bay. We silently saluted the hard work and patriotism of the people of Manila who had toiled so tirelessly to restore their shattered city as well as the beautiful new Dewey Boulevard.

The next morning in the meeting with President Magsaysay we had a chance to express our gratitude and admiration for his leadership, which had brought his nation forward to a recognized position in Southeast Asia. He opened the conversation immediately, "I have been fully briefed on your mission, and I look forward to receiving its members here at the palace. Is there anything more I can help you gentlemen with?" He listened carefully to Gordon's presentation, which centered on the four Japanese with our international delegation. Gordon said, "We totally understand the sensitivity of this situation and hope that you can help by looking favorably upon this request." There was silence as he stared out of his window across the bay. It did not look very hopeful, but he suddenly said, "I'll see what's possible." We thanked him. As I turned to leave he said, "Mr. Belk, I understand you were in the Navy here in the Philippines at the end of the war, and I want to thank you for your service."

Gordon and I were both impressed with the visit and the president's statesmanlike qualities, and we agreed with the recent press that featured him as the "George Washington of the Philippines." Our conclusion was that we had a fifty-fifty chance of the Japanese being given permission to enter the country. We sent that word to Peter Howard on Okinawa.

Much later, Gordon confirmed that they were indeed granted entrance. At the show in Manila, he told us an audible shock went through the crowd when the Japanese delegation was introduced at the end of *The Vanishing Island*. At the first word of Japanese being spoken, there was an angry murmur from the audience. When Yukika Sohma interpreted the humble apology of Japanese Diet member Nirō Hoshijima it was totally still, and then the audience erupted in thunderous applause.[1] Gordon himself said he was near tears—it was such a memorable moment! It was definitely the courage of the Japanese that had brought this about.

Unfortunately, we had to miss this moment because we were hopping forward to Burma while the mission team continued in the Philippines and Thailand. Burma was a new experience for Betty and me, our first in a Buddhist country. The Shwedagon Pagoda stood out in all its majesty as we drove in from the Rangoon airport. Everything was green and lush, but of course we had landed in the middle of monsoon season. We were met by a welcoming committee consisting of five Burmese women dressed in their colorful national dress. They were all carrying multicolored notebooks tied tightly with ribbon. One of them spoke a little English. She said to Betty, "All the plans for your 'Statesman's Mission' are here" and pointed to her notebook. We had to take her word for it because not one of the women opened their notebooks to expose what was inside. Betty whispered to me, "Go with it!" And we did just that for the next four days! To our amazement it all worked out. The tallest of the women, who seemed to be in charge, talked constantly to Betty as we drove into Rangoon. Betty turned to me and said, "I think she's trying to say that they're taking us to the home where we will be guests."

Betty had heard correctly because within the hour, we were being introduced to a charming Burmese couple and their three young daughters, who were peeking from behind their mother at the strange people from America. We learned later that we were the first Americans who had ever been in their home. Betty learned from the women in charge that our host, Dr. Chan Taik, was the leading eye doctor in Rangoon. We sat around their kitchen table and enjoyed homemade pastries and hot Burmese tea. The three daughters occasionally got up the courage to take a quick look at us and just as quickly disappeared.

The women heading up the host committee made it clear that all of the preparations had been taken care of. They were not going to share the details with us, so we decided to simply trust them and enjoy our host family, who wanted to show us the city and meet their friends. It was a delightful break from our nonstop schedule hopping from country to country.

The evening that the rest of the team of the Statesman's Mission arrived was calamitous. Betty and I were standing with the women's welcoming committee to meet the airplanes. It was the height of the monsoon season, and it seemed to have saved its biggest punch for that moment. The rain was coming down in torrents with lightning flashing and cracking across the skies and thunder so loud we could hardly hear the women speak. To make matters worse, the torrential rains created a river out of what had been the road leading to the hotel. With the doors of the hotel flung open to receive the guests, water was pouring into the first floor and some of the rooms had already flooded. The hotel was brand new, and the city had opened it early as a gift for our mission. Everything was in place except for glass in the windows, which would be put in later! Fortunately, the welcoming committee was on full alert and met the crisis head-on. They had already housed most of the first planeload on the second, third, and fourth floors. We did not dare to ask them where the second and third plane loads would go because we were sure they had that in hand.

Suddenly, Betty disappeared and within a few minutes reappeared, saying, "We have a problem. I just heard someone crying." Betty and I went to investigate and it was a friend from New York City, elderly Mrs. Tessie Durlach. She was sitting on the bed with her feet in the running water. Understandably, she was crying. But the committee swiftly went to work and instructed men to get her baggage and whisked her away to a dry room. We thanked the committee and went to bed. We learned the next morning that in the end, the whole team was safely placed in homes or hotels.

The next night we escorted our host family to the premier show of *The Vanishing Island*. The three small daughters loved the music and all the national costumes. They enjoyed meeting some of the different young people from other countries, and their parents seemed to enjoy the show as well. They had taken very good care of us.

After our week in Burma, we rejoined the mission and flew to Ceylon (now Sri Lanka). In Colombo the prime minister came to see the show. Soon afterwards, we were on our way to India where President Rajendra Prasad received us. *The Vanishing Island* played to packed audiences in New Delhi, Madras and Calcutta. Then on to Pakistan and Iran where Mohammad Reza Pahlavi, the Shah of Iran and Queen Soraya welcomed the delegates in the summer palace gardens. Magnificent Persian carpets were spread on the grass with a mountain stream running through the middle of the garden. The waiters were everywhere offering delicious Persian food and drinks. It was a party the likes of which few of us had ever experienced. At one point one of our delegates was so excited that he stepped off the carpet into the mountain stream without even noticing it. He was finally coaxed back to terra firma! A special stage had been built for our command performance for the Shah and the Queen. The next two nights in a rare happening the summer palace was opened to the public for two more performances.

To our surprise, Peter Howard asked Betty and me along with Charlie Howard to fly ahead to prepare the way for the tour in Kenya in East Africa. At that point Kenya was living through the turmoil of the Mau Mau uprising, so it was both an exciting and dangerous time to go there. Our anxiety about where we would all live was alleviated immediately when we were ushered into the home of Dr. and Mrs. G. W. Anderson, a pioneering English surgeon who welcomed both Black and white people into his clinic. When they heard that Betty and I were traveling with Charlie, they sent word they would like to host all three of us. We had adjoining rooms.

Everyone dressed for dinner, with Charlie and I seated on either side of the doctor. Charlie was moved by Dr. Anderson's work and said to me on the side, "We need more doctors like that in America." Betty and Robin, their daughter, were seated on either side of Mrs. Anderson. The candles were lit and the silverware was glistening, and Mrs. Anderson made a lovely toast. She thanked us for coming and hoped that the mission might bring the country a little closer together during this critical time. We all lifted our glasses and Dr. Anderson repeated, "Hear, hear!" Precisely at that moment a very tall Black Kenyan servant dressed in white entered from the kitchen with shining carving knives held in each hand. We were momentarily startled but relaxed slightly when he presented the two knives to Dr. Anderson with a sweeping bow. There was an audible change of atmosphere! Dr. Anderson immediately endeared himself to Charlie by saying, "We know of your efforts in your civil rights struggle in America. It's an honor to have you as a guest at our table." Charlie was visibly moved and said to me later, "I never expected to hear words like that from a Kenyan citizen." The more Charlie and Dr. Anderson compared notes on their common struggle for equality regardless of race or nationality, the more they seemed to enjoy one another. Toward the end of the dinner Dr. Anderson said in a rather matter-of-fact tone, "Speaking of the Mau Mau, we have just been alerted that there is a small Mau Mau encampment at the end of the valley that runs below our home." I could see and feel Charlie jump but at the time I didn't know what brought that about. Mrs. Anderson and Robin escorted us to our rooms and asked us what time we would like tea in the morning. It had been a good beginning.

As Betty and I were preparing for bed there was a loud noise coming from the next bedroom. At first we thought Charlie was just rearranging his bed, but as the scraping and noise increased I felt I needed to investigate. There was no response to my first knock so I waited a few moments and knocked on his door with more authority. I heard a rather distant voice saying, "Who's there?" and I answered quietly, "It's me, Blanton, your traveling partner and your next-door neighbor." There was quite a long silence and then the door suddenly creaked open. When Charlie saw it was actually me, he told me of a rumor that he had picked up earlier in the day. Apparently the Mau Mau had pledged to get blood from an American Black man. Since he felt he was the only one that fitted that bill in Kenya, he needed to beware and take precautions. That's what he was doing! I also realized I was not going to change his mind so I helped him move some furniture near his door. When I went out I could hear him finishing the job as the other bed was pushed against the other door. Fortunately we were all alive the next day, and Charlie never mentioned it again.

For the next two days we were given the grand tour of the wildlife and the great parks under and around Mount Kilimanjaro. It was awe inspiring, but we never totally relaxed because of the underlying tension between the races. The third day we came face to face with reality. We were taken with our delegation to visit those in the Mau Mau detention camps. They had been captured and incarcerated in a large open area. It was completely enclosed with a high fence, a guard tower with a spotlight, and armed guards.

It was here we were welcomed by one of the more impressive statesmen we met on our mission, Colonel Alan Knight, the colonial officer in charge of the Mau Mau detention camp at the Athi River near Nairobi. We had been fully briefed about Colonel Knight, who after meeting MRA members in college found vision and direction for the rest of his life. He had felt compelled to do something that was unheard of in the civil service in Kenya: he openly sought forgiveness from the detainees that were under his charge. Such apologies were unimaginable and unheard of. Knight apologized in Swahili for his and other whites' brutality, racism, and arrogance. He acknowledged that it was such attitudes that gave birth to the Mau Mau rebellion against British rule in Kenya. He then pledged to work with everyone to rebuild Kenya.

Colonel Knight led us on a short walk to their soccer field where a stage and chairs had been placed for the detainees to see *The Vanishing Island*. Our whole team was seated on the sides. Colonel Knight introduced the show and paid special tribute to the number of nations involved. When he came to the United States, he mentioned that Black and white people from our country were involved, and Charlie and I waved. Charlie told me later he was very nervous with that introduction since it identified him for the Mau Mau. There were giant screens above the stage for simultaneous translations into Swahili, and the audience came to life as they listened to the music and followed the dialogue. They certainly loved the production, but even more than that they were fascinated with all the different people that made up the delegation. The show led to a boisterous ovation when the last melodies ended.

Colonel Knight seemed extremely happy things had gone so well. As he was making his way through our delegation, he spotted us and came over to talk. Charlie immediately grabbed the occasion to thank him for his words. At that point I was pulled aside but left Charlie in conversation with the colonel. Charlie told Betty and me later how affected he had been with the whole day, especially with the vision of the colonel. Charlie was certainly terribly troubled by the way the Mau Mau detainees were herded like cattle into these big pens. But he also underlined how grateful he was that they had a man in charge like Colonel Knight. He hoped someday to have Alan Knight come to the US and give his convictions.

In late July we flew from Iran to Iraq for a four-day visit. Former Prime Minister Fadhel Jamali and US Ambassador Loy Henderson facilitated the performance of *The Vanishing Island*. However, there was one more performance—a special one written for the occasion paying tribute to the US Air Force and the planes and pilots that had carried us around the world. This was done on the tarmac with pilots and crew standing in front of their planes. The title of the special song was "Swing Those Propellers, Fellows." At the first notes they were very polite, nodding their heads and clapping in appreciation, but soon afterward they broke down in laughter and all sense of military decorum disappeared. When we ended there was applause and great shouts of "encore, encore!" The effort had been worth it, and there were lots of hugs and thanks from both sides. The planes and pilots had flown the delegates on the route I've described; however, in order to cover more of the area, small groups had taken off independently to visit Taiwan, Korea, Singapore, Vietnam, and Thailand. Then we boarded our flight to Cairo, Egypt, where the mission were guests of President Lieutenant Colonel Gamel Abdel Nasser. We went to Alexandria, a beautiful city on the Mediterranean Sea, before returning to Cairo for our flight to Istanbul, Turkey. In Istanbul, *The Vanishing Island* was very warmly received. We had a chance to tour Istanbul and visited the Sultan Ahmed Mosque, also called the Blue Mosque—it was breathtaking. In Ankara, the mission were guests of honor at the Hippodrome on Turkey's Victory Day, August 30, 1955. We saw 5,000 troops demonstrating Turkey's military strength. From Istanbul we flew to Switzerland and on to Caux at the beginning of September 1955.

At Caux we reconnected with our friend Gordon Wise, who we hadn't seen since we had said goodbye at the airport in Manila on June 30. We had hopscotched over or behind one another on our trip. We sympathized with him when he told us how exhausted he felt, and we all decided to take a break. Betty said she would like to stay in Caux.

When I informed Charlie that I wanted to take a break he said, "That's great news because I have a proposal. Why don't we find a car and drive to France. Let's find the farm near Verdun where my company was pinned down by the Germans in the First World War." It seemed like a tall order after all the years gone by. Fortunately for us, when Dr. William "Bill" Close heard the news, he said he would accompany us. This was the break we needed. Bill had been raised in Paris, spoke fluent French, had a car, and was familiar with the country. He drove and Charlie sat next to him, studying the maps, while I was most happy to relax in the backseat. We were like kids out of school and thoroughly enjoyed ourselves. Bill even located small French restaurants that delighted us. Charlie kept commenting that the food was nothing like the food that the Army had given them when he fought here many, many years ago! Bill even learned from a service station attendant of a delightful inn off the main road and made reservations. This trip was already turning out to be the R&R we all needed after our race around the world.

One morning, I got up early, and after a couple of cups of lovely French coffee went for a walk. I was impressed with the beautiful tilled farmland—a far cry from the horrors of two world wars that had rocked Europe. When I returned to the inn I found Bill and Charlie engrossed with their very ample breakfast. Meanwhile, I slipped out down to a nearby bakery for fresh croissants, cheese, and *jambon* for our picnic lunch. Charlie was obviously nervous. He said to us, "The closer I get to this battleground, the more I keep reliving it as if it was yesterday." We assured him that we all understood. Amazing as it may seem, Charlie had carefully studied the map and was able to direct us clearly to the farm where his last battle had been fought. Here he insisted that we stop the car so he could walk the long dirt road to the old barns and house. We walked behind him. There he stood in this abandoned farmyard, staring out across the valley to the far hills. It was obviously a spiritual moment, and no one said a word. Charlie turned around and motioned for us to come forward, and then he described how the battle had unfolded—not many personal details but broad strokes of how the Germans, entrenched on the hillside with their artillery, had them pinned down. Charlie then added, almost under his breath, that his orders had been to clean them out during the dark of the Moon. He lost a lot of his platoon. At Charlie's request, Bill took a photograph of him looking across the valley at the hill and then we left. At dinner that night Charlie thanked us all saying, "That was an important moment and closure on an awful memory."

When we arrived in Sweden in November 1955, Charlie, Betty, and I received an official invitation along with a small contingent from *The Vanishing Island* to visit the Arctic Circle. We would meet with the Sami people at their annual reindeer roundup. Before we flew to the north, we along with a small international group from the cast were given a full briefing. They underlined for us that the Sami people, the reindeer herders of northern Sweden, had a mystical sense of kinship with the reindeer like no other human-animal bond. The reindeer have been part of the Sami culture for thousands of years. Above all else the reindeer were considered kindred spirits that shared the harsh yet beautiful northern landscape with them and gave them life.

We were hosted with the most delightful couple. They immediately took Betty, Charlie, and me in as family. November is a time when Sami set up camp, round up their reindeer, check their health, the size of their herd, and mark their calves. It is the time when they harvest the reindeer they need. All the family, no matter the age, participates. When the roundup is finished, the remaining reindeer are released to the wild once again.

Our hosts were relieved that we had heavy clothing and Betty was relieved when she decided she would stay with this nice hospitable family in the warm home. The next morning they awakened Charlie and me before light with a mug of hot tea. Then we put on our layers of clothes, our stocking hats, and heavy neck scarves. Betty was up and joined us around the candlelit breakfast table. Torsten, our host, grabbed the occasion with much humor to brief Charlie on what he thought might be the reaction of the Sami people to him. Charlie took it all in stride and said, "Of course, I will be studying them while they're studying me." Everyone laughed. It was a good send off and we needed a good one when we hit the bone-chilling morning air. Torsten drove us to the rendezvous to meet our guide who turned out to be a most delightful personality. He had a red peaked hat and Sami national dress and a lovely face filled with humor and mischief. We responded to him immediately. He didn't speak a word of English but fortunately, Torsten had decided that he would stick with us as our interpreter. As we set out on foot, he informed us that the guide said it was only a half a mile to his family camp. Torsten explained to us that a Swedish mile is equivalent to 6.2 US miles. Charlie nearly turned back but we both sucked it up and charged forward! We had three miles to go to our destination.

It was all worth it. When Torsten introduced us, most of the young children stood motionless staring at Charlie. He was like no other person they had seen before and he was wonderful in playing his part. They had been busy gathering their reindeer. It was a great atmosphere. To the best of my memory, lunch was served. It was hot venison stew with many mysterious ingredients. Charlie finished his quickly and said to Torsten, "That was so good, I think I'll have another dish." And he did. Soon after, Torsten whispered to us that we needed to thank them and head home because it would be dark soon. As we started to leave, the whole family stood around and sent us off with a loud goodbye song. We waved our goodbyes as we trudged out into the snow. Charlie suggested to Torsten that perhaps we could ride a reindeer home. He did it with great humor and we thanked Torsten for a memorable day.

It was dark when we got home. Both Charlie and I skipped more food and fell into bed and I think Torsten did the same. Tomorrow would come soon enough!

11

Meeting Dr. Martin Luther King Jr.

"Does It Really Matter"
Judging not by the color of the skin
It's the content of the man
The character that stands
Shining from within.

In March 1957, Betty and I were with Charlie Howard in Atlanta, Georgia, staying with friends, T. Guy Woolford Jr. and his sister Frances. I felt that the time had come to try for an appointment with Dr. Martin Luther King Jr., who was fast becoming a central figure of the civil rights movement. Charlie was the key; he telephoned Dr. King's secretary and requested an appointment for the two of us. The following day, word came back that Dr. King would receive us in his office the following week in Montgomery, Alabama.

The Woolfords offered to loan us one of their cars, a big black Packard, so we could make the drive from Atlanta to Montgomery to meet Dr. King. At that moment, Montgomery was the focal point of the civil rights struggle. History had been made when Rosa Parks, a seamstress and civil rights activist, refused to sit in the back of a city bus. In another country such a thing would have minor significance, but here in the United States in the mid-1950s, it was something gigantic—especially in the South. Mrs. Parks had deliberately stepped across the line marked "Colored Here" and "White Here," and all hell was breaking loose. For the state of Alabama this was illegal, and Rosa Parks had been arrested and put in jail.

Dr. King lived in Montgomery at the time, where he served as the pastor of the Dexter Avenue Baptist Church, his first and only full-time pastorate. He had taken on the mantle and the civil disobedience methods of Mahatma Gandhi. He and Coretta, his wife, had traveled to India and studied Gandhi's nonviolent tactics. Black leaders in Montgomery, who had founded the Montgomery Improvement Association to organize and lead a bus boycott, chose Dr. King as president. During the boycott most Black citizens and many white citizens of Montgomery refused to ride the city buses. The bus company lost up to 40,000 riders per day. Nearly a year later, the boycotters finally won the right by law to sit anywhere on public transportation. On November 13, 1956, the Supreme Court declared Alabama's bus segregation laws unconstitutional. The bus boycott resulted in a victory that reached far beyond Montgomery. Nonviolence had won.[1]

Charlie's and my enthusiasm seemed to blind us temporarily to the true situation in the South. We had lost sight of the reality that we were living in a totally segregated country. Racial tensions were very high, and you had to be extremely cautious. There we were, two idealistic men, one Black, one white, together going across rural Georgia in that big black Packard into rural Alabama. A white man driving with a Black man sitting next to him was a recipe for violence and possibly lynching. Luckily, we managed to arrive in Montgomery without mishap.

While the bus boycott had ended some months previously in December 1956, it was obvious that it had not healed the city. Still, Charlie and I were excited if apprehensive. We located Dr. King's office, a small, single-story, white wood-framed building on a side street away from downtown. We were received cordially by his secretary, Maude Ballou, and told that he would see us shortly. We were alone in a small waiting room, without magazines or coffee. It was a quiet, frugal setting. Charlie and I sat looking at each other, wondering what was next. An hour ticked slowly by, and then another half hour, and we heard nothing. I said to Charlie, "Maybe we should go." Charlie emphatically answered, "No, we should stay." We did, for another half hour. It was almost noon when the door opened and his secretary announced, "Dr. King will see you now." He greeted us at the door cordially but guardedly. I'm sure he'd been sitting there, probably on the phone, trying to find out who I was and what we had come for. As he and Charlie exchanged small talk about their many mutual friends, I looked at Dr. King. My first impression was of a man small in stature, five feet seven inches tall, and big in vision. He was totally serene and at peace with himself. This man, I thought, is only 27 years old yet think what he has done and risked already for his people and the country.

Charlie thanked Dr. King for receiving us. He knew who Charlie was and his record on civil rights. He trusted Charlie. The unknown factor in the room was J. B. Belk. What was this guy's motive? Dr. King began to focus on me. "Mr. Belk, what brings you to Montgomery with Charlie?" he asked. I answered as best I could that Charlie and I had met in Chicago. We were both veterans—Charlie an officer in the Army in World War I and I an officer in the Navy in World War II. We shared a passion to do something about the relationship between the races. We bonded as friends. Then, Dr. King asked, "But what are you two men doing together?"

"We've been speaking at the Black colleges and universities, such as Morehouse, Tuskegee, Fiske, Tennessee A&I, and Lincoln," I said. "We hope we might be an example to the youth that as a white Southerner and a Black militant it is possible for the races not only to get along together but to enjoy each other."

"That's a good mission," he said. "But what are you telling the young people?"

I told him our basic conviction that character is more important than color and our hope that if we can lift the character of the people, someday we might have a color blind country. He seemed to ponder that, and then he said, "I like that, and I fully agree but, Mr. Belk, what moves you to do this with Charlie?"

"Yes, Dr. King, that's a good question," I answered. "I was born, bred, and raised in the South, and I am ashamed to say I took segregation for granted. My father was a Presbyterian minister, and he encouraged me to make a difference with my life."

"So," he said, beginning to relax. "I knew it, I knew it! We have something in common. We are both PKs [preacher's kids] and bad boys in our youth!" There was laughter, and Charlie added, "Yes, you can say that again!" Dr. King sat in his chair and quietly contemplated what I had shared. "I can identify with all you have said," he told me, "and I congratulate you and Charlie for your efforts." There was silence. The atmosphere changed. Then he suddenly said, "What are you two men doing for lunch?" Charlie was quick to reply, "We have no plans for lunch. Breakfast was a long time ago back in Atlanta!" Martin laughed and said, "Yes, Charlie. We must feed you." Then he picked up the phone and called his wife. "Coretta, set two extra places. I'm bringing my two guests home."

We followed his car to his house, set on quite a large lot, surrounded by a fence. In the yard, sand and dirt had been raked bare so there was no underbrush anywhere. The trees held floodlights. As we walked through the fence and up the driveway, two FBI agents with very small cameras were in the yard behind the trees, filming our approach. We learned later that J. Edgar Hoover, head of the FBI, had ordered them there for protection and security purposes, but they were also there to find out who was visiting the Kings.

I was very impressed with Coretta Scott King, a most gracious woman. She was born and grew up in Alabama. The couple had met in Boston where she was studying at the New England Conservatory of Music and he was getting his doctorate at Boston University. They married in June 1953. She was obviously a partner for Dr. King in every way. I don't know to this day how Coretta prepared such a sumptuous meal between the time her husband telephoned and our arrival. The four of us were seated at the dining room table. After Martin said grace, he said to Coretta, "These two men have been speaking in quite a few of our Black colleges and universities underlining that character is as important as color. And if we could lift the character of our country we just one day might have a color blind country." Coretta looked at both Charlie and myself and said, "Congratulations, I buy into that vision." We enjoyed the most wonderful Southern meal. We even had pie for dessert. We all relaxed and talked about family and friends. Martin was interested that I was a cousin to John Belk, who ran the Belk's Department Stores, which stretched throughout the Southern states. By this time he seemed to take us into his confidence. There was animated conversation spiced with humor and seriousness. He spoke frankly about his hopes and his frustrations. He looked at Charlie and me with a twinkle in his eye and said, "You know I've been thinking about character, and I've been wondering what in the world brought you two unlikely characters together." There was a lot of good talk and laughter around that lunch table. Then with quite a lot of emotion, he shared with us his experiences and convictions about the bus boycott. "Now," he concluded, "my people can sit wherever we wish on public transportation, but our city and our country are more divided than ever before. This is a great sadness for me. We must find a way—and we will."

A friendship was born that long ago day in Montgomery. We met as strangers and parted as friends and allies. This friendship would never have happened without my own friendship with Charlie Howard. I am convinced that our friendship is what captured Dr. King's interest. There was no question in my mind when we left late that afternoon that we had become friends. When we finally said goodbye, we were Martin, Coretta, Charlie, and Blanton. Perhaps that is all we accomplished that day, but in retrospect, the building of that friendship seemed very significant at that moment in history.

As Charlie and I drove out of Montgomery late that afternoon, we were elated about our visit. Both of us hoped that our time with the Kings would have some long-range ramifications. In fact, we were so absorbed in reliving the visit that as we drove through a town, we hardly noticed a convertible loaded with young white men following us at every turn and through every traffic light. Too late we realized that we were a target—a car with Georgia license plates, with a white man driving and a Black man sitting in the front seat. Charlie caught sight of them first in our side mirror, and without turning around to look back he said, "There are some young white guys right on our tail—and they will stop us." I stole a glance in the mirror and saw the convertible with the top down, packed with five or six people. Charlie sucked in his breath and whispered, as if they could hear him, "If they cut us off and make us stop, I'm getting out to confront them. You are staying in the car, and you are locking the doors." I'm sure his heart was racing as fast as mine. In those days in the South, it was not a pretty picture when a group of toughs decided to make an issue of race. Charlie was certain they would stop us and there would be a confrontation. It was a heroic act of friendship for him to suggest that I stay in the car while he faced threatening strangers by himself. He knew the potentially deadly peril of being the lone Black man in that situation, or a Black man in the company of a lone white man in an out-of-state car. We were sitting ducks for violence, and we knew there was plenty of that in the South then.

"Keep your same steady pace," Charlie said. "Don't look back. Don't give them any hint that we see them, or that we're worried about them." The minutes crept by as we maneuvered through the winding streets of that Alabama town, with the convertible glued to our bumper. I stole another quick glance in the mirror, and the boys seemed to be in an ugly mood—or so they appeared to me. They tailed us for about 25 minutes, long after we drove out into the remote countryside.

Time stood still, and I expected that any minute they would dash around us and block the road. Finally, however, they slipped behind us but still kept us in sight. What were they planning? Would they come back with reinforcements? Charlie and I didn't speak for a long time, wondering what they would do. Suddenly Charlie said, "They've stopped. Keep going." We kept our speed steady, and they sat on the side of the road watching us go over a hill and around the next curve. That was it. Finally they were gone. We heaved a great, joint sigh of relief and gave a solemn prayer of thanks.

Two months later, in May 1957, Charlie and I were thinking about the planned Prayer Pilgrimage in Washington, DC, on May 17, and whether this would be a chance to see Dr. King again. Charlie decided to stay in Atlanta, but I flew to Washington three days before the march. I was welcomed again at "2419," the Elys' home, and read in the *Washington Post* that there was to be a press conference on the day of the march. I wanted to see Dr. King, so I talked my way into it. A. Philip Randolph, Roy Wilkins, and Bayard Rustin as co-chairs discussed the march and rally at the Lincoln Memorial. It was called a Prayer Pilgrimage for Freedom and was to be a nonviolent demonstration. This would be Martin Luther King Jr.'s first speech at the

Lincoln Memorial and would set the agenda of voting rights as an important part of the civil rights struggle. I sat at the back of the room at the press conference but didn't have a chance to speak with Dr. King.

After the press conference I went to find a parking space. Most streets were closed off, and the police had been warning people on the radio to beware of racial violence. There was none; the atmosphere was peaceful. The three-hour demonstration, which started at noon, proved to be a happy occasion. The organizers had hoped that 50,000 people would come, but the press and police estimated after the event that some 25,000 people participated.

The rally was organized on the third anniversary of the 1954 *Brown v. Board of Education* decision by the US Supreme Court banning segregated schools. A number of civil rights advocates spoke or sang, including Mahalia Jackson. Dr. King was the last speaker. His topic was "Give Us the Ballot." The crowd followed every word, and there was a tremendous ovation when he finished. Reporter James Hicks, writing about the event in the New York *New Amsterdam News*, declared, "King emerged from the Prayer Pilgrimage to Washington as the number one leader of 16 million Negroes in the United States, at this point in his career the people will follow him anywhere."[2]

After Dr. King's powerful speech, I made my way through the crowd and was standing at the bottom of the steps of the Lincoln Memorial. Everybody was attempting to get up the steps to speak to him. I finally made my way until I was standing just outside the circle of admirers. Martin somehow saw me. He yelled, "Blanton! Come on in!" He gestured for me to come and say hello. The crowd parted, and I shook his hand and congratulated him. He said, "What did you think of my speech?" Before I could answer, someone else had grabbed his arm and was trying to get his attention. I knew I only had a second, so I said, "Martin, what are your plans for dinner?" He turned to Ralph Abernathy, his right-hand man and the cofounder of the Southern Christian Leadership Conference, and asked, "Ralph, what are our plans for dinner?" "We don't have any plans," Ralph replied. I quickly said, "I have a house at my disposal. Please bring your party for dinner."

So it was arranged that they would come for dinner at 7:00 p.m., and I gave Ralph the address. I finally found my car and got to the house as quickly as possible. By then it was after 4:00. I rushed into the house and said to my friends Rachel Jackson and her sister, Harriet Addison, who were the cooks at the house, "Guess who's coming to dinner?" They had been listening to the rally on the radio, and when I told them "Martin Luther King," there was dead silence and then peals of laughter. "Blanton, you've always been a joker. You've got to be kidding," Harriet said. They refused to believe that I was serious. I was getting a little desperate, but I finally convinced them, and what a meal they prepared! They went into overdrive, cooking a wonderful dinner for this very special guest and his friends although we had no idea how many to expect. When the doorbell rang around seven, Martin, his father, and 16 or 17 others flocked into the house. Many of them signed a page in the guestbook on the way in, and to this day, I am happy to have a copy of that page in my possession.[3]

Everyone was excited by the response to Martin's speech, and everyone was enormously hungry. After Martin had introduced me to all his friends, he took me by the arm and said, "Sit with me, Blanton, at the end of the table. I want to hear what you thought of my speech." When I asked him to say grace, Martin turned to his father, the Reverend Martin Luther King Sr., and asked him to give thanks for this miraculous day. Then, everyone was talking and eating at once. Martin asked me how I thought the white community would react to his speech. "Obviously, all the people were touched by your words," I said. "But even more than your words, they were touched by your total sincerity and passion as a person. They were moved by your speech. Most of all they were moved by *you*. That is what moved me." We talked about politics in Washington and our predictions about what would happen next in the civil rights movement. After dessert, when the lemon meringue pie had been devoured, Martin called for Rachel and Harriet to come from the kitchen. They beamed as they met our guests, who saluted them with a boisterous ovation. Each of the guests came by with thanks for a wonderful dinner party. The last two were Dr. King and his father, the Reverend King, who said, "You gave us a perfect ending on a miraculous day." Martin said after I shook his hand, "We must meet again and talk." We did just that.

12

Washington, DC, and Eisenhower

"Freedom Isn't Free"
Freedom isn't free! You got to pay a price,
You got to sacrifice for your liberty.

Washington, DC, in the 1950s was an exciting place to spend time. The economy of America was booming. Thousands of veterans had returned home and were energizing universities, businesses, and politics. It was peacetime, and there was even bipartisanship in Congress. I had made many friends in the House and Senate, some through family connections, others via my work in MRA. I enjoyed myself as a volunteer intern for Congressman Charles B. Deane of North Carolina, a good friend who took me on so I could learn the political workings of our government.

One day my father called from Richmond and suggested that I introduce myself to one of his classmates from the University of South Carolina, Congressman James P. Richards, who was chairman of the Committee on Foreign Affairs in the House of Representatives. He invited me to lunch in the congressional dining room with his wife. We had hardly settled down to the traditional white bean soup when his wife turned to me with a big smile and said, "Are you really the son of Fuzzy Belk [my father's college nickname]?" When I answered that I was, she replied, "But he was such a tall, good-looking man." I felt like crawling under the table.

Not all of my DC adventures were so light-hearted. I happened to be in the Capitol Building on the day the press considered "the wildest day in the history of the US Congress,"[1] March 1, 1954. On that day, four Puerto Rican nationalists opened fire from the House gallery on the congressmen below. I had been asked to escort a labor leader from Great Britain who was visiting Congressman Deane, and we were sitting in the gallery just across from where all hell broke loose. There was loud shouting, the unfurling of flags, and what sounded like fireworks going off. We were both startled, and my labor leader friend stood up just at the moment a bullet crashed into the woodwork over our heads. I grabbed him and pulled him down behind the barricade as he babbled, "What was that?!" Another bullet slammed into the gallery just to the right of us. I told my friend to follow me and stay down. We quickly crawled up the stairs and headed for an exit that I knew about from working with Congressman Deane—a small circular staircase that took us to the first floor and out. Fortunately, we made it outside just before Congress was cordoned off. Even when we got to the bottom of the staircase we could hear the shouting and shooting that was still going on, but there was little security in those days to rush in and help.

Sometime later I received a letter from my labor leader friend saying that his first visit to the US Congress had left an indelible imprint that he would never forget. I could say the same, and I can shut my eyes and see the blood staining the carpeting around the congressmen who had been shot, some seriously wounded but nobody killed, thankfully. The one or two policemen who were on duty did extraordinary work in capturing the four Puerto Rican nationalists, but that event was the beginning of new security for Congress.

Despite this tragedy, I continued to build friendships with members of Congress. Another representative I got to know around this time was Charles E. Bennett from Jacksonville, Florida. He was a decorated US Army officer who had served with distinction as a guerrilla fighter during the invasion of the Philippines. Although he was a bit slowed down by the permanent use of crutches, the result of contracting polio during the war, it didn't dampen his spirit. He was full of life and a senior member of the House Armed Services Committee.

During late winter of 1961, former President Eisenhower was hosting a reception for some of his close colleagues from Britain. This was at his Gettysburg farm and home in Pennsylvania. These men had been his comrades when he was supreme allied commander of the Allied Expeditionary Force in Europe during World War II. The head of the delegation was Rear Admiral Sir Edward Cochrane of the British Navy. How I ended up in Gettysburg at Eisenhower's home with such notable military leadership, I can't recall. Perhaps I had driven Congressman Bennett to the meeting. In any event, there I was seated at the back of the room at this distinguished gathering. The conversation was lively and humorous as they talked about the many experiences they had lived through together. It was heady stuff. They talked candidly about Winston Churchill, Franklin Roosevelt, and Charles de Gaulle, and all of them paid tribute to the character of the young men and women who had been under their command. I was mesmerized and felt smaller by the minute.

Towards the end, to my utter surprise, General Eisenhower pointed to me and said, "Young man sitting back there, what did you do during the war?" I blurted out that I had served on a PCC boat in the Philippines. Thinking I had said PT boat he replied, "Why aren't you in the White House?" I quickly retorted, "Because my boat didn't sink, General!" He and his guests roared with laughter, and Eisenhower said, "It must've been political for that very fast PT boat to be run over by a much slower Japanese destroyer." Again, much laughter. On the way out, General Eisenhower gave me a thumbs up as he passed. This was the beginning of a lifelong friendship that helped shape my life.

Earlier, in June 1960, a massive group of militant Japanese students, the 120,000-member All-Japan Federation of Student Self-Government Associations (Zengakuren), had protested the Security Treaty between the United States and Japan. The violent demonstrations in and around Tokyo led to the death of one female student and countless injuries. This coincided with a planned visit by President Eisenhower, who was touring Asia to promote the treaty.[2] His White House press secretary, James C. Hagerty, was in Tokyo to arrange details of the visit when the Zengakuren students mobbed his car at Haneda Airport. Fearing for his life, Mr. Hagerty had to be rescued by a US Marine helicopter and President Eisenhower's visit was called off. The incident ultimately led to the resignation of the Japanese prime minister,

Nobusuke Kishi.

A month later, 40 of the Zengakuren leadership traveled to an MRA conference in Switzerland. While there they had a chance to ponder the recent demonstrations in Japan. They decided that they had been right in demonstrating against the corruption in the Japanese government. On the issue of the Security Treaty, however, they concluded that they had been manipulated by militant anti-government, anti-American groups. They channeled those feelings into a show they wrote called *The Tiger*, which demonstrated the ideological struggle for the youth of Japan.[3] These students definitely had a change of heart, and they wanted to come to America and apologize to President Eisenhower personally. The people working in MRA in the United States, including myself, invited them to come, and they arrived in February 1961 in New York City, where we had arranged for their first performance to be in Carnegie Hall. My friend David Carey was a colleague of James Hagerty, who had been press secretary to President Eisenhower, and invited him to meet with the Japanese prior to their first show. David told me that on the way to the dinner James Hagerty became very nervous. David could feel Hagerty's apprehension when he told me that he kept a piece of rock on his desk that had come through the helicopter windshield at the Tokyo airport. It could have caused the helicopter to crash. David assured him that it would be safe, and the students gave such a moving apology that James Hagerty volunteered to introduce their show in Carnegie Hall a few days later.

On February 21, Carnegie Hall was packed for the first American performance of *The Tiger*, and it was quite a moving experience for the audience when James Hagerty appeared on stage for the introduction. He described his original meeting with the students at the airport in Tokyo and the frightening experience he had with them. When he turned to the students on the stage and described their apology to him and to America there was loud applause.

I awoke the next morning after the show thinking, how do we get the Japanese students to meet President Eisenhower? I seemed to be the only link after that brief encounter with him at Gettysburg. However, the link was quite tenuous, and I went back and forth, debating with myself what would happen if I tried to make contact. I came to the conclusion that I had to try. When I put a call through into his office at the Odlum Ranch in Indio, California, a secretary answered. I quickly introduced myself, saying I had met General Eisenhower at a reception in Gettysburg. She quickly said, "You need to talk to General Eisenhower's military aide, General Robert Schulz." She transferred the call, but there was a long pause before the booming voice of General Schulz came over the phone saying, "I remember you! You had the back and forth with the general because your boat didn't sink in the Philippines and you are not in the White House! What can I do for you?" I started to breathe again! I briefed him on the situation and especially the time with James Hagerty at Carnegie Hall. A message came through the following day saying that General Eisenhower would look forward to meeting the Japanese students on March 29 at the El Dorado Country Club in Palm Desert, California.

After New York City, the 40 students took *The Tiger* on tour to Washington, DC, Detroit, and Los Angeles. From Los Angeles they went to meet President Eisenhower in Palm Desert. He was in a relaxed, jovial mood, and after shaking hands with all the students he said, "I can't tell you how very happy I am to have you people come and tell me about the changes that have taken place in your lives because of the incident back in June. I am for you 100 percent!" Speaking on behalf of the students, Koichi Morita, chair of the Zengakuren, apologized to the former president and to the American people for the riots in Tokyo. It had not only divided Japan and America but done serious damage to the unity of the free world. The students promised President Eisenhower and the American nation that they would fight alongside them for freedom in the world.

United Press International, which covered the event, reported that President Eisenhower was beaming with obvious pleasure over the meeting with the Zengakuren students. CBS TV and radio, the Associated Press, and the *Los Angeles Times* all covered the 45-minute interview, easily the longest the general had granted since coming to Palm Desert. The major Los Angeles press carried front-page stories. News and photographs of the event appeared in newspapers across the country, and it was broadcast on nationwide television. The story was also widely reported by radio stations throughout Japan. It was carried by the national dailies of Japan and by all of the English-language newspapers. The Far East Network radio for the American Armed Forces broadcast the recording of the conversation between President Eisenhower and the Zengakuren students. In his final remarks, President Eisenhower urged the Japanese students to take their magic with *The Tiger* to Brazil: "I am convinced that you can have a great impact on the militant Brazilian students rising up across that country." Then he said, "I hope to go back to Japan in the fall but I don't expect to see you there. I expect to see you in South America and other places taking this message there." He added, "This is the last act in the June riots, and it has a happy ending!"[4]

13

The Tiger

"We Will Stand"
We're the voices of change that cannot be denied

Some weeks later Peter Howard heeded the suggestion of President Eisenhower to take *The Tiger* to Brazil. He called a meeting in Miami, Florida, in early April 1961. Quite a powerful delegation came from Brazil, led by General Hugo Bethlem and businessman Alberto Kovaric. *The Tiger* was invited to come and perform at the meeting. They were a hit. When the Brazilian delegation learned that President Eisenhower had suggested the cast go to Brazil, the Brazilians immediately went to work. They secured an official invitation from their country for the students and their play to come. When they invited Peter Howard to accompany *The Tiger*, he asked Betty and me to go with him. By the time we arrived in São Paulo, Brazil, the Zengakuren students had been featured prominently in the press. The news of their meeting with President Eisenhower had preceded them. Within the first few days Peter Howard was interviewed extensively on Brazilian TV and radio. Assis Chateaubriand, the head of *O Globo*, the largest media group in South America, received us saying, "I have learned of your mission with the Japanese and former President Eisenhower's request that you come here, and I'm here to tell you that our media entities will fully back your mission."

After 10 days Peter Howard had to return to London. When he left he said, "I'm leaving you in charge of this mission. You're the friend of General Eisenhower, and you can keep him posted." I was pleased but overwhelmed, thinking, "How are we going to move this international delegation of nearly

100 people?" I came to the conclusion that since President Eisenhower had suggested we come here, perhaps we should visit with President Jânio Quadros and ask his advice on how best to operate. General Bethlem liked the idea, and within 10 days we took a small delegation to be received by President Quadros in his office in the new capital in Brasília. At Bethlem's suggestion, we picked people from various countries, including Jerry von Teuber, an American who was our very skilled interpreter; Alberto Kovaric, a Brazilian business executive and one of our hosts; a professor and former Communist from India named R. Vaitheswaran; Dr. Toyotane Sohma, a Japanese medical doctor; William Pawley, an American businessman from Miami; and two of the student leaders of *The Tiger*. We asked them all to be prepared to share their convictions with the president. General Bethlem presented our delegation of eight, representing four countries, and when Professor Vaitheswaran was introduced, the president asked him, "What are your thoughts for my country?" The professor responded by saying, "I can assure you Mr. President that communism is not the best way for a country—democracy could be the way, if it is free of corruption." The president pounced on that, replying, "I'm sure all of you know that I ran my campaign with two brooms tied to the back of my pickup truck with a slogan, 'Let's get together and sweep corruption out of Brazil!'" The president also questioned us about President Eisenhower's involvement in *The Tiger*. After the two Japanese students spoke, President Quadros urged them to reach out to as many students in his country as possible, especially in northeastern Brazil.

General Bethlem introduced me as a former officer in the US Navy and the leader of the delegation. I thanked him for his gracious hospitality in receiving us and added, "I would like to say to you, Mr. President, that we are here in your great country to learn all we can from your people. We would like to build as many solid friendships as we can in our common effort to build a more peaceful and understanding world."

President Quadros got up from his chair and came around to shake each of our hands and thank us for our words. When we prepared to leave, he turned to General Bethlem and said, "How are you getting back to São Paulo?" Bethlem replied, "We have a bus waiting for us." But the president said, "Nonsense! I'll fly you back in one of our military planes." Then he turned to a colonel who was his aide and said, "Get me the secretary of the air force on the telephone." The president motioned for us to stay seated while he talked to the secretary. Afterwards President Quadros said, "I am taken with what you're trying to do for my country and especially the students. I have directed the secretary of the air force to put air force airplanes at your disposal as you go from city to city. I have also instructed him to give you hospitality in our military barracks if not enough families come forward to host your delegation." He then turned to General Bethlem and said, "I have directed the secretary of the air force to coordinate details with you." Something definitely clicked with President Quadros, and he said as we left, "I'll make arrangements to see *The Tiger* presentation as soon as it's convenient. I want to thank all of you for your care and concern for my country." Without a doubt this visit was a tipping point for our time in Brazil. Soon after, an invitation came to General Bethlem for *The Tiger* to perform in a new theater in Brasília where President Quadros and his wife, Eloa, members of his cabinet, and others could attend. That turned out to be a most memorable evening.

The Tiger, with the convictions of the young Japanese, was a phenomenon throughout 12 great cities in Brazil. The response from the youth was overwhelming, and the young Japanese in *The Tiger* were treated like rock stars. Marshal Juárez Távora had been captured by the passion of the young Japanese, and he volunteered to introduce them to the country. He was a national hero of the Brazilian people who received an enthusiastic reception everywhere we went. In Fortaleza some weeks later, he and Marshal Henrique Teixeira Lott, the former Minister of War and a political rival, had found reconciliation following years of animosity after attending *The Tiger* performance together. Their handshake was front-page news across Brazil.[1]

When we arrived in the northeast region of the country where President Quadros had urged us to concentrate, we were received by Archbishop Hélder Pessoa Câmara. On that occasion, Marshal Távora informed the archbishop that in his estimation *The Tiger* was doing important work with Brazilian youth. The archbishop thanked him and the Japanese students and offered a special blessing to Marshal Távora and Marshal Lott saying, "That handshake spoke to all of us and inspired reconciliation with all the people of Brazil." The archbishop then turned to me and said, "When a man has a dream it remains a dream until 10,000 people participate and then it becomes a reality." That became a reality for me some years later when we reached the milestone of our 10,000th student participating in Up with People.

The final Brazilian performance of *The Tiger* was in Manaus, the old rubber capital of Brazil, which lies 1,000 miles up the Amazon from the coast. At that point the river is 12 miles wide and the heart of the Amazon basin. The word had gone out far and wide from the military in charge of that area, and a tidal wave of people, thousands strong, packed the soccer stadium for this last show in Brazil. One member of our delegation estimated 50,000 or 60,000 but the general in charge said it was closer to 90,000— whatever it was, it was a hell of a crowd and a tumultuous response when Marshal Távora introduced the evening. The celebration continued into the early morning even as we gathered on the tarmac to fly to Peru, our next stop. The military general of the region with his staff, the mayor of Manaus, and quite a few host families gathered to say goodbye. We were all moved. Not only had *The Tiger* and the young Japanese touched the Brazilian people, but Brazil had touched all of us. Something permanent and lasting had taken place. We gave a special thank you from all of us to the pilots and staff of the Brazilian Air Force who had flown us and looked after us in such a wonderful way and made the whole trip possible.

The Peruvian Air Force met us in Manaus and provided planes to fly the mission over the Andes. The snow-capped Andes is a memory that no one forgets. We also will not forget the small tubes that supplied oxygen on the trip. We landed in Talara, on the west coast of Peru. A Peruvian military bus picked us up for the trip along the Pacific Ocean on the Pan American Highway. In quite a few places sand dunes had blown across the road, which sloped in spots nearly 30 degrees. The drivers would stop so we could all have a look, and then with a roar they would pass over these spots. Those on the right side would be looking down 1,000 feet to where the Pacific Ocean was crashing on the rocks below. We were tired but no one slept on this trip. We stopped for lunch in Cabo Blanco, Peru, a famous fishing venue of the 1950s. This had been a mecca for giant black marlin and other billfish. Naturally I skipped lunch and took a quick tour of the Cabo Blanco Fishing Club.

Later, after we arrived in Lima, we were saddened by a cable from Peter Howard saying that Frank Buchman had died in Germany on August 7, 1961.[2] Betty and I were asked to come as quickly as possible for the funeral service in his hometown of Allentown, Pennsylvania, on August 19. After the funeral in Allentown, Peter Howard asked me to drive him to Washington, DC, where we had some days together discussing what lay ahead. He had to return to London, but he encouraged me to rejoin the delegation in Brazil where a final celebration of *The Tiger*'s tour would be held at the Quintandina Stadium in Rio de Janeiro. Peter assured me that he would come to this show and support the celebration.

When Betty and I got to Rio in September, we were informed that Peter had had to change his plans and was sending Rajmohan Gandhi to represent him instead. This was deeply concerning to me. Not all of the leaders of MRA were happy with what we'd been doing with the young people and *The Tiger*. I definitely felt a withdrawal of their support. I didn't know it then but it was the beginning of a separation that would eventually become a full-fledged break from MRA. We did the best we could, and for this final performance in Rio, even Hannah Nixon, former Vice President Richard Nixon's mother, came to pay tribute to the Japanese students. Cowboy actor Roy Rogers and his famous horse, Trigger, came from Los Angeles and made a big hit when they led the Japanese students into the stadium. Peter sent a cable congratulating us and inviting us to come to Copenhagen and confer.

It was especially touching to say goodbye to the Zengakuren students. What a noble group. Many years later when I was in Japan, Dr. Sohma took me to the Japanese Diet to renew my friendship with Tokuichiro Tamazawa, one of the leaders of the Zengakuren. He had just retired as Minister of Defense for Japan. I got a large embrace from Mr. Tamazawa as he thanked me for the trip to Brazil. He said, "That experience changed my life and left me with a great desire to serve my country." There is no doubt that the Japanese students touched Brazil and Peru, but perhaps the lasting legacy of the trip was its effect on students like him. I thought to myself, here is one of the young men who demonstrated against his government over the Security Treaty between the United States and Japan, and he turns out to become minister of defense.

After the show, Betty and I flew from Brazil to Copenhagen to talk with Peter. We were met by a friend who tipped us off that not all the British were happy with my leadership of *The Tiger*. Some were unhappy with Peter Howard for leaving me in charge. This friend said, "As you know, some of them are very anti-American and they think you as a young American have gotten too much power and need to be curbed—so be careful." There must be some angel that looked over us because I avoided any further criticism. Somewhat conveniently, I came down with a severe case of malaria and had to go away and recuperate for seven weeks. We were offered a chalet in the Swiss Alps or a fisherman's cottage on the west coast of Ireland. I finally persuaded Betty that a fisherman's cottage was just too tempting, and we accepted. After seven weeks of good exercise, salt air, and the never-ending warmth of the Irish people, we started to feel fit again, and my malaria was cured.

To our surprise a letter that had been following us around arrived from the former president of Brazil, Jânio Quadros, who had been so helpful with *The Tiger*. The letter informed us that he and his wife, Eloa, were traveling by ship to England. Having heard we were in Europe, they were hoping we might meet again. But by the time we received the news, their arrival was just a week away. I went down to the village and made a phone call to Peter Howard in London. He said, "Come immediately, and I'll have a dinner party in their honor!" We had burned through the whole winter's supply of turf (peat blocks for fuel) for heating in seven weeks, so it really was time to go. Our lovely and faithful next-door neighbor May Grady and Betty assured one another that we would certainly return again.

Peter Howard and his wife, Doë, arranged a dinner party covering all the important details, even having the cooks prepare a Brazilian meal of *feijoada*. Betty and I joined the Howards and welcomed the president and his wife. I think to the surprise of quite a few of the British MRA old-timers, the president gave me a Brazilian embrace. By that time all sense of criticism of our leadership in Brazil seemed to have vanished, probably with the word that President Quadros had asked to see us in London.

Peter and the former president made wonderful remarks at the end of the dinner party. Peter underlined President Quadros's incredible contribution to such a successful tour and thanked him for his personal backing and the outstanding contributions of the Brazilian Air Force in providing transportation throughout the country. Speaking in English, President Quadros thanked Peter and his wife for their gracious hospitality and offered a special thanks for a delicious Brazilian meal with all the trimmings. He then went on to pay tribute to MRA and their backing for the Japanese students. Quadros also paid tribute to President Eisenhower, saying he had been right on target with his vision that they could help with the militant students in Brazil and South America. He underlined that he had received constant reports that they had done just that, and that there had been no violent outbreaks or demonstrations from the students of Brazil. Then he very graciously turned and thanked Betty and me for our leadership, and added with a twinkle, "Blanton, as a former American naval officer, made his way with all of our Army generals, including Marshal Távora. At the end of their travels together they had dubbed him 'O Capitan.'" I was flattered by his words but also secretly happy that Peter had been exonerated. A wonderful atmosphere had been created, and many of the guests mingled and talked with President Quadros and Eloa and thanked them for coming.

Two days later, Betty and I were finally returning to America aboard the RMS *Queen Elizabeth*, headed for New York City in the spring of 1962. We had good talks with Peter before leaving. It might have been the heavy fog and cold weather in London but Peter told us, "I'm coming to be with you soon in sunny Tucson, Arizona." He went on to say that he believed without a doubt that "the youth of America are coming to a boil and they could be the key to something new developing for the world. We shall see!"

In late November I was in New York City and I had a breakfast appointment in the Pierre Hotel with two friends, Boots Adams and Bill Keeler,

Chairman and CEO respectively of Phillips Petroleum in Oklahoma. Both of these men had heard of my earlier meeting with General Eisenhower in Gettysburg, and Boots was a close personal friend of the general. When I told them I had recently escorted a group of militant Japanese students throughout Brazil at the general's request. Boots said, "Have you reported this to the boss?"—meaning General Eisenhower. I said I hadn't yet. Boots pulled out his wallet and gave me a private phone number, saying, "Call this number, use my name, and get an appointment." I called and received a call back from Eisenhower's aide, General Robert Schulz, the next day. He said, "You're lucky! General Eisenhower will be in New York City next week and suggested you come next Wednesday, December 5 at 10:00 a.m. and visit with him at his suite at the Waldorf Towers."

I had 45 minutes with General Eisenhower in his sitting room, and I had an excellent 10 minutes with General Schulz while waiting. When I walked into the sitting room there was Ike sitting with his tie off, his feet up on the desk, chewing on the end of his glasses with a definite homespun character reminiscent of his early Kansas days. The general seemed keen for the latest news on the Japanese students. He listened intently when I told him I had been in London and went to a dinner party honoring Jânio Quadros and his wife. At the end of the dinner President Quadros had thanked us for what *The Tiger* had done for his Brazilian students. "He also paid tribute to you, General Eisenhower, for urging them to go to Brazil." He said, "I appreciate that, but why don't you send more of these plays around the world—more than two companies on the road? I first heard about MRA in 1935 when I went to a home in Washington, DC, to meet Frank Buchman. Later on, I was told during the war that it was pacifist. I unfortunately didn't read enough nor study enough to know the facts until you visited me last year in Gettysburg. It was Shigeru Yoshida, the former Prime Minister of Japan, who also told me, 'My God, these people aren't pacifists!'" General Eisenhower continued. "Too many people equate military disarmament with Moral Re-Armament. You have got to get a new understanding in Washington." When I thanked General Eisenhower he said keep your eye on the young people, that's our future.[3]

14

"Tomorrow's America" Conference

"Let the Rafters Ring"
You got to sing! You got to shout to make the rafters ring!

By the mid-1960s, youth demonstrations were building in America. Young people were angry about the escalation of the Vietnam War and were starting to protest against it. At the same time, they felt deeply about the racial situation in the country that was exploding city by city, and were involving themselves in the civil rights struggle. No one seemed to know what to do, and the youth were certainly not listening to their parents, clergy, or teachers. They had a common retort: we can't hear what you're saying because the way you're living is shouting in our ears!

Early in 1964, Donald "Don" Birdsall—my close associate—and I felt strongly that we should get involved in the youth explosion. It was exciting, challenging, and a bit frightening since their hue and cry was "don't trust anyone over 30"—and we were both over 30. We met with Peter Howard, who had become the world leader of MRA. He immediately hopped on the idea, saying, "I fully agree! You two take the leadership role and I'll back you up. Go for it!" This led to the first Mackinac Island conference for young people in the summer of 1964 called "Conference for Tomorrow's America."[1]

We were in the midst of the turbulent 1960s, and the consciousness of America was changing. The once quiet college campuses of this country were becoming the focal point of a new voice—the voice of youth. The University of California, Berkeley had exploded, but much more significantly, the whole Baby Boomer generation had exploded. It was not a local or even national phenomena but one of global proportions and significance. Half of the American population was under 25, as was half of the Soviet Union, and the average age in a country like Brazil was 18. What caused these changes? Doubtless, there were hundreds of factors coming together by chance and evolution at that point in our history. However, two reasons stand out above the rest. The first was prosperity. Particularly in America but to some extent elsewhere around the world, the younger generation had been freed from the immediate task of survival, freed to let loose their imaginations. The second factor was the exposure they received through technology—young people were exposed through television to war, violence, deprivation, and disaster. By the time they were 17 they had seen places and things that most of us at the same age only dreamed of. Most importantly, this generation had developed a concern for problems that in our own younger years seemed far away indeed. They had a global awareness that was unprecedented at their age. The cry was, "We want part of the action now!" Don's and my thinking was that when you touch youth, you touch parents, grandparents, the world, and the future. We had one basic belief: that if this searching youth were given a global setting, they might say things from which we all could profit. And of course, if they could say it in the international language of music, everyone would understand it.

So word went out across the country for a new conference that summer on Mackinac Island, Michigan. One newspaper wrote, "Evidence keeps coming to light that a great many of our young people are concerned—spiritually, morally, and intellectually—with the future of our country and the world."[2] Young people needed a chance to discuss and find solutions to these issues. The response was instantaneous, as if someone had opened the dike and let the ocean in. During the summer of 1964, over 2,000 young people descended on Mackinac Island. It was truly a happening: uncontrollable and loud but terribly exciting, not only for the young people but for all of us who were there.

During the days, various inspiring speakers shared their wisdom and experience with the students. And in the evenings there was a hootenanny. The hootenannies happened frequently but on Saturdays they would showcase the best of the music written that week—everyone wanted to say something with music, so there was always a lot of songwriting going on. There were also plenty of performances of standards and inspiring songs of the day. Everyone was encouraged to participate. Naturally, some of the new music was better than others but it all felt a part of this happening.

Peter Howard was definitely the centerpiece of the conference, and he captured the young people with his eloquence. Besides being a columnist, a former captain of the All-England rugby team, he was also a well-known author, playwright, and charismatic personality. He spoke the young people's language; they were captured by him, and he was captured by them—their spirit and passion to make a difference brought out the best in him.

Many different personalities were invited to speak to the young people. Some of those who came were politicians like Representative Gerald Ford of Michigan. There were sportsmen like NCAA basketball star (and later senator) Bill Bradley of New Jersey, Stan "The Man" Musial of the St. Louis Cardinals baseball team, and Caroll Rosenbloom, owner of the Los Angeles Rams football team, who presented us with a check for $50,000. There was General Lewis Hershey, director of the Selective Service System. Finally there was the actor Sidney Poitier, who came as my guest.[3] At daylight each morning there were vigorous calisthenics, and Sidney and I joined in—or tried to. One morning he dropped out. I found him sitting under a big tree, saying as I went by, "I'm definitely going to write my congressman!"

There was a large delegation of First Americans in full ceremonial dress. Governor Abel Sanchez of the San Ildefonso Pueblo in New Mexico walked the island, giving his traditional blessing. From California, three young brothers named Colwell came: Steve, Paul, and Ralph. They had already started a successful career singing on various television and radio programs, and they quickly took the lead in organizing talent nights at Mackinac. They really became the musical leaders of our fledgling program along with Herbert Allen, a superb musician. Herb was child musical prodigy from Seattle, Washington. Since he played the xylophone he reached out to work with the steel band who had come from Trinidad and Tobago. There were also gifted dancers among the First Americans and First Nation participants.

With all this talent an idea arose that they could build a showboat and take the musical demonstration to the port cities near Mackinac, such as Harbor Springs, Kincheloe Air Force Base, and Sault Saint Marie. Teams of workers turned a barge called the *Beaver* into a first-class showboat. They built a superstructure and put sides on the barge to create a workable theater. At the last port of call in Harbor Springs, the city council cleared the main dock, supplied electric power, and brought in bleachers from the local ballpark. It was a huge success.[4]

Peter had also invited some of the leaders of MRA in Britain, but they were less enthusiastic. Still, the conference ended with Peter challenging everyone to go home and make a difference in their own communities. The conference laid the groundwork for the following year, when Sing-Out/Up with People was launched at the "Conference for Modernizing America."[5]

Following the 1964 conference, many colleges and universities across the country invited Peter to come and speak. He asked me to accompany him, which I did, and this gave us a lot of opportunities to talk. He was greatly concerned about the malaise that was turning MRA inward after having worked so diligently to bring Germany and Japan back into the family of nations. Much had been accomplished, and now the question was, what was the new mission? Peter kept saying, "We need momentum and new ideas." He was looking for fresh ideas, and we were on the verge of discovering several.

We went from Dartmouth University in New Hampshire to the University of Southern California in Los Angeles, and Peter was in his element on his speaking tour. He was in his finest role as a political analyst. Everyone responded to his convictions. When we drove into the small town of Las Vegas, New Mexico, a group of young people from MRA with creative ideas hosted a dinner for Peter. There was Bob Fleming and John Hallward from Canada, and Stu Lancaster, Frank McGee, and Malcolm Roberts from the United States. They proposed starting a magazine geared to young people. Peter again said, "Go for it, and I'll arrange for you to use the MRA headquarters on South Flower Street in Los Angeles to pioneer your magazine." Accordingly, they started *PACE* magazine, and for five years it highlighted events and pioneers of creativity. Issues covered topics such as gender, race, political corruption, the Cold War, the Vietnam War, environmental developments, the space race, and the counterculture movement.[6]

After this latest tour, Betty and I headed back to Tucson, which had been our home since 1957 when Frank Buchman invited us to spend the winter with him there. Now in 1964, it was a good place for a break and a little R&R. Don Birdsall and I sat down with Peter, and Don outlined an idea we had been talking about—how to use our headquarters buildings at Mackinac Island. He suggested that we might consider beginning a college there. Peter agreed, commenting that he had been thinking along the same lines. He thought it might give challenging work for some of the scholars in MRA like Dr. Morris Martin and Basil Entwistle. Thus was born Mackinac College, under the leadership of Dr. S. Douglas Cornell, who had recently retired as the executive officer of the National Academy of Sciences. The college would be officially chartered in 1965 and the freshmen class admitted in 1966. Eventually, it would be staffed with highly creative, passionate, and experienced professors and staff. The college lasted for just four years but has a very proud and active alumni group.[7]

While in Tucson, Peter was preparing to go to South America in early 1965. He looked quite gaunt and weary, and I encouraged him to rest a while, but in typical Peter Howard fashion he said, "They have invited me, and I must go." Before he left, he bypassed some of the older members of the MRA USA board and established me as chairman and executive director.[8] This was done publicly, and when he left for South America he said, "Now you are in charge of America, take care and stay in touch."

When Peter arrived in Lima, Peru, after a heavy schedule of speaking engagements in Brazil and Argentina, he fell ill. Morris Martin, who was accompanying him, sent me word that Peter was in the hospital but it looked like a minor infection. Several days later Morris telephoned me with the sad news that Peter had died on February 25, 1965.[9] I was poleaxed and stunned. A message came to me from his widow, Doë, urging me to come as soon as possible to London when Peter's body arrived. I contacted a good friend, John Hallward, who was the publisher of *PACE* magazine, and we flew through the night. John slept, but I found it impossible. I mourned Peter's passing and wept silently as the hours went by. What kept going through my mind was, what do we do now? Frank Buchman had died four years earlier and now his heir apparent was suddenly taken from us. I saw no one on the horizon who could step into Peter's shoes. And there was no contingency plan in place for such a leadership void. The question "What to do?" kept repeating itself in my mind. Then, the thought hit me: go to the public, the wider public who were not a part of MRA, people who had some knowledge of the program, and ask for their advice. Since I was going to Europe, the elder statesman Chancellor Konrad Adenauer of West Germany came into my mind immediately. This was definitely a crisis, so why not give it a try?

John and I arrived in London in time to be at the airport when Peter's body arrived. Doë came right over to welcome us along with her daughter, Anne, and two sons, Philip and Anthony. We were all in shock.

A friend living near Hill Farm, the Howard's family home in Suffolk County had thoughtfully arranged for our hospitality. He had brought his car to drive us. John and I were totally bushed but after a cup of strong English tea and biscuits we came back to life. Our host loaned me a phone, and I put a call through to Ernst Reinecke, a friend who I had first met when *The Good Road* was in Germany. He was now in charge of MRA in Germany. He immediately wanted to help in getting me an appointment with Chancellor Adenauer. Ernst Reinecke's enthusiasm over the project gave me a much-needed boost, but he tempered that by saying, "I'll do my best but four days is short notice!"

The next day dawned bright and sunny—not an ordinary occasion in England. We walked to Hill Farm following careful directions from our host. By that time, the Howard home was a bevy of activity with flowers and messages pouring in from friends and leaders from around the world. Peter's casket was placed in the living room, looking out over the rolling farmland. Peter Howard had made his mark on the world, and now he had come home to his family and country that he loved so dearly. I had a private moment standing at the head of the casket and the tears came as

I silently thanked Peter for what he had meant to Betty and me. We had known and loved the best of England!

At Doë's request, we had brought a copy of a film of Peter speaking to the Massachusetts State Senate and being introduced by Senator John E. Powers, president of the senate. The film captures Peter and his eloquence and the response of an American audience. All who came to pay their respects also stopped to view the film in the adjoining room. John and I were stationed in the room to answer any questions. We compared notes at the end of the day, and we both agreed that while most people were totally friendly, a few were not—in fact, they were quite cool. They had been part of the older British delegation who Peter had invited to witness and perhaps more deeply understand the youth explosion at the Mackinac conference the previous summer. Peter's family, however, made up for any small slights with their warmth and inclusiveness.

The third morning we again gathered at Hill Farm and from there walked behind the casket, carried on a horse-drawn farm dray, to the Anglican church in the village of Lavenham. Dr. Morris Martin, who was one of Peter's oldest friends from Oxford University, gave a beautiful eulogy at the funeral and was most eloquent in his tribute to Peter, sometimes eliciting tears and quite often laughter. At one point Morris compared Peter's passing to the death of a knight and the knight's sword lying where it had fallen. The challenge seemed to be who would have the courage to pick up the sword and continue the battle.

Following the funeral service there was a dinner party honoring those of us who were attending from other countries. I was seated across from Dame Flora MacLeod of MacLeod, whose ancestral home was the famous Dunvegan Castle on the Isle of Skye. We had become close friends during her visits to Tucson. One of her grandsons, Patrick Wolrige-Gordon, also my friend, was a member of Parliament and married to Peter's daughter, Anne. I'm sad to say the seating turned out to be a set up. From the moment I sat down, Dame Flora was challenging me, saying, "I'm sad that you've reneged on the commitment you had with Peter and that you're now trying to make MRA a youth program." I realized it was part of a planned strategy when the two senior men sitting next to Dame Flora also spoke, saying they had been part of the British delegation Peter had invited to the Mackinac conference and had seen this happening. They had even warned Peter. I thought to myself, what a shame it would be for me to be baited into a debate, especially at Peter's funeral. So for once in my life, I stayed quiet and nodded while they berated me. John was close enough to hear the whole conversation, and it was an eye-opener for him to realize the opposition we were facing in trying to bring new life to MRA. When we parted, Peter's words were ringing in my ears. He had given me fair warning: "Beware! Unbridled enthusiasm is an anathema to the British!" He knew that something like this might happen with his British MRA contemporaries.

John and I left early the next morning for the airport where I said goodbye to him. He left for Los Angeles and wished me lots of luck with my visit with the chancellor in Bonn. When Ernst picked me up from the Cologne-Bonn Airport some hours later, I felt a great sense of freedom. After a good German lunch of springtime white asparagus and sausage, I felt even better. Ernst's constant good counsel and briefing on Chancellor Adenauer was a tonic. I was still too naive to grasp the depth of opposition from the British but we were to learn more in the ensuing months.

When we entered Chancellor Adenauer's office he stood up from behind his desk and shook our hands. He said, "Please bear with me for a few minutes, I'm listening to the election results in northern Italy on the radio. At the moment, the communists are losing." So Ernst and I sat there studying the chancellor. His face looked like it had been chiseled out of marble but came to life when the announcement was made that the Christian Democrats were winning in Bologna. I was struck by the strength of character emanating from this man. I could see why many considered him the George Washington of the new Germany. He had a big smile on his face when he turned off the radio. Facing us, he said with a twinkle in his eye, "Now tell me young men how did you ever get along with that pious old man Frank Buchman?" We were both temporarily stunned and speechless. That was not the story we'd heard of Dr. Buchman's and Chancellor

Adenauer's relationship. I regrouped and said, "Dr. Adenauer, I've read one of your recent speeches in which you say how much the new Germany needs America, and I would like to say to you, as a young American, how much America needs Germany."

He really came to life when we told him of our recent youth conference at Mackinac Island and the enthusiastic response of the young people. He immediately said, "There is your focus. It is my greatest concern here in West Germany that our young people have grown up knowing nothing more than National Socialism under the dictatorship of Adolf Hitler. I have recently been visiting our university presidents across West Germany, urging them to be more creative in explaining freedom and democracy to their students. Please make them your focus here in Germany! If you will do this you will have my fullest backing and support." As we left we thanked him for the visit. He asked us to keep him informed and that he would back us in our efforts—which he certainly did!

With Konrad Adenauer's strong backing I felt that we were on the right track. I went back to the States with renewed energy to plan with our staff another summer conference at Mackinac——one that would mark the real beginning of Sing-Out/Up with People.

15

Sing-Out Explosion

"Up with People"
If more people were for people,
All people ev'rywhere
There'd be a lot less people to worry about,
And a lot more people who care.

When I got back from Europe, I knew I wanted to focus on the youth movement. The question was how. The thought Don Birdsall and I shared was, "What if we could capture the energy of young people and inspire them to use it in demonstrating what they are for and what they want to build for their future?"

The challenge was how to begin. The key turned out to be two great athletes, both gold medal winners in the Olympics, both attractive and articulate. Richard "Rusty" Wailes had graduated from Yale and been captain of its crew, and John Sayre had graduated from the University of Washington and captained its crew. These two men had won three gold medals between them in the Olympics. They had played a pivotal role in the "Conference for Tomorrow's America" in 1964.

With a Herculean effort, John and Rusty had spoken at 60 universities and colleges. As a result, eight student leaders came to meet with a group of us in Tucson, Arizona, on April 12, 1965, to discuss the upcoming conference. Those present were Jim Bell from Clemson University, Don Reed from Oregon State University, Ellis Fisher from Duke University, Roger Buchholtz from Western Michigan University, Ed Livermore Jr. from the University of Oklahoma, John Seeley from the University of Colorado,

Steve Roberts from the University of Wyoming, and Dave Neely from Southwestern State College.[1] It was a dynamic group, some of whom had been part of demonstrations at their colleges, they were caught up with the concept of finding a new voice to show what they stood for. Together, we thought, we could make a difference in the world.

This turned out to be a turning point. Jointly with these youth we planned a conference at Mackinac Island, which started on June 14, 1965. In the end, over 3,500 delegates from the United States and around the world gathered that summer in Michigan for a program we called "Modernizing America."[2]

They came from everywhere. There were 350 First Americans and First Nation Canadians and 10 charter flights from all over the United States, two planeloads from Europe, and a delegation from Africa. Over 120 came from Asia and 100 from Latin America, as well as groups from Australia and New Zealand. It was as if somebody had taken the cork out of the bottle, and they came pouring out. It was a happening, it was exciting, and it was uncontrollable.

Music was the medium of the time. We were most fortunate to have the involvement, again of Herb Allen, a superb musician and composer, and Steve, Paul, and Ralph Colwell—creative songwriters and motivators of young people. As Paul Colwell reminisces: *Back in June of '65 my brothers Steve, Ralph, and I were on the road. We were somewhere near the Indiana-Michigan border on the way to Mackinac when we came up with the idea for the song, "Up with People." Against the backdrop of the tumultuous '60s we wanted to add an all-inclusive note into the mix. In the years since our car ride, there's been no greater privilege and I speak for all the songwriters, than to have had young people from so many countries singing our songs around the globe. Beyond the songs, the enduring message of our common humanity is reflected in the cast members themselves. When people see these youth from so many nations and backgrounds performing with one voice and one spirit, it lifts their hopes for a world that could work together.* They had traveled the world with MRA and were excited by this new challenge. Once a week what started out as the Colwell Hour became by the second week the Sing-In, "Up, Up with

People" show. It was named for the song that in time became our theme song and eventually the name of the organization.

They were the inspiration and glue that cobbled together this musical demonstration. By late July they called the show Sing-Out '65. It was a creative explosion and a big hit with all the youth. Each day from June 19 through September 13, the ferry from Mackinaw City was kept busy bringing participants to the island for the conference. Each day there were morning calisthenics, speakers, rehearsals, sports, and competitions. The First Americans outran everyone, and the Latin American and Caribbean soccer players gave a challenge to just about everyone else. Everyone was involved in making the work of the conference happen. One group was even building a showboat, as had been done at the 1964 conference.[3]

Every evening there was a show of some kind. Once a week there was a semi-polished performance showcasing the amazing talents of the delegates. Everyone was eager to share their skills. As the summer waned and the conference was coming to an end, people were returning to their homes, jobs, and schools. Still, no one seemed eager to move on, especially the 180 students who were participating in Sing-Out '65. They were ready to go out into the public with their demonstration. John Sayre and Rusty Wailes, the Colwell brothers, Herb Allen, and all of us were of the same mind. We were relieved and excited that the gathering seemed to have been a success, but what next? Pauline McChesney, a delegate at the conference who had a home in Cape Cod, Massachusetts, suggested we bring the show there where she could help with hospitality. We enthusiastically agreed and proposed sending several of the cast with her to prepare the way. So, off they went to the Cape. There was a loud cheer from the Sing-Out '65 cast when they heard the news.

From Paul Colwell's recollection: *As successful as the show was at the conference, we knew it needed the eye and skill of an experienced artistic director to pull it together and make it "road ready." British friends contacted Henry Cass, an acquaintance of theirs, and a well-known theater director in London's West End. Cass and choreographer Bridget Espinosa arrived at the conference in mid-July. Cass's initial reaction on seeing the show was that he didn't want to touch it. He was hesitant to tamper with the authenticity, spontaneity, and unfettered energy of the youth, which he saw as the main appeal. Nonetheless, the reality was that a professional touch was essential to the production's success out in the general public. And Henry and Bridget went to work.*

Ten days later, the rest of the cast flew to Westchester County Airport near the New York/Connecticut border. Friends from Connecticut, John and Barbara Newington, had heard of the development of the show. They offered to sponsor two performances at the Ezio Pinza Theatre in North Stamford, Connecticut, on August 7 and 8. Twenty-eight hundred people came to those first two shows.[4] Then we went on to Cape Cod.

Cape Cod was busy with tourists and permanent residents, and the enthusiasm of our cast fit right in. The young people also seemed to draw attention wherever they went. Somehow, they found an old barge and made it to replicate the showboat they had at Mackinac. We never asked where it came from, and no one ever said. They proceeded to take it to different ports and put on shows for the residents and summer visitors. The news traveled swiftly around the Cape that the demonstrating youth of the 1960s had arrived and were inviting all to witness their demonstration.

They came—on foot, by bike, car, several yachts anchored nearby, and even a canoe or two. They sat on the grassy banks or anchored their boats nearby. The show was an instant hit. A group of senators was visiting the Kennedys in Hyannis Port, and they came to see the show and loved it. Congressman Durward Hall of Missouri cornered us at the end of the performance, saying, "Washington must see this! Before you end your summer conference, come to Washington. We'll put together an invitation committee from Congress." They did, and 95 Democrat and Republican members of Congress sponsored the first show at the Hilton Hotel on Connecticut Avenue in DC. On opening night 5,000 people came. From the moment the cast ran down the aisles and up onto the stage, the crowd was with them. There was great excitement in the air, both with the cast and the audience. The demonstration of Mackinac had landed in Washington, DC.[5]

The words of their songs seemed to carry special significance in the capital of the United States, and indeed in that time the capital of the free world. In the midst of the civil rights struggle, here were young people of all races singing to America, "What color is God's skin? / Everyone's the same in the Good Lord's sight." Some of the young men in the cast, later would go on to fight in Vietnam, sang a song they had written: "Freedom isn't free, / you have to pay a price / and sacrifice / for your liberty." In Washington they asked, "Which way America?" Their hope and spirit seemed to energize the audience. Several in attendance said to us at the end, "I believe in the future of our country again."

Sitting there, I was overwhelmed with the response. One could feel it growing and building to a united standing ovation. I was moved and humbled that we had been entrusted with such a gift of the young people on fire with their convictions. We felt challenged to keep it alive and growing for the future. I kept thinking, "This must go to the world." The cast and our leadership must have been on the same wavelength, because when I went backstage to thank the cast, they immediately said, "Mr. Belk, we have something going. Did you see Senator Fulbright, a Democrat from Arkansas, and Senator Goldwater, a Republican from Arizona, standing together for the ovation? We want to stay on the road! What do you think?" Without hesitating I said, "Let's do it!" And so the journey began, and what a journey!

We heard that the next day in the US House of Representatives, several members of Congress recognized the presence of Sing-Out '65 in Washington. Representative Frances Bolton of Ohio and Representative Robert McEwen of New York said, "Last night was the most moving performance I have seen. I would hope we in Congress could make it possible for the cast to stay in Washington for a further performance, this time in the open air where everybody who could not get in last night could see the show." Representative Spark Matsunaga of Hawaii declared, "I have never seen a show which inspired me so much. It showed young Americans joined in an effort to put forth a new patriotism. It is a show every American should witness."[6]

Word went out far and wide that Sing-Out '65 was going on the road. Almost immediately, invitations came from some who had been at the conference in Mackinac. First came an invitation from Supervisor Warren

Dorn of Los Angeles County, saying, "Please bring your cast, and I'll arrange a performance in Watts," a neighborhood in South Los Angeles that had just burned during race riots.[7] The second came from Dr. Toyotane Sohma in Japan, who had been responsible for the students on *The Tiger* tour of Brazil. He had witnessed the positive influence that students could have on a whole nation. He and Masahide Shibusawa of MRA Japan wanted to invite Sing-Out '65 to Japan and Korea. We accepted both groups immediately. The cast was thrilled with the news. Even the thought of California seemed to interest all of them. They were further excited when we said we would travel by train across the country. Many had never been on a train before.

What a wonderful experience it was to be on the "Sing-Out Express," heading west with this very noisy but interesting group of young people. They were determined to reach out to anyone and everyone to enlist them in their mission of building peace through understanding. At every stop they poured out of the train with a guitar or two and serenaded whoever was there. Once in a small town in Kansas, they were filled with laughter when they climbed aboard again. I heard them yell, "Can you believe that? Our cast was larger than the population of the entire town!"

An operation of this size needed a great deal of coordination. There were two couples who volunteered to travel with the cast, Jim and Carol MacLennan and John and Pat Sayre. Teams of students handled the logistics such as baggage, food, and hospitality. Multiple donors supported MRA USA, which provided the funds used to finance the operation. During that summer, Betty was in Tucson welcoming our eldest daughter, Jenny, into the world but she was certainly with us in spirit.

Everyone who saw the students' performances seemed uplifted by their spirit and passion. They landed with a bang in Los Angeles the second week of September 1965. Supervisor Warren Dorn and Don Birdsall met them at the station. The cast was visibly excited. Some were housed in private homes and others lived in the former Women's Athletic Club at 833 South Flower Street, an MRA facility. Dorn welcomed them on behalf of the supervisors of Los Angeles County, who, along with Mayor Sam Yorty, wanted to receive them later that week. Don Birdsall then calmly dropped a bombshell in their midst: "The Hollywood Bowl has been booked for a performance while you're here." The roof came off, and the train station shook. The Hollywood Bowl? My god! Beyond their wildest dreams. I said to Don, "We're still ahead of them, let's keep it that way!" After all this, the cast calmed down when they realized they had the challenge of a show at Jordan High School, a predominantly Black school in Watts, first on September 16.

The 833 South Flower Street location was a perfect setting to invite people in to meet the cast. Host families and friends came to the facility to learn more and talk with the students. It became an information center for friends and future supporters. In between these meetings, the students were rehearsing like mad for their big show at the Hollywood Bowl on September 19.[8] That performance proved a huge success with 15,000 in attendance. Everyone wanted to hear from young people who actually had something positive to say and seemed to know where they were going with their lives.

One of the men who was captured by what he experienced at the Hollywood Bowl performance was Patrick Frawley, the CEO of Technicolor and Schick Razors. He was concerned whether we were socialists, and he came to 833 South Flower Street to talk with me personally. I assured him that we were neither left nor right but up with people, all people. He was reassured. Mr. Frawley was keen to invite his friends and colleagues to a private performance at his beautiful home in Beverly Hills. Quite a few came from the business community, as well as Hollywood. Betty and I were seated at a table with Barron and Marilyn Hilton of Hilton Hotels. Our friendship with them started that evening and lasted until Barron's death in 2019. The cast performed on the outside patio of the Frawley's home. Patrick introduced them and spoke of how inspired he was after experiencing their Hollywood Bowl performance. He repeated our conversation, saying, "I was a bit concerned whether they had socialist leanings, and I went and talked to the president, Blanton Belk, sitting here. He said, 'We are neither left nor right but up, up with all people.' I like that."

He then introduced me saying, "Please tell our guests here about the success the cast had at Jordan High School last Thursday." I thanked the Frawleys for their gracious hospitality and gave special thanks to Supervisor Dorn for the sponsorship of the Los Angeles County Supervisors and his initiative in having the cast perform at the high school. I think it's fair to say that all of them were astonished that we had gone into Jordan so soon after the race riots. I said what a challenge it had been to our young people, but they had performed magnificently and won their way with a very skeptical audience. Mr. Dorn then spoke up, underlining how happy he was with their response. He observed, "I don't know of any other group who could have done what they did with the students." He also paid tribute to Rosey Grier, the former college football All-American and NFL star, who had introduced the cast at the high school. That moment had resonated with the Black students, and afterward they seemed to listen intently to the words of the songs. By the end, all of the students were standing and clapping.[9] It was a great beginning for Sing-Out '65 in Southern California.

After about 10 days in California, the cast was ready for their first overseas trip on September 21. There was some apprehension when we arrived in Hokkaido Prefecture for their first show in Sapporo, Japan.[10] Some of our cast members and even our staff were wondering how the Japanese would receive Sing-Out '65. One thing that proved most helpful was that before we left the United States we had much of the show translated. The parts that weren't sung or spoken in Japanese were projected on a large screen. We really shouldn't have worried. By the time we got to Tokyo, television and radio had announced the arrival of over 130 international students, identifiable by their Western outfits with cowboy hats, and we were off and running. In fact, in the Ginza district of Tokyo, when our cast walked around, students and others would come up and welcome them personally, often trying out their English.

Another concern was whether enough Japanese families would offer hospitality and take in our students. Fortunately, Takasumi Mitsui, part of the famous Mitsui family, had been involved with MRA Japan and spoke up on our behalf. This provided us with many host families. So many wonderful relationships and stories evolved during the visit, and our students could not get over the heartfelt hospitality of the Japanese families.

One of the first places we tested the waters was at Waseda University, a private university. Some of their student body had led the way in demonstrations against the Japanese government. They were keen to build a link with youth from other countries. The words and music of Sing-Out '65 translated into the Japanese grabbed their attention and they took it all in. At the finale, the students were stomping and standing and demanding more. They were keen to make contact personally with the international cast, though they were most eager to make friends with the Americans. We also were invited by Nihon University, the second largest university in Asia, and by Sophia University, a major Catholic university in Japan. The response was similar at both these universities. It was a true mixture and coming together of many different cultures.

Something quite unusual happened at that point. An invitation came from the prestigious Kabuki-za Theater in the Ginza district for Sing-Out '65 to perform there. Our Japanese hosts told us that, to their knowledge, no foreign group had ever performed there before. This was an entirely different audience from the one at the university—representatives of the arts, politics, and business all filled the venue. Again, it was a huge success.[11]

After this very successful tour in Japan, the cast was welcomed in South Korea. Unfortunately, I was not able to stay for most of this part of the tour, but I was invited to a memorable visit with Prime Minister Chung Il Kwon at his office followed by a luncheon. The cast spent a week in South Korea traveling from Pusan (now Busan) to Seoul. In Seoul they performed for Prime Minister Chung and his family.[12] The cast members ended their visit with a performance for the officers and men of the 2nd Infantry "Indianhead" Division of the US Eighth Army stationed at Panmunjom on the 38th parallel north. The cast used a railway flatcar as a stage. It was well-received by the soldiers. An excited group of students returned to California just in time to tape the show for TV. As Patrick Frawley had promised, it was sponsored by Schick Razor and broadcast as a one hour coast-to-coast special on NBC TV the following spring.

16

Chancellor Konrad Adenauer

"Keep Young at Heart"
Old Father time can't catch up with you,
So keep young at heart

Chancellor Konrad Adenauer was a major influence on my decision to focus on young people. So it made perfect sense that one of our earliest tours would be to West Germany. Therefore, we were thrilled in 1966 when Chancellor Ludwig Erhard, with backing from former Chancellor Adenauer, sent an official government invitation for Sing-Out '66 to fly to Bonn. They would reach out to the youth of West Germany. This invitation, which included all expenses paid by their government, was accepted and the international cast of 150 started their tour. They were met by Chancellor Erhard and members of the cabinet at the Palais Schaumburg, the official residence of the chancellor. My friend Ernst Reinecke met me at the Cologne-Bonn Airport. After the welcoming reception for us and the cast, I presented Chancellor Erhard with a cowboy hat. The cast broadcast part of their show live from the Palais for public radio. Following that event, they went for lunch as guests of President Eugen Gerstenmaier of the Bundestag, the West German parliament.

In the meantime, Ernst and I went straight to the Bundestag where Chancellor Adenauer had his office. He received us most cordially. I was struck again by his strong personality that had led West Germany out of the depths of despair at the end of the World War II into a respected place in the family of nations. He turned to me and said, "Mr. Belk, I have just returned from America. I had a most valuable visit as the guest of President and Mrs. Johnson on their ranch in Texas." He broke into a smile, saying, "Lady Bird wears the trousers!" He was grateful for the opportunity to thank President Lyndon Johnson and America for the outpouring of assistance and aid that had helped put West Germany back on its feet.

Dr. Adenauer continued, "At my 90th birthday celebration, I had the opportunity to meet and hear from your students in Sing-Out '66. They sang a special song for me, 'Keep Young at Heart.' I assured them I was working on that daily. When I thanked them, I underlined that they would be in West Germany at a very important time in the life of our young people, since they have grown up knowing very little else than National Socialism. I urged them to reach as many of our young people in high schools and universities as possible, hoping you can encourage them to put aside any feelings of guilt about our past and build for the future."

During our meeting with Dr. Adenauer, Ernst briefed him on the effect that Sing-Out/Up with People was having on the German university students traveling with the cast—100 members in all from nine newly formed local Sing-Outs representing various cities in West Germany.

A group of these students would later speak about "the cast's pace, discipline, and enthusiasm for their idea, which has lifted them out of their cynicism and noninvolvement."[1] In Hamburg, the *Hamburger Abendblat* there described the hot discussions that went on in the foyer of the auditorium after the show, observing, "The Sing-Out challenged people with the power of irresistible conviction. Sing-Out forces people to think." Another newspaper, *Welt am Sonntag* reported, "There was a roar of applause for 'Deutschland, mein Heimatland' ('Germany, My Homeland')." The article continued, "These are the roots of this new youth action. 'Homeland,' 'fatherland' are new words for teenagers. Freedom, action, responsibility for other people, and democracy are not only musically new notes. These are new ideas.[2] Earlier in the year, in the city of Neuss, the *Neuss Grevenbroicher* newspaper wrote, "The success was unusual. The fresh vitality of the young Americans won the hearts of the German youth. Spontaneously a German-American friendship was cemented. The audience were literally yanked out from their seats."[3] Ernst then had a chance to give Dr.

Adenauer a briefing. When he mentioned that some 350 young people had just been involved in a new expression called Sing-Out Deutschland '66, a big smile appeared on his craggy face and he said, "Congratulations! That's what I hoped."

During our time with Dr. Adenauer we found out that he had recently traveled to Spain. This gave me an opportunity to get his advice on an invitation that had come to Sing-Out/Up with People from the Department of Culture in Madrid. When I told Dr. Adenauer that some of our Scandinavian friends had advised us not to accept, saying we should not visit a country that was under a dictatorship. He roared with laughter and replied, "For goodness sake, they have a benevolent dictator to what we had under Hitler—go to Spain, perhaps you can play a part in encouraging them to connect themselves once again with Europe." We welcomed his opinion since the potential trip to Spain was imminent.

Chancellor Adenauer was in a relaxed mood and underlined for us the special relationship he had built with General Charles de Gaulle and the French. "Four years ago, General de Gaulle invited me to Paris. There we made peace and started a friendship that is fundamental to the future of Europe," he said. "Please inform him what you're planning for the youth and that you want to include the French youth. My secretary will give you his personal phone number. Call on my behalf for an appointment." As we got ready to leave, Chancellor Adenauer spoke to us in a fatherly fashion saying, "I have been thinking a great deal about Sing-Out/Up with People, and I believe it represents something new. I would advise you not to pour this new wine into old bottles—stand on your own!" We thanked him and assured him we would take his thoughts seriously. And we did.

In the next few days we were tempted to reach out to President de Gaulle using the private number that Dr. Adenauer had given us, but language was an issue. Ernst briefed the MRA office in France and asked if they would help us make the call, but they refused. We had assumed they would be as excited we were. In retrospect, we should have figured out a way to do it ourselves.

On June 10, 1966, at the Westfalenhallen in Dortmund, 20,000 people packed the biggest hall in West Germany and demanded 20 minutes of encores while they stood with glowing cigarette lighters swaying back and forth to the beat of the music. Sitting directly in front of me was a large group of MRA full-time workers from England who had flown over at my invitation. Through all this loud response they sat there with hands on their laps. I was shocked to see such behavior. They must have been directed. How sad. What a mistake. It was one thing to be against me and the new young people's program but not in the neighbors' living room. I flew home sick at heart, realizing suddenly what we were up against. I thought again about Peter Howard's warning to me to be careful: "Unbridled enthusiasm is an anathema to the British."

Less than a year later, in April 1967, an invitation embossed with the official crest of Germany arrived from the Adenauer family for me to attend the funeral services for Chancellor Adenauer. I was honored and of course accepted. I flew to Bonn where Ernst Reinecke met me at the airport and informed me that Prince Richard of Hesse-Kassel, Colonel Eric Peyer of Switzerland, and Ernst and I were some of the few outside guests to be a part of the funeral party. These other two gentlemen were our friends and longtime associates and friends of Dr. Adenauer.

Morning coat was the dress for the two services—one in the Bundestag and the other in Cologne. We had all come prepared, but I was missing a top hat. I acquired one, but it was much too large, coming down over my eyes. After we folded part of the *Frankfurter Allgemeine Zeitung* newspaper inside, it fit perfectly. The four of us looked quite dignified in the official photograph, but without a doubt Prince Richard of Hesse-Kassel, a great-grandson of Queen Victoria of Great Britain, gave us class!

The next morning we were seated in the front row of the gallery in the Bundestag. They were wonderful seats looking down on the packed hall; the two front rows were reserved for heads of state, royalty, and representatives of other governments. We could see President Lyndon Johnson talking with Chancellor Erhard and President Charles de Gaulle, who seemed to tower over all the others. Quite a few were gathered around General Lucius Clay, who had administered the Berlin Airlift during the occupation of

Germany. When the organ started playing there was silence and everyone stood in tribute to the Adenauer family as they were ushered into their seats. At the end of this moving service, Konrad Adenauer's casket, draped with the German flag, was escorted by the military down the aisle and taken by hearse to a gunboat standing by. It had been Chancellor Adenauer's wish to be buried in his hometown of Rhondorf near Cologne. I thought as the gunboat slowly went up the Rhine River that the whole world would miss the wisdom and statesmanship of this man. I personally owed him a debt of gratitude for his vision and encouragement in the development of Sing-Out/Up with People. I felt humbled to call him a friend. Historian Charles Williams wrote in his book *Adenauer: The Father of the New Germany*, "The father of the new Germany had come home to his rest."[4]

We drove to Cologne for the Requiem Mass in the cathedral. It was packed. Again world leaders were there to say their goodbyes. Later, we stood on the banks of the Rhine and watched the motor launch, accompanied by three naval patrol boats, moving slowly upstream past the thousands who stood in silence on both banks of the river. The casket on the afterdeck was visible to all of us as it made its way up the river to Rhondorf. Afterward, I shook hands and introduced myself to the gentleman standing next to me. It turned out to be General Lucius Clay.

On the 25th anniversary of Chancellor Adenauer's death, we wanted to honor his important role in the founding of Up with People. In May 1992, Professor Pieter van Vollenhoven, husband of Her Royal Highness Princess Margriet of the Netherlands and Up with People Board member, and I joined Chancellor and Mrs. Helmut Kohl in Bonn for the presentation of Up with People's Founder's Award.

We knew that Konrad Adenauer would have been pleased with all of the progress Up with People had made in the 25 years since he had encouraged us to forge a new path for young people in the world. Chancellor Adenauer would have felt that his charge to me had been well fulfilled by the creation of two national casts of Sing-Out Deutschland and the 12 local sing-outs.

17

Growth and Incorporation of Up with People

"The Beat of the Future"
The sound of tomorrow's ringin' in our ears.

There was a dynamic at the heart of Up with People. Hard to put your finger on. It was quicksilver and combustible but out of it came a global strategy that inspired everyone. It was the coming together of like-minded people with a shared passion to affect the world. It was not group thought. It was freedom to turn your mind loose and let it soar. It would sometimes start with a small issue, building and expanding as one after another put forth their ideas and thoughts. The process was that we are many but we are one. It had something to do with the people involved. We were brought together because we shared a common mission. We were friends who completely trusted one another and had respect for what each brought to the table. It excited us and the excitement ricocheted down to the students, to our sponsors, hosts, and public. We were at home with one another, we liked and treated each other with respect, and each played his or her distinctive part.

I gloried in these informal gatherings and I think I was at my best. I would listen until a thought generated in my soul. Often I would be able to bring it all together with an idea that was nowhere on the horizon when we started. It was our creative powerhouse. Strategy for our casts emerged, ideas for fundraising, people to be enlisted, themes for our shows, ideas for new songs, and relevant issues to be focused. Everything was brought together by these gatherings and everyone was inspired and uplifted. We came together knowing that we were reaching for things which none of us could achieve on our own because our reach was longer than our arm.

In Paul Colwell's words, *We were engaged in a nonstop think tank and songwriting collaboration. We looked at what was going on in the world and tried to create material that tapped into the culture and trends of the times and also addressed some of humankind's inequities and injustices. In one of these sessions, Blanton commented that "this is an unfinished world." We songwriters jumped on it and "Unfinished World" became the finale number of the show we later took to the Soviet Union.*

It was becoming increasingly clear that Sing-Out/Up with People was not just a happening of the 1960s. Instead we, the leadership, believed it could become something permanent for the future. Sing-Out/Up with People was being welcomed in countries around the world. More students were applying to travel than we had space for in the buses and on the stage. Fortunately, the Colwell Brothers and Herb Allen had caught the vision of what Sing-Out/Up with People could do and stayed on the road with us. They continued to write music and lyrics and impact show production as well as help develop a road staff to maintain the quality of the show.

Families were opening their homes for homestays in every city and country. The interest was so great among those young people who were not able to be part of a traveling international cast but wanted to participate, therefore it was decided to publish a book inviting anyone to start their own local Sing-Out. *How to Create Your Own Sing-Out* was published in 1965 and was the first of many editions. Editors David Allen and Robin Hoar said, "Thousands have expressed a desire to put on their own Sing-Outs. Dozens of casts have already sprung up. This book was written by us—the members of the [international] cast—so that you could join us in what has been the greatest adventure of our lives."[1] In 1965 we could not have imagined that over 230 local Sing-Outs had sprung up by National Sing-Out Day on April 20, 1968. Celebrating the spirit of the local Sing-Outs, 14 governors and 139 mayors issued proclamations. However, the Sing-Out explosion was not only in North America but also in Europe, South America, the Caribbean, Asia, Africa, and Australia. By fall of 1968, there were 716 local, national, and international Sing-Outs.[2] We had an explosion on our hands; it was exciting and uncontrollable!

After the creation of a second cast in late February 1966 and the astonishing growth of the local and international Sing-Out program, we felt the need for another conference. The center at Mackinac Island was being prepared to become Mackinac College, a four-year liberal arts college. So we decided to make Estes Park, Colorado, the conference site. Summer 1966 was a great time to gather students who were on vacation. The two existing international traveling casts met in Estes Park. They called their month-long demonstration "Action Now." After it ended on July 2, several hundred youth went to Douglas, Wyoming, to work on the show production and a third cast was formed. Then, three international casts of about 500 students covered the Unites States and Canada. In mid-August, the three casts reconvened in Long Island, New York, and I met them and heard their stories and experiences. I told the casts that in the coming months that one cast would be on the West Coast, one in Canada, and one would travel to Puerto Rico, Panama, Jamaica, Venezuela, and México City. By the time we met again in Santa Fe, New Mexico, for Christmas and New Year's they would have touched the whole North American continent.

Early the next year on February 12, 1967, the cast performed for a standing-room-only audience at the Holiday Inn Riviera Hotel Convention Center in Palm Springs, California. The next day's *Desert Sun* newspaper carried two front-page pictures and a write up of Mamie Eisenhower attending the performance of Up with People. The article stated, "A musical hurricane swept through the convention center last night," and quoted Mrs. Eisenhower as saying, "I wouldn't have missed this. The general is one of your biggest boosters. You are the best ambassadors that America has."[3]

The next morning, General Eisenhower entertained the cast. They performed for him at the Cochran-Odlum Ranch in Indio, which he had often used as the Winter White House. So here we were with an international cast of over 150 on a beautiful California day, and chairs had been arranged on the lawn for President Eisenhower and special guests. President Eisenhower, obviously very moved by the performance, asked to speak to the cast. "...If I thought they would accept me, I would go down to a recruiting place. Yes, I assure you, I am young enough at heart." He said that the first time he heard the song "Freedom Isn't Free" was right in the middle of the battlefield of Gettysburg. "It was a very, very appropriate spot," he said, "where so many, many thousands of men died, so it made it a very meaningful thing to me as an old soldier, and made me proud of those youngsters, as I am of you. I wish there were six million of you instead of 600 as one of your directors told me…. I just can't tell you how proud I am and how thankful I am that youngsters like you will make the sacrifice to go out and carry this message everywhere."

He then added, "If we could wake up people to think of the sentiments, to reach out again for the kind of sentiments that you have been singing about this morning, this would be an almost perfect country. We would understand the world of men because of our brotherhood under God and as sons of God. We would really have such a nation that has never been on Earth and could stand as an example for all, reaching out a helping hand intelligently and usefully and making us all a happier and finer people."[4]

We thought everyone would be as thrilled as we were by all this great success, but we were too naive. Within MRA Britain, there was a growing resistance from the traditionalists. They seemed to be against any change or anything new. They thought it was just American enthusiasm and would die out, that there was no substance to it. I had hoped from the beginning that this explosion would be the answer to a malaise in MRA that had turned the organization inward. More and more it was becoming clear this was not to be. I still had a foot in both camps since I was the chairman and executive director of MRA USA, but I was pouring my time and energy into the creation of something new with Up with People. When I discussed all of this with my associate Don Birdsall, I told him I wanted to try one more time to confer with MRA Britain before we made the move of breaking away and incorporating separately. I had heard that there was to be a meeting in London of the young international leadership of MRA. So I sent word to Roly Wilson, one of those in charge of MRA Britain, saying, "I would like to come and meet with this group to discuss how we should handle this explosion of young people." A message came back:

"There is no meeting. Roly will fly to confer with you in Tucson." He and his wife Mary arrived in March 1967 in Tucson. We welcomed them and hosted them in our home.

The next morning on our telex machine was a message for Roly from the London office of MRA Britain. My secretary Barbara Sack gave me the telex which was addressed to me since my name was copied on it. It read, "For your information all the young leadership is gathered here in London to plan for the future." I was furious and felt completely conned! They were going ahead and making their own plans, even as Roly was supposed to be meeting to discuss the situation with me. After breakfast, we met in the living room and I confronted Roly and showed him the telex, which he read and he turned completely red in the face. I said, "Roly, you lied to me! You told me there was no meeting planned. And now this." There followed a heated discussion, he and his wife left the room and they left Tucson the next day. I asked my associate, Don Saul, to drive them to Denver for their return flight to London.

When I informed Don Birdsall and showed him the telex and described our meeting with Roly, I said, "That's it! Enough is enough; we're going to break and run free." I then said, "From the beginning, I felt this whole emergence of Sing-Out/Up with People had been a gift from God. There is a certain precious substance here. The decision we are facing is whether to go along with MRA Britain and let this die, or forget them and keep this alive? There's no question in my mind which way we should go. I want you and Bill Wilkes, our assistant treasurer, to go to Los Angeles as soon as possible to see our attorney, Deane F. Johnson at O'Melveny and Myers. Please talk to them about the process of incorporating Up with People as a charitable and educational nonprofit corporation 501(c)(3)." The conversation had started and I felt we were on the right track.

One month later I took a break in México to take in the salt air and enjoy some fishing. I flew back to Tucson in a private plane, landing in Nogales, Arizona, to go through customs on April 17, 1967.[5] As we taxied up to the front of the terminal, which at that time was only a barracks building, the woman who ran air traffic control came running out, red in the face, waving her arms, exclaiming something we couldn't hear. We opened the small window and asked her what was going on. At that point, the propellers were still slowly turning. She said, in a most excited voice, "President Eisenhower is on the phone for Mr. Belk!" I was startled but immediately got out of the plane and followed her at a loping gait to her small office. To this day, I do not know how President Eisenhower knew I was arriving on a private plane at that point from Guaymas to Nogales, but he did! She handed me the phone and sat down in the corner, listening to the conversation. She seemed mesmerized.

His voice came booming over the phone, and he immediately came to the point, "I've been thinking about your program, and I have some thoughts for you. As you know, I'm an old military man, and I believe in the chain of command, so I'm passing on these thoughts to you."

As a former lieutenant (j.g.) in the US Navy, I almost saluted but said instead, "Yes, sir, general, I do know that." He continued, "Well, I was talking with one of your Japanese students, Emiko Chiba, the granddaughter of one of my old friends from Japan." Then he said, "Are you still there?"

"Yes, sir!" I answered.

"Well, I have something else," he said. "I want you to incorporate your program, making it totally independent, apolitical, and nonsectarian, and available for the youth of the world. Did you get that?"

"Yes, sir!" I answered. I began to feel that I was in an officer's briefing room during D-Day, so I answered "Yes, sir!" again, then, "I will certainly do that!"

He said, "Fine, but I'm not finished yet. Emiko tells me you have a big performance coming up in Washington, DC, in Constitution Hall. I have a thought about that. I think you need bipartisan support as you get this mission going, so I was wondering if you would mind if Mamie and I invited President and Mrs. Lyndon Johnson to join us for this occasion. What do you think?"

I quickly thanked him and said, "We would be greatly honored to have such support."

Then he said, "It's a done deal! Now, remember, with your young people, you are talking about the essence of freedom, which is self-responsibility and service to others. It is a precious substance, freedom, so treat it as such." I thanked him again and said his remarks and convictions were so timely. President Eisenhower was a visionary who felt keenly, as Chancellor Adenauer had felt earlier, that the time had come to stand on our own.

Upon my return from attending Konrad Adenauer's funeral I flew to Panama City, Panama, in early May 1967. The Panamanian government wanted to bestow on me the Order of Vasco Nunez de Balboa "in gratitude, by the government and people of Panama for the admirable job the cast of Up with People has been doing in our country."[6]

In mid-May 1967 the US Department of the Army had turned over Fort Slocum/Davids Island to the City of New Rochelle, New York. Two years earlier, Fort Slocum had ceased being used as a military installation. Our staff proposed to the New Rochelle City Council that we have use of it for our World Sing-Out Festival that summer of 1967. They agreed to rent it for a handsome fee of one dollar for the summer and the deal was done. Then, the real work began. A cast with great energy went to work to make the facilities ready for the World Sing-Out Festival a few weeks away. The day before the official opening we graduated the Class of 1967 of Sing-Out High School on the Island. As the opening day approached, delegations began pouring in from Brazil, Panama, Puerto Rico, and Venezuela. Fourteen African nations were represented by the casts of Harambee Africa and Springbok Stampede. From Asia came the 100-strong cast of Let's Go '67 representing Hong Kong, Indonesia, Japan, Philippines, Republic of China, and South Korea. The Europeans arrived in force from Denmark, Finland, Netherlands, Norway, and Sweden including the 200 members of Sing-Out Deutschland. We regretted that India Arise and the British musical *It's Our Country, Jack* were not able to accept the invitation that was sent to Roly Wilson by me. Also, we were disappointed that the Australian musical *Wake Up, Matilda* was unable to come because of prior commitments. Later that summer at the Festival when I made the announcement of the decision to incorporate Up with People as its own nonprofit corporation, there was great applause.

During the next summer, we spent time with longtime friends from Connecticut, Dr. Bill Close and his wife Bettine. Bill was a young doctor and had a desire to help the emerging new countries in Africa, especially the Congo. He could move freely there being fluent in French. So in 1960 he went to Leopoldville (now Kinshasa) to practice medicine. He was the sole surgeon operating during those desperate days of the revolution for their independence from Belgium. He befriended a young soldier named Mobutu, who later became president of the Democratic Republic of the Congo in 1965. For the next 17 years, Bill divided his time between Connecticut and Kinshasa while being the personal physician to President Mobutu Sese Seko. Their daughter Glenn was in the cast of Up with People and he could see the value of the training the students were getting and wanted to make it possible for the young Congolese to know what they were experiencing. In consultation with the president, an invitation was sent to me for the cast to perform at the Eighth Independence Day celebrations. It would be followed by a three-week tour of the country. Naturally we accepted.

Meanwhile, all the casts were gathering at Fort Slocum for the World Up with People Festival, which was due to open on June 30, 1968. The cast flying to the Congo departed on June 23. Their first open-air performance, presented in French and Lingala was filmed by Radio-Television Nationale Congolaise. It was repeatedly shown during the next weeks and months on Congolese TV. After a four-city tour, the cast returned to the World Up with People Festival to great acclaim from all of the assembled Sing-Outs and delegates. Then, on to the next challenge which was filming the NBC TV special sponsored by the *Reader's Digest* and Coca-Cola and hosted by entertainer Bob Hope. The filming began immediately in Washington Square Park in Greenwich Village and on the streets of Upper Manhattan. After three days of rehearsals and the final taping at Madison Square Garden, the cast finished filming at Fairleigh Dickinson College in Madison, New Jersey. The show was colorcast on the NBC TV Network on August 23, 1968. After a spectacular summer, the three casts fanned out across the United States and Canada.

While all of this was happening in New York, another whole chapter was opening in California. We had met Mervyn and Kitty LeRoy at a dinner at Patrick Frawley's home in 1965. Mervyn was an Oscar-winning director and producer and Kitty was a mover and shaker of Hollywood society. They decided to chair an evening at the Dorothy Chandler Pavilion of the Los Angeles Music Center on December 11, 1968, where Governor Ronald Reagan and his wife, Nancy, were the honorary chairmen. Bob Hope hosted the evening. It was a star-studded occasion and all 3,200 seats were filled. Governor Reagan, who had met with the cast before the show and had asked for an opportunity to speak, said "...these young people are the most hopeful thing that has happened in this century." At the end of the show there was thunderous applause from the audience demanding encores. At the request of Kitty LeRoy, as Chairman of the Board and President of Up with People, I stepped on stage and told the audience, "...I believe that America is absolutely ready for what we have seen on stage tonight... The world is reaching out for this."[7]

All three casts, some 700 members, met together in Santa Fe, New Mexico, that December. We were welcomed by Governor David Cargo, Archbishop James Peter Davis, and Mayor George Gonzales. It was refreshing for everyone to interact and we performed our shows for each other because each show was unique.

After Santa Fe, an unusual thing happened, the governors of three states—Oklahoma, Missouri, and Arkansas—invited all three casts of Up with People to blanket their states with performances the first months of 1969. The interest and hunger for what they had to say seemed to be insatiable.

In the spring of 1969, all three casts converged on Europe. One cast went to Italy and performed in all the major cities. At the Vatican, they were recognized in a general audience of Pope Paul VI. Another cast went to Spain sponsored by the Ministry of Information and Tourism. They had a chance to perform in the *Festivales de Espana 1969*. The third cast went to Belgium and France for the first time. They performed in the Palais de Beaux-Arts in Brussels and for Their Majesties King Baudouin and Queen Fabiola in the Royal Arboretum. Those three casts stayed in the homes of 6,000 host families and made lifelong friends. It was the emergence of Up with People Europe. During those three months, Up with People reached more than 90 million people in six countries and 53 cities via live performances, radio, and television coverage. One of the casts visited Paris as part of their tour.

Sargent Shriver was the US ambassador to France at the time. I had met him when he was head of the Peace Corps and also had met his wife Eunice Kennedy Shriver. Ambassador Shriver sent a private message to me asking whether a cast could perform at the Cité Universitaire in Paris. That performance happened on May 9, 1969. It turned out to be a memorable and terrifying experience for all of the cast and for the packed audience.

Ambassador Shriver got up to introduce the show. As he started to speak, the whole balcony erupted with Viet Cong students unfurling Viet Cong flags. The Viet Cong were South Vietnamese who supported the Communist cause in North Vietnam. They were shouting and yelling, trying to drown him out. The shouting started in the main balcony but very soon it was echoed by everyone shouting their opinion. It was bedlam. The ambassador, to his credit, stood his ground and continued his introduction. He and his wife had refused to have any security in the auditorium. They thought it would put a damper on the evening. There Betty and I were: I was sitting next to Mrs. Shriver and their children; Betty was sitting on the aisle and experienced first-hand terror when a man ran by her up the aisle with a smoking package headed for the stage. Of course, we all thought it was a bomb. He set it down at the front of the stage and I was terrified that we were going to witness another Kennedy family tragedy. We found out later that the package was harmless but the moment was terrifying. We discovered, after the fact, that the Viet Cong students had barricaded all the doors. Little did we realize that we were prisoners inside.

The show started but the din continued on and off, eventually putting fire in the cast's performance. At one point in the show, soloist Dan Broadhurst—a wounded Vietnam War veteran who had served in a tank company—stepped forward with his guitar, alone on the stage, to sing in French and in English, "What Color is God's Skin?" This song spoke to the racial conflict in the '60s and would become one of Up with People's signature songs. His sheer presence and passion and his anger at the disruption from the audience slowly started to quiet the students down, and they began to listen. That was the turning point in the show. Mrs. Shriver later described it as an extraordinary moment. The Shrivers were impressed with the courage of the cast and how their energy and enthusiasm affected the crowd.

At the end of that show, some Viet Cong students came down to the front of the stage and many of them spoke to our students and even apologized to the cast. They thought that, given the sponsorship of the Shrivers, we were part of the US government not just students from all over the world representing their hopes and values. Many of them were very taken with the concept and the ideas in the show that young people were trying to demonstrate in this fashion.

Through all these weeks and months, the MRA USA Board, from which I had resigned as chairman and executive director, had been entirely helpful to us. They even went to the point of encouraging us to form an international educational corporation and stand on our own.

In 1970, H. Kenaston Twitchell Jr., the Chairman of the Board, and Skiff Wishard, Managing Director of MRA USA, came to me privately with a proposal. They said, "What you're doing best represents the next phase of MRA USA, and the board made a decision that we'd like you to consider. We would turn over to you for Up with People our financial portfolio, which as you know includes quite a few lifetime pledges." I was completely surprised and flattered at the same time. I sent my sincere thanks and gratitude back to the board and said that I would need to think about it. I felt compelled to talk this over with Deane Johnson, our attorney, to ask for his advice and I went to Los Angeles to see him and to explain the situation. He sat and pondered for a long time. Then he said, "Blanton, this is your decision. You have to make this by yourself." The more I considered it, the more I came to the conclusion that, although it was financially compelling, these monies had been left for an ecumenical Christian organization. It would be wrong for the monies to come to Up with People without the full agreement of each of those donors. So we declined. When I went back and told Deane Johnson of my decision, he said, "Congratulations, I believe you made the right decision."

Sadly for all of us, on his trip back to Washington we heard that President Eisenhower had a heart attack and was taken to Walter Reed Army Medical Center. He had a number of additional attacks before dying on March 28, 1969. That was of course a poignant moment for all Americans. I was glad that I had followed through with his suggestion, as I promised, and we incorporated Up with People as he had urged.

After General Eisenhower's death, Mamie Eisenhower was one of the first to agree to accept my invitation to join the Up with People International Advisory Board. In February 1974, I flew to Palm Springs to escort Mrs. Eisenhower and her friend to a show and green room before the show. Green room was a theatrical tradition which Up with People adopted and was a chance for the whole cast to come together and reflect. Both of these women were much taken with the candid expressions of the young people. The following day Mrs. Eisenhower sent me a handwritten note accepting my offer to join our International Advisory Board. She accepted not only for herself but in honor of her husband and the hope he found in the mission of the students. She also included a check with a notation, "Ike always paid tribute to Up with People as the greatest ambassadors that America has."

18

The Further We Reach Out

"The Further We Reach Out"
The closer we become.

Throughout my time building and running Up with People, I sought out those who had the same motivation that I did to make a difference in our world. Sometimes they were college students or people in the business world. Sometimes they were visionaries like General Dwight Eisenhower and Chancellor Konrad Adenauer. That included others who were willing to back our vision with financial resources and give us ongoing advice on how best to develop a sustainable organization. Here are some of their stories.

On the way to Chancellor Adenauer's funeral in April 1967 I stopped overnight in New York City to visit Sing-Out '66, which was performing in the Pierre Hotel. The ballroom of the hotel was filled. The performance ended with a standing ovation, and the cast came off the stage to talk with the guests. At that point, a gentleman approached me and said, "My name is DeWitt Wallace, and I'm very taken with what I've seen tonight and in my talks with the young people. I was wondering if you would accept my invitation to lunch with me tomorrow. I'll send a car for you if that's possible." Not having a clue as to who this tall, stately man was, I said I'd be happy for a rain-check but that I was on my way to Chancellor Adenauer's funeral in Germany. Fortunately for all of us, Don Birdsall had learned that DeWitt Wallace, with his wife Lila, were the founders of *Reader's Digest*. The magazine with the biggest circulation in the world, read by millions in their own languages. Don interrupted the conversation and said, "Mr. Wallace, I'm sure we can change Blanton's flight so that he can accept your invitation for lunch." So the next day Mr. Wallace sent his driver with a blue Cadillac to pick me up at the hotel and take me out to the guesthouse at the *Reader's Digest* headquarters.

Mr. Wallace greeted me at the door and introduced me to Hobart Lewis, the CEO and Editor-in-Chief of *Reader's Digest*. Mr. Lewis had not seen the performance the night before but had heard high praise about it from Mr. Wallace. It was interaction with the international cast, however, that really caught Mr. Wallace's attention. His father had been the president of Macalester College in Minnesota, and Mr. Wallace (who I was soon calling Wally) said, "My father struggled with how to pass on character to his students. Last night I honestly felt the character and stability in these young people."

Mr. Lewis fixed me with a beady eye and said, "Blanton, this is all well and good but how are you going to finance this operation? I'm sure you have dreams of expanding it." I replied that we hoped we were doing something that would get backing from the public. Already many people were helping by offering to be host families for our students. Wally stepped in saying, "I've been thinking about your financing overnight, and I have a proposal. What would you think if the Reader's Digest Foundation gave you $40,000 a month for the three casts you have already on the road? If you like the idea, we could do that and you could recognize us by saying Up with People is brought to you in part by a gift from the Reader's Digest Foundation."

Swiftly moving into unknown territory and not knowing how to respond, I said nothing. Wally quickly said, "Are you thinking that's not enough?"

"No, no," I quickly replied, "that would be an enormous boost to our program at this moment." So with handshakes all around the deal was done! He was most solicitous and walked me out to the car to head back to Manhattan. As we were saying our goodbyes, Wally said, "What I saw last night, my wife and I have dreamed about—international youth united with a message of peace for the world. You are doing what we are trying to do with our magazine and perhaps someday we can unite!" This was the beginning of a lifelong friendship.

There was great excitement back in Tucson at the news of Wallace's donation. This pledge was definitely a tipping point!

Shortly after I arrived back from Konrad Adenauer's funeral, there was a message from Wally that he was sending me a draft of an article on Sing-Out/Up with People. He had requested that one of his top editors have it ready for the May issue of *Reader's Digest*. In fact, he did several articles on Up with People over the years. At the time of this first one, we were still associated with MRA. To the best of my recollection, it had an ending that quoted MRA's founder, Frank Buchman. This really annoyed Wally. When he called me about it, he was incensed, almost blaming me, and considered canceling the whole thing. The editor of the story was in line for a lot of fire and steam. Wally wanted the article to be about Sing-Out, not MRA. As he continued to complain, I went to work and got a quote from former President Eisenhower instead, which then appeared at the end of the piece.[1] Wally frequently told me, "Blanton, you've got to get away from this dreary image of Buchman and MRA. You have got to incorporate and make this an independent organization on its own."

Wally welcomed the news of the World Sing-Out Festival at Fort Slocum in 1967. He said, "This will allow us to become more acquainted with your program." Wally visited us several times at Fort Slocum, and I enjoyed picking him up in the motor launch that had been donated to us by our friend John Newington. Usually Wally came with guests and he greatly enjoyed being in the midst of all the young people. At one particular session, we had over 1,000 on the island with Sing-Outs that had come in from Brazil, Kenya, Japan, Germany, and different cities across America. During that first summer in 1967, we had over 5,000 young people attend the Festival.

Wally arranged a special performance on August 18 at the *Reader's Digest* headquarters in Chappaqua, New York. They built platforms in their large parking lot and some 2,300 people came that evening. Betty and I joined the Wallaces for dinner at their home, High Winds. Wally was very sporty and drove me over in his convertible before the show. Lila brought Betty in another car. I remember Wally bouncing up those steps to introduce the show and give his conviction about the program. He said, "Speaking for the Reader's Digest Foundation, it is a rare privilege to be partially supporting appearances of this…cast of Up with People. Looking across the stage from face to face—such dedication, enthusiasm, happiness, animation, and spirit are a joy to behold. The world has all too little of these qualities. It is a safe assumption that more and more people will get these qualities as this group moves through the country. The first time I saw the show, I thought of a Greek philosopher who told us to lead the good life until habit makes it pleasant. My conviction about this cast is that they have discovered the good life is the happy life. …In conclusion, I want to say, and I'm sure I echo the sentiments of everyone in this audience, we are deeply indebted to this group for the profoundly gratifying fashion in which they are serving their fellow men."[2]

Wally was fascinated that we had taken 1,000 students from Fort Slocum to Washington, DC, where they were welcomed as guests into the gallery of the US House of Representatives. On August 23, Speaker John McCormick paid tribute to Sing-Out/Up with People. In fact, when he did this, the students erupted with loud applause, so much so that he had to gavel them back so that other members of Congress could pay their own tributes.

In September 1967, we had our first performance of Sing-Out/Up with People at Carnegie Hall in New York City sponsored by the Reader's Digest Foundation. Betty and I invited the Wallaces to be our special guests. The whole audience came to their feet at the end of the performance. Wally and Lila seemed thrilled. Members of the cast came off the stage and presented them with a record album and made them honorary members of the cast. Betty told me later that after I introduced the show, Wally had turned to her and said with a sly grin, "He is so eloquent. How do you live with him?"

In 1968, *Reader's Digest* and Coca-Cola co-sponsored an NBC TV show featuring Up with People.[3] Wally, Lila, and Hobart Lewis and his wife came to the taping. Wally had asked that I speak in place of one of the *Reader's Digest* commercials on the show. He came that night when I did the taping in front of the cast. I remember saying something about the violence that was taking place across the country and what effect Up with People could have on that. After the show aired on August 23, Wally called me. He had seen the show and he thought it had gone over well.

A little over a decade later, in early March 1979, we had an important luncheon for the future of Up with People. Before I left for New York, Betty had said to me, "You really ought to ask Wally for $2 million." Well, I had never done such a thing and I was quite nervous on my drive to the *Digest* office. However, I got an immediate boost from Gordon Davies, Wally's nephew who ran the Reader's Digest Foundation. On the way in from the parking lot, Gordon said, "Blanton, I think the time has come to ask Wally for endowment money for your program." Gordon joined Wally and me for lunch, and at the end of the meal, Wally asked, "Do you have any endowment for this program?" The door was opened. I replied, "We don't, but I was wondering if you would make a gift toward one." He asked what I had in mind. With fear and trembling I said, "I was wondering if you would give me $2 million toward the endowment."

Wally dropped his fork and turned to Gordon. The maid came rushing in from the kitchen to see if there was a problem, just as Wally said to Gordon, "Where in the world would I find $2 million?" Fortunately, Gordon jumped in and said, "I think we could find it, Wally." Wally started asking me how much I needed to raise every year. At that point in our budget I think I had to raise about $700,000 besides what we brought into the program from the performances. So Wally got out a paper and pencil, wrote some notes, and looked up and said, "Well, if you'll raise $5 million, I'll give you $2 million and that will give you $7 million to initiate an endowment."

I remember leaving that meal totally elated. Driving back to Manhattan, I stopped at a phone booth and called James "Jim" G. Boswell, a member of Up with People's Executive Committee of our board and a mentor. He was thrilled with the news and said immediately, "I'll give $1 million to match his challenge because we must seal that deal, and the deal is not sealed until the first challenge comes in." Wally had given me three years to find the $5 million, and now I had to find only $4 million. There was a great celebration when I notified Betty and our staff back in Tucson.

How were we going to raise $4 million over the next three years? It came down on my shoulders as president, and I assumed responsibility. I concluded the best way to find the money was to get people to see a performance, meet the students, talk with them, and find those who were really interested and build friendships. It had worked with Wally, and I had faith it would work with others. Wally's challenge grant and Jim Boswell's gift lifted everything to a new level and opened many doors. Not all of them matched the challenge, but all of them who were touched by this news did something. With many visits and miles traveled, we reached the $5 million match before the three-year period was up.

It was during this time that Betty and I decided we would have a luncheon to honor Wally for all of his backing and support. Since we had initially met at the Pierre Hotel in New York, we decided to make that the venue. We had a cast available for the event, and I worked with Gordon Davies and Lila Wallace's secretary to get a list of his best friends to invite to this luncheon. Of course, the line given by his closest friends was that over the years many people had attempted to honor Wally; he would accept, but then he would never appear. They even had bets that he wouldn't come for this luncheon.

On the morning of April 22, 1980, Betty and I drove out to High Winds and found Wally standing in the hall with his raincoat on saying, "I'm ready to go." We went with Wally and his driver to the Pierre Hotel. A Cadillac followed us all the way into the luncheon; I learned later it was the magazine's editor, Ed Thompson, who was checking to see if Wally would direct the car to turn around.

When we got to the Pierre Hotel, Wally wanted to go around the back, not through the crowd gathered in the vestibule, and we took him through the kitchen area into the hall. When the doors were opened there was great surprise when they saw Wally standing there to welcome them. He invited as his special guest Laurance S. Rockefeller, a prominent third-generation member of the Rockefeller family. I had invited Dr. Landrum Bolling, CEO of the Council on Foundations and a peace activist, especially in the Middle East. I also had a chance to introduce all the members of the Up with People Board who were present. We paid tribute to DeWitt Wallace, what he had put into the program, and what it had meant to us. He thoroughly enjoyed these accolades and led a standing ovation when the 60-member cast ended their performance. Mr. Rockefeller kept saying to him, "Why have I never heard about this before?" And Wally kept replying, "That's right, Laurance, where in the world have you been all these years!" This led to a lively discussion.

The cast gathered around Wally's table and sang "Keep Young at Heart," which got him to his feet again, and he said a few words of thanks to the cast. Without a doubt it was a tremendous success. Wally was just thrilled and talked about it all the way back to High Winds.

Later, I did follow up and visit Laurance Rockefeller several times, and he said to me, "I want to contribute to what you're doing with these young people." He handed me a check for $50,000. He was a director at the Reader's Digest Foundation and a great backer of Wally's commitment to our program.

The Wallaces wanted to meet our daughters, Jenny and Katie, and invited us to visit in June 1980. Our schedule was such that we only had a chance to go for lunch, but they hosted a beautiful luncheon and particularly enjoyed talking to Jenny and Katie, who at that time were 14 and 12. High Winds was a magnificent home surrounded by beautiful gardens. Lila Wallace had restored the Monet House and Gardens in Giverny, France, and had an impressive collection of his paintings as well as many by Degas.

On other occasions, we would have drinks together before dinner; Wally particularly liked Jack Daniels on the rocks, and Lila loved her martinis. Lila had a 4,000-year-old gold cup that had been given to her by the wife of President Anwar Sadat on behalf of the Egyptian government. Lila had helped to save the ancient Egyptian temples on the Nile by giving over $1 million to the American Committee to Save Abu Simbel. When Betty and I used to get together with the Wallaces, we always had a toast: "Here's to the four of us, thank God there are no more of us!" I've often pondered how Wally and I bonded so quickly, especially since he was 35 years my senior (he was 77 and I was 42). We were both preacher's kids and troublemakers in our youth. Fortunately, we were both saved by our impossible dreams and our commitment to bring them to reality, he and Lila with the *Digest* and Betty and I with Up with People.

Every time I was with Wally, the first thing he would say was, "Tell me again all the news of Up with People. Where are the casts? What are they experiencing? How many are applying to travel with you and what are your future plans?" During these years I constantly updated him by sending out detailed reports of the casts and their exciting performances. Some of them were in the Congo for the Congolese Independence Day (June 1968), others met and performed for Their Majesties King Baudouin and Queen Fabiola of Belgium at the Royal Arboretum (June 1969), at the Boy Scout Jamboree (July 1969), in Paris at the Olympia Music Hall (January 1970), at Expo '70 in Osaka, Japan (May 1970), at the Governors' Conference at the White House (February 1971), at the Munich Olympics at the time of the tragic massacre of the Israeli team (September 1972), on our first visit to China (May 1978), for the General Electric Centennial Tour (fall 1978), and at Super Bowl XIV (January 1980). These exciting events thrilled Wally and Lila.

In March 1981, I had a call from Gordon Davies that Wally had fallen ill and was now in the Columbia-Presbyterian Medical Center in New York City. I flew from Tucson to see him. I was told that no visitors were allowed, but I went to the hospital anyway. I said I was part of the family, went straight up to his floor, and walked right into his room. He was dozing in a chair. He woke up and said, "Blanton, how in the world did you find me here?" We had an animated conversation, and he said, "Wait a minute!" He called in the doctor and the nurses and said, "Sit down, I want you to hear about this program, Up with People." Then he had me start all over again and tell him what was happening so they could be a part of it. After the doctors and nurses left the room, I had a few private minutes with Wally and took the opportunity to thank him and inform him that his $5 million challenge grant was near completion. His wholehearted support of Up with People had been an inspiration to all of us. I thanked him again and told him how much his friendship to Betty and me personally and to the program had meant to us. We said our goodbyes and I left. That was the last time I saw him.

Wally died peacefully two weeks later in his home. I was in México at the time and received a call from Gordon Davies with the news. There was going to be a small private family memorial service and there was no need for me to fly back. Gordon said how much Wally had enjoyed his friendship with me and Betty through the last 14 years of his life and what Up with People had meant to him. Yes, it is true that Wally gave generously financially, but more than that, he gave wholeheartedly and generously of his mind and spirit. For Betty and me, he was one of the "most unforgettable characters" we ever met. In many ways the young people and Up with People were the elixir of life for him. Gordon became an absolutely loyal friend and fan of the program and was a tremendous help throughout those years.

Several years later, while we were planning the 25th Silver Anniversary Celebration of Up with People, I went to visit Christine DeVita, president of the Reader's Digest Foundation and a dear friend, to inform her of our upcoming celebration. She said, "It's so good to see you again and to hear the program is strong." She said to her staff, "We always love to see Blanton. His motives are so pure." Later, when she informed her board of our 25th Silver Anniversary Celebration, she telephoned to say they had unanimously voted to give us $1 million in honor of DeWitt Wallace's conviction about Up with People. She came personally to Denver during the celebration to present the gift.[4]

Another great friend of Up with People was Barron Hilton, who I had the good fortune of meeting soon after Sing-Out/Up with People burst on the American scene. It was 1965, and Betty and I were at Patrick Frawley's dinner party in Beverly Hills, California, seated at the same table with Barron and his wife, Marilyn. We hit it off right away. We had both served in the US Navy during World War II, and we chatted about football and duck hunting. At that point, Barron owned the San Diego Chargers football team. It was the beginning of a great friendship, and he became a generous supporter of Up with People. Every year he also entertained members of our board of directors at his Sunday brunch on the morning of the Super Bowl. Sometimes there would be four or five and sometimes 15. Barron had the welcome mat out as a perfect hotelier.

Barron did much more than provide funding and entertain folks connected to Up with People. He was proud that his phone call to Pete Rozelle, commissioner of the National Football League had resulted in Up with People performing at a Super Bowl halftime. This eventually led to our unprecedented four halftime performances. At all of these games our board of directors was fully in attendance with seats to the game, some on the 50-yard line. My job was to secure tickets, not only for the game but to two big parties—one hosted by Pete and Carrie Rozelle, known as the NFL Commissioner's Party, the night before the game, and Barron Hilton's Sunday brunch. Everyone was attempting to secure these tickets, and somehow, I managed to get them. Sometimes, at the very last moment, Don Weiss, the executive director of the NFL, would slip me the tickets. One year my tickets for the Hilton brunch had not arrived in the mail. There we were at the entrance to the party with 20 of my board members and spouses and no tickets—and the guard on the door was not yielding. Fortunately, he did agree to take word to Barron that we were stuck at the door, and to our amazement, about 10 minutes later, Barron personally came to the door. He said, "Blanton, what are you doing out there?" We had made it again! Several times when the cast was there to perform at the halftime, Barron would have them run in to his brunch party and perform, which they loved doing.

In late fall of 1988, my longtime secretary and top assistant Ola Cook Henry, who was the epitome of propriety, came into my office holding the phone at arm's length, red in the face. She said, "Mr. Hilton is on the phone and is he mad." I took the phone, and she was right. He was very agitated. He said, "My God, Blanton, get these guys off my back!" I asked what he was talking about. He said, "You know, I got you $1 million but Gene Cernan and Jim Boswell have been bugging me that that's not enough, so I got you $2.5 million. Goodbye."

Several times when we were visiting, Barron would say to me, "You know, you're the only one during the Cold War who came to me saying we've got to find a way to reach behind the Iron Curtain and build some friendship with the young people for the future." He responded to that concept and funded our first tour of the Soviet Union in 1988 and also sponsored the first Ukrainian students to participate in our 25th Silver Anniversary Celebration in Denver in 1990.

Barron was a great human being and a superb hotel man. He called one day inviting me to come over and join him for a weekend of duck shooting at the Venice Island Duck Club in the Sacramento Delta in California. Shortly afterward, his secretary telephoned saying, "Barron wants to know if you like cold lobster for lunch before you fly up to the club." I started to say facetiously "I never have cold lobster on Thursday," but I thought better of it. So I said, "Certainly, that would be great," and it was. The duck hunting was superb, and Barron and I had a friendly competition with our shooting. We agreed in the end it was a draw; still, we did have fun.

Before we celebrated the 50th Anniversary of Up with People in 2015, Betty and I felt the responsibility to go personally and thank donors and celebrate that the program was still going strong. We started with those who had supported us through these many years. We drove to Los Angeles to start with Barron. I went in alone to see him while Betty waited in the sitting room. As we were leaving his office together, his longtime secretary heard my voice and came out. She asked, "Blanton what's happened to Up with People?" to which Barron quickly replied, "You won't believe this but they're celebrating their 50th Anniversary. We gave them some of their first seed money, and we're proud of that." When Barron said hello to Betty, he told us to go and visit with his son Steve at the Conrad N. Hilton Foundation headquarters in Agoura Hills, California. We were very glad to have a chance to also thank Steve and the foundation for all their backing, so we drove out to the valley, where Steve took us to lunch at the country club. Halfway through the lunch he said to me, "Blanton aren't you going to ask for money?"

I replied, "Steve, I know your protocol and I can't ask for money from your foundation unless you request it."

At that point, Steve stood up and said, "Here, in the presence of your wife, Betty, I officially ask you to ask us for money!"

I said, "I'm flattered but I don't know where to start."

So he said, "My father and I want to give you $1 million in tribute for the 50th year celebration of Up with People. Not many nonprofits that started in the turbulent 1960s are celebrating 50 years!" Betty and I were flabbergasted but told him what a great kickoff that would be for our 50th celebration. I said to him, "Thank you and your father and the Conrad N. Hilton Foundation."

Some people's contributions to Up with People were more about inspiration and personal support and less about money, which are equally important. Sometime in 1966, I picked up a rumor from our cast—probably untrue—that one of the students was the niece of Arthur "Punch" Sulzberger, publisher and owner of *The New York Times*. At that point I was so enthusiastic about the development of Up with People that I wanted to meet Mr. Sulzberger. How was I going to do it? The only place I could find any connection was possibly through the military. I had also read that he loved salmon fishing and had fished the Restigouche River in New Brunswick, Canada, which I too had done. Since I couldn't think of a go-between, I made a call directly and was put through to his secretary. She turned out to be a very tough, protective woman and the chance of an appointment seemed slim. However, some days later, I had a call from the secretary saying that Mr. Sulzberger would like to meet me in his office on a certain date. When we met I was struck with what an urbane gentleman he was. He had some knowledge of Up with People and said he had read about us and seen us when the Schick TV special had aired in May 1966. It was a beginning, and we quickly developed a relationship.

In February 1967, Punch instigated an invitation for Sing-Out/Up with People to perform at the American Newspaper Publishers Association at the Breakers Hotel in Palm Beach, Florida. Punch invited me as "part of the family" to lunch with his wife, Carol, and editors of *The New York Times*. Soon afterward, he sent another invitation for a cast to perform again at the American Newspaper Publishers Association gathering on April 24,

1967, at the Waldorf-Astoria Hotel in Manhattan. These events did more than anything to make Up with People known in the United States. As a result, many newspaper publishers sponsored casts in their cities.

In the fall of 1967, Punch helped us out of another potentially difficult situation. I was back in my office in Tucson when he telephoned, saying, "I've run into a situation that needs your personal attention, and I think it's important enough for you to fly to New York." When Don Birdsall and I arrived at his office in the New York Times Building the next day, he met with us immediately. He told us, "I've learned that CBS and *Esquire* magazine are planning an exposé article on Frank Buchman and MRA, and they're pulling Up with People into it." Punch went on, "I know you don't want this to happen, and I'm suggesting you go right away to see my friend Frank Stanton, the president of CBS, and present your facts." He picked up the phone and called him, and Stanton said, "Send them over."

Frank Stanton received us cordially but he was all business. We underlined for him that MRA USA had helped us initially with funding. However, with the encouragement of General Eisenhower and others, we were in the process at that time to become a completely independent global educational program and a 501(c)(3) nonprofit. We then told him of the positive message the young people were taking around the world. He seemed to ponder this for quite a while, and then he said with a grin, "What you're telling me is a separation of church and state!" Then, to our great relief, he said, "Leave it with me, I'll take care of it." And he did— nothing more was heard about it. When we reported this back to Punch, he said, "I can assure you that Frank does not take any wooden nickels, and he studied you men as well as your facts, and you obviously impressed him with your sincerity. Congratulations."

In the summer of 1975, I invited Punch to join our International Advisory Board. Quite to my surprise he accepted and took it seriously. The next year he arranged for a cast to perform at the Associated Press Luncheon on May 3, 1976, during the Bicentennial Year Celebration. Punch sent word that it was a great success and that he was impressed with the professional quality of the performance, but then he added, "Your literature is far less impressive, so give me a call." When I called him back he said, "We can help you with your publicity; send a couple of your most able young people and we'll put them into training with our people." And we did.

One time when I was in New York City I visited with one of our board members, Hubert Turner "T." Mandeville, a distinguished attorney who had his office in the Pan Am Building. He was the most hospitable gentleman, and he always put me up either at the Union League Club, the Union Club, or the Yale Club. We met in an interesting way. I was lunching with DeWitt Wallace in the Sky Club in the Pan Am Building, and since both of us were losing our hearing we were talking loudly. Mr. Mandeville at the next table was listening to our conversation. When we got up to leave, he came over and introduced himself to me. He had been listening to our loud, shouted conversation. That was the beginning of a friendship and later I invited Mandeville to join our Board of Directors, which he did in early 1979. After my meeting with T. Mandeville, I telephoned Punch to suggest we get together. He said, "I'm extremely busy, but why don't we meet for a drink at your hotel? By the way where are you staying?" When I told him I was staying at the Union Club, there was quite a pause, and then he finally said, "Okay, I'll come by around 5:30." He did come by and we had a drink, but he seemed agitated and left early. Only later did I learn that there were no Jewish members in the Union Club. When I talked to Punch he said, "That's the first time I've ever been there." He urged me when in New York to consider staying in the Stanhope Hotel around the corner from his home instead.

In 1980, Super Bowl XIV was in Pasadena, California. The 20-minute performance of the cast received a great response, and Carrie Rozelle was full of thanks and praise. When I canvassed our board there was unanimous approval that I should invite her personally to join the board. That occasion presented itself on a scheduled trip I already had to visit with Punch in New York. Carrie invited me to lunch with her at the 21 Club. She was immediately enthusiastic but had one caveat: she and Pete had made a pledge never to be a night apart during their married life. She wondered how that would fit with our board meetings. I assured her that the board was flexible and we could accommodate her schedule. That satisfied her, and she said how honored she was to be invited and how enthusiastic she was about our program.

That afternoon when I met with Punch in his office in the New York Times Building he was quite interested that I just came from a luncheon with Carrie and that she had agreed to join our board. He was intrigued that she had urged her husband to invite Up with People to perform the halftime show at the recent Super Bowl. Punch commented that he had watched it on TV and thought it was outstanding. As I got ready to leave he said he would very much like to meet Carrie. He said, "Why don't you invite her to lunch on my behalf? If she accepts, please come with her and we'll dine in my private dining room."

When I informed Carrie she was very interested, saying she would very much like to meet Mr. Sulzberger. Punch was delighted, the date was set. I was honored to be a bystander watching old New York meet new New York. Punch immediately charmed Carrie with his immaculate manners and his Old World charm. She, on the other hand, captured him with her enthusiasm and eagerness. She wanted to learn from Punch how he and the Sulzberger family had built such an enterprise. When they got to Up with People, they both agreed that it would be appropriate if they sponsored a private show for their friends and others in the New York area. They both came to the conclusion that the theater in the Asia Society would be a perfect setting for such an invitational performance. I was given the job of finding out if and when the theater might be available. I can tell you, when I went in to meet the CEO of the Asia Society, he was flattered that Punch Sulzberger and Carrie Rozelle wanted to use their theater for a private performance. He immediately agreed.

Over 200 of their friends attended. There was great enthusiasm when the two of them took the stage together to welcome and introduce the show. They were a show themselves as they danced around humorously, trying to decide who would go first. Carrie said, "Punch, you're the senior here, you should go first." And he said, "You're the best looking here, you should be first." They both turned facing the audience and started to talk simultaneously and broke out laughing to the applause of their friends. At the end of the cast's performance the entire theater was on their feet clapping and cheering.

Looking back at my association with Punch, he was so helpful when we expanded the program to Europe in the mid-1960s and opened an office in Brussels in 1971. At that point, Punch had alerted the publisher of the *International Herald Tribune*, the newspaper owned by *The New York Times*. It covered Europe and was popular with English-language speakers. Then in 1979, Punch introduced me to the publisher, Lee Huebner. He became a great friend and attended the performances. The newspaper covered Up with People with articles over the years.

At one of our meetings, Punch said with a twinkle in his eye, "Let me show you something in my back room." There on the wall was a framed blessing signed by Pope John Paul II. Punch said, "As you know, I'm an observant Jew but I don't want to take any chances!" Punch lived with a global vision, and his friendship came at a critical time in the development of Up with People.

19

A Show at the White House

"With Everything Changing"
With ev'rything changing
Does anything stay the same,
A hope you can cling to,
Someone who needs you…

It was 5:00 a.m. in early October 1970 and our home phone was ringing. Who in the world was calling so early? I picked up; it was Bob Cook, who was in charge of our Up with People office in Washington, DC. He said immediately, "I'm sorry to call so early but late yesterday Perle Mesta telephoned me at the office. She was formerly our US ambassador in Luxembourg and now a political hostess in Washington." He told me that she and Nellie Connally, the wife of John Connally, the Secretary of the Treasury and the former governor of Texas, were hosting a benefit in Washington. It was to be in November 1970 featuring the composer Marvin Hamlisch. Nellie had seen an Up with People performance in Texas earlier in the year so she and Perle were suggesting that Up with People perform as the opening act for Hamlisch. Furthermore, time was running out on printing invitations and programs. She asked Bob to let her know by 11:00 that morning whether such a thing was possible. I encouraged Bob to accept if a cast was available. Bob added that Perle had also said she had heard that I was the president of Up with People although we had not met. She would like to have Betty and me as her guests at this function.

At that moment, Betty needed to be with our young girls, but she urged me to go, so off I went. The ballroom of the hotel was filled, and the short performance of Up with People was well received. Marvin Hamlisch paid tribute to them when he took the stage. In fact, that was the beginning of a friendship that later led to Marvin joining our board of directors. His presentation was just wonderful as he sat in front of the audience on a high stool alternately playing the piano, singing, and speaking. Perle had arranged for the students of the cast to be seated among the audience, and she had very thoughtfully seated me with President Richard Nixon's secretary, Rose Mary Woods. Miss Woods asked me many questions about where the students came from and what we were doing. At the end of the evening, she volunteered that perhaps we could perform in the White House. She gave me her card and said, "Here is my private number, give me a call and I'll see what I can do." When I made the call the next day, she told me, "Hold on to your hat, I'm transferring you to Lucy Winchester, the social secretary who handles special events and entertainment for the President and Mrs. Nixon."

Fortunately for me, when the call went through the social secretary acknowledged that she was familiar with Up with People because she'd seen a performance on TV. She added that Rose Mary Woods had been very taken with the evening and that her enthusiasm would be helpful in trying to arrange a performance in the White House. She added, "I can recommend such a commitment to President and Mrs. Nixon and let you know their decision."

Several weeks later, a telephone call came from the White House to Bob Cook requesting that Up with People be the special entertainment at a reception for the governors and their wives during the National Governors' Conference. An official letter arrived confirming the invitation and giving the date two months ahead with a request that we perform with entertainer Bob Hope for 45 minutes.[1]

Betty and I flew to Washington for the black-tie event in the White House on February 23, 1971. It was a festive occasion, and President Nixon introduced the small cast of Up with People. He congratulated them on their mission to build peace through understanding. The show was a hit, and the standing ovation was led by Governor Jimmy Carter of Georgia.

He was almost lifted out of his seat by the final song called "Take Me There." Then Bob Hope stepped onto the stage from where he had been sitting with President and Mrs. Nixon. He turned to the cast and said he was very moved and wanted to thank them personally for what they were doing for America. Then, we had a humorous incident. Bob Hope said to the young man leading our group, "Join and sing with me, 'Thanks for the Memories.'" We almost had a disaster on our hands when the young man replied quietly, "I've never heard of it." Fortunately, the president and the governors didn't hear this conversation. One of our other students stepped forward and said, "We can certainly sing that song with you, Mr. Hope." Bob Hope then invited the governors and wives to sing his theme song with him, which they did. The generation gap almost reared its ugly head, but a crisis was averted.

I was sitting there with Betty greatly enjoying the moment with the cast spread out talking to the governors and their wives and White House staff. I said to Betty, "Isn't this amazing? Here we are in the White House, and it was only five and a half years ago that our first public show of Sing-Out '65/Up with People was across town in the Washington Hilton Hotel." The journey had begun then, but we had no concept of where it would lead us.

I greatly enjoyed my time with Perle Mesta. She was sparkly and full of life, and even though she had become an international figure, she was still a daughter of Oklahoma. Once I was in London attending a wedding, and Perle was there for the Queen's Garden Party. I telephoned her secretary hoping that Perle might be free for lunch. Sometime later, a call came from her secretary saying that Perle would like it very much if I would escort them to the famous seafood restaurant, Prunier. When I went over to check, it was sold out for the evening. However, when I explained who Perle Mesta was to the manager, he arranged to put a table right next to the dance floor. He personally welcomed Perle when we came in. As usual it was a delightful evening with much humor as well as superb seafood.

Perle's secretary was a wonderful woman and completely committed to looking after her. She accompanied Perle wherever she went. When the evening ended, I hailed a cab and dropped them off at the US Embassy where they were staying. They both said how much they had enjoyed the evening and gave me pecks on the cheek.

The next morning I telephoned Perle to thank her for the evening. She immediately said, "You are an admiral aren't you?" When I answered that, no, I had been an officer in the Navy during World War II but not an admiral, she replied, "Well, you're going to be an admiral this evening when you escort me to the Queen's Garden Party. I have officially notified the queen's aide-de-camp that Admiral Belk will be escorting me to the party." When I told her I was flattered but booked that afternoon to fly back to the US, she was not a happy camper. She said very strongly, "That's impossible. It's a done deal, they're expecting us! Change your flight plans." I'm sad to report that neither the admiral nor the lieutenant (j.g.) appeared at the Queen's Garden Party. Her secretary told me later that Perle explained my absence by saying the admiral had an emergency call to return to Washington immediately! Sometime later, all was forgiven and we were on good terms again, but Perle was not an easy woman to say no to.

Over the next couple of years, I kept her up to date with all that was happening with Up with People. When I sent her a report in September 1972 of what Jesse Owens and Up with People had done for the athletes at the Munich Olympics after the massacre of the Israeli Olympic team, she telephoned me saying, "Why isn't that front-page news here in America?!" Shortly after this, Perle fell quite ill and was hospitalized in Oklahoma City. Her secretary telephoned me: "Perle does not have much longer to live." The rumor was that it was terminal cancer. I tried unsuccessfully to reach Perle on the phone but did reach her secretary, and she passed on to Perle all our love and gratitude for what she had meant to Betty and me personally and to Up with People.

20

Jesse Owens and the Munich Olympics

"Can We Sing a Song of Peace?"
...in a world that's full of fear,
Can a melody of hope ever hope to dry a tear?

I had one of the most frightening moments of my life at the Munich Olympics in 1972. Up with People had been scheduled to perform at the opening ceremony and at several other venues in the Olympic Park. I was to accompany the cast and had invited Jean Wittouck and his daughter Beatrice Lunt Wittouck to join me in Munich. Of course, Up with People Board Member Jesse Owens, who was a member of the US Olympic Committee was also present. The event had been planned to perfection. Germany was committed to countering the image of their last Olympics in Berlin in 1936 with Adolf Hitler in the stands. The weather was perfect, the countryside was in bloom, and everyone was impressed with the friendliness of the German people. Everything was running on time. The famous Munich beer halls were packed, and there was a festive spirit of celebration everywhere.

Then all hell broke loose. On September 5, 1972, without warning, the Olympic Games came to a sudden halt. The Olympic Village was shut down. Athletes could neither go in nor come out. Sirens were blaring all over Munich with military helicopters overhead. Many tourists, still in the Village, rushed to get out. It was pandemonium. Nobody seemed to know what had happened. Rumors flew. Some had heard that terrorists had attacked. Others claimed it was a terrorist attack on the whole of West Germany. It was the unknown that created such fear and panic.

We learned later that eight members of Black September, a militant Palestinian group, armed with assault rifles, pistols, and grenades, broke into the apartment building housing the Israeli Olympic team at 4:00 a.m. A wrestling coach and weightlifter were killed early on, and many hours of terror followed for the other nine captives. During the day the West German government offered to negotiate and pay for their release. One of the terrorists' response was, "…the purpose of our mission was to fight for the rights of our people and raise the profile of our cause, not to make money."[1] They demanded a trade for 234 Palestinian prisoners being held by Israel and two West German terrorists being held in a West German prison. The Israeli government, following its longstanding policy, refused to negotiate. That night, in a botched rescue operation at the airport, the remaining nine Israeli athletes and coaches were murdered. The police killed five terrorists and three others were captured. By 12:30 a.m. on September 6, the 20 hours of terror were over.

We were informed that the cast were much shaken with the news. Some of the cast wanted to attend the memorial service, which was held in the Olympic Stadium later on September 6. One of the cast members, Jean Weathersby Wysocki, said later, "The service that morning was the first official assembly since the murders. I've never experienced such emotion in a stadium filled with 100,000 people—the feeling of sorrow, terror, anxiety, perplexity, and dying hope ran through the hearts and minds of everyone there to the extent that I thought I could see it just hanging like a cloud over the stadium. During the speeches, you could've heard a pin drop, it was so quiet. I cried."[2]

Earlier on September 5, Jesse Owens had taken part in the decision to immediately send the Jewish swimmer and Olympian Mark Spitz, back to the US. He had just won seven gold medals at the Games. Spitz was in the Olympic Village watching the drama unfold on television when a group from the committee came into his room and said they were sending him home that day. We were equally concerned with how to keep our Up with People group safe, especially our six Jewish cast members. Cyndi Jarrett, a cast member, remembered that the cast had a meeting in central

Munich the morning of September 5, as the hostage crisis was still going on, to discuss whether or not to send our Jewish cast members home. One of them, cast member Marcie Lipschutz Ward, recalled, "Our year had just started in July in Vermont. None of us wanted to go home. We had a mission."[3] Our mutual conclusion was that, for now, we would closely monitor developments but all stay in Munich and perform.

On September 6, I made my way to Jesse's hotel room. His whole mind and spirit was preoccupied with the Olympic athletes cordoned off in the Olympic Village. He kept saying, "I know what they're going through—they are the forgotten hostages. They have spent years sacrificing, training, competing, living, and dreaming for this moment, and now it may all be over. I've been thinking about what I could do to help, and I have an idea." Jesse turned to me and said, "You guys have to go in there. Come with me—we must go see Stefan von Baranski, my friend," who was the head of entertainment for the Olympics. We took off on foot toward the Village, and I challenge anyone to keep up with the fastest man on earth when he's on a mission!

Security was tight but von Baranski had paved our way. Even with all that was going on, the Germans at the security gates were startled when they saw Jesse Owens's passport. They all wanted to shake his hand. When we got to Stefan von Baranski's office it looked like a war room. People ran in and out, and papers were scattered on the floor. They had been there all night. Since time was of the essence, Jesse dove right in, presenting his plan to have Up with People perform for the athletes in the Village. Stefan von Baranski sat back startled and stared. Jesse broke in and said, "I know what you're thinking. What would happen if some of the students were taken hostage." He continued, "I'll be responsible if it comes to that and if you want it in writing, you've got it." Mr. von Baranski seemed to relax and then said, "Let's do it. I'll arrange the theater in the Village. Also, I will need the passports of your 150 students immediately." Security by that point had become ironclad. We would become the only outsiders allowed inside the Village. Nobody else would be permitted in.

Mr. von Baranski asked the cast to do one show in the Olympic Village

Theater. All other entertainment had been canceled but he felt that, in his words, "Up with People would give a needed gift." On the evening of the show, representatives of the 130 Olympic teams crowded the venue. The atmosphere was tense. There was little conversation, and none of the normal joking around. There was jostling for seats among the few hundred coaches and athletes, all visibly confused and helpless. As always tickets were given out proportionately to all delegations, but for the first time the theater was packed, and hundreds were turned away. The athletes were identified by the names of their country on the jackets or shirts—there was the USSR, USA, México, Great Britain, Sweden, North Korea, Cuba, and the always anticipated great long-distance runners from Kenya. It was a global village.

Jesse did not want Mr. von Baranski to introduce him at the show so the three of us sat in the back row. When the cast started the performance, neither the performers nor the athletes were relaxed. There was so much tension you could cut it with a knife. There was not much response to the show. But the cast persevered, and slowly the tide turned. At the end of the first half they launched into "Annemarieke," a Belgian drinking song that always received a boisterous reaction. Halfway through the song, the cast started a conga line up and down the aisles of the auditorium, inviting the audience to participate. I held my breath, wondering if anyone would join in. At first, no one did. A glance at Jesse told me he was still confident. It looked bleak but suddenly a Cuban coach was moved by the beat and motion and told his athletes to get in the line. No coach wanted to be left out so the same thing happened throughout the audience. All the coaches turned to their athletes and said, "Represent us in that line!" Hundreds of athletes danced through the aisles and several ended up onstage, arms linked with our cast and each other, swaying back and forth to the music, singing that drinking song and laughing. It was an amazing sight to see Cuban basketball players, Soviet gymnasts, and Americans from all teams clapping and stomping side by side. The cast instinctively extended the song longer than normal to accommodate the rush of emotion. "It was the conga line that changed everything. The athletes connected with us and with the message," said cast member Jean Weathersby Wysocki.[4] A thunderous ovation greeted Jesse's intermission announcement that because of popular demand, Up with People would run another night. The ice was broken. The atmosphere changed. It was as if a great sigh of relief had taken place. We had lived through an historic happening. It was more than that. The show ended with wild applause and a standing ovation.

Some 10 days after the Olympics ended, Jesse and Stefan von Baranski went to visit Chancellor Willy Brandt in Bonn. A picture of the three of them together appeared in the newspaper *Abend Zeitung*. They were all smiling, and Stefan von Baranski said to the chancellor, "We owe a debt of gratitude and thanks to this great American athlete, Jesse Owens, for bringing Up with People to the Village. The students brought a sense of unity and oneness back to the athletes with their two performances." In my view, Jesse was extraordinarily courageous with what he initiated. It was true statesmanship. He had won four gold medals at the Berlin Olympics in 1936, and it might have been fitting to give him a fifth one for what he did at the 1972 Olympics. In early fall of 1973, Jesse Owens was officially recognized and presented the Bundesverdienstkreuz 1. Klasse (Federal Cross of Merit, First Class) by the German consul general in Los Angeles in the name of the German federal president, Gustav Heinemann.[5]

Jesse was diagnosed with lung cancer in 1979 and treated at the University of Arizona Medical Center here in Tucson. On one of my visits to see him, he said, "I'd dearly like to see astronaut Captain Gene Cernan again." They had gotten to know one another through their service together on our board of directors. I telephoned Gene, and he flew his own plane out from Houston. I picked him up, and we went straight to the hospital. When we went into Jesse's room, he lit up at seeing Gene, but he was very weak. He didn't have much energy to speak but he said, "I want you men to stand by my bed and take my hands." He said to us, "I really don't want to die. I think about Up with People. They've already meant a lot to the people of the world but it's only a beginning of the effect they're going to have on the future." Gene and I were both in tears and Jesse also. He died the next week, on March 31, 1980, and late that night, his wife, Ruth, phoned me. She said, "Jesse has gone. He went peacefully in his sleep. Could we have a small cast to sing his favorite song, 'Where the Roads Come Together,' at his funeral?" We assured her that we could, and in a packed Rockefeller Chapel at the University of Chicago, the cast sang that song and a few others in a tribute to that special man. When he was finally laid to rest, one of our alumna, Cyndy Watson, sang "Amazing Grace" at Ruth's request.

After the service, I had the opportunity to meet Jesse's three daughters, Gloria, Marlene, and Beverly. I thanked them personally for what Jesse's life had meant to the thousands of young people who traveled with Up with People. His three daughters continue to carry on his work with the Jesse Owens Foundation.

At Up with People's 25th Silver Anniversary Celebration in 1990, before 5,600 alumni and friends, I was proud to present the Founder's Award posthumously to Jesse.

21

Moving to Brussels

"Pays de Coeur/Hartelijk Land"
Je revien toujours à ta joie et ta chaleur
Belgique/Belgie, pays de coeur...

In spring of 1969, a tour of Belgium was being planned by Up with People. Jean Wittouck, Chairman and CEO of the Tirlemont Sugar Refinery, had been captivated by recently meeting the young students of Up with People and seeing the show. He wanted to meet me. There was an immediate rapport when we met. On one of my later visits to Belgium, Jean Wittouck urged me to come with Betty and the girls and live for a while in Brussels. He said, "Unless you live in Europe we will always think of Up with People as a very attractive group of young Americans with their song and dance production. They'll never know that is only the tip of the iceberg. If you spend time in Europe, they will get to know you as the founder and your vision and convictions for an educational program." So we decided to go. By September 1972, we had sold our house in Tucson, met with our staff, and explained our move to Europe to my parents and Betty's mom. Up with People would continue to have its main office in Tucson, but Betty, the girls, and I would base ourselves in Europe for a couple of years.

We flew first to New York's Kennedy Airport; when we arrived to check in with Pan Am we were greeted by a vice president of the company whom I had met earlier on a visit. He was most cordial and he said with a twinkle in his eye, "Our tourist section is sold out and, I hope you don't mind, we've moved you, Mrs. Belk and your children to first class." It was fortunate this happened because when our flight attempted to land in Brussels, the airport was locked in fog and we had to be diverted to Amsterdam. At that point the head steward came and visited with us and said that it would be some time before we could fly to Brussels. He said, "We're going to fly first to Vienna, Austria, and we can put you and your family up in a hotel here in Amsterdam or you can remain with the plane." Our two little girls, Jenny and Katie, were sound asleep so we stayed on the plane, and after some 20 hours we finally arrived in Brussels on November 2, 1972. Jean Wittouck, who was known by his friends as Johnny, met us in his brand-new Citroën. He drove us at breakneck speed through the city to the apartment that his daughter, Beatrice Lunt, had rented for us. At the time, Beatrice's husband, Lawrence "Larry" Lunt, was imprisoned by Fidel Castro in Cuba.

During the drive from the airport, Jean informed us that he had been very successful in starting an Up with People Belgian Board of Directors. Jean Rey, president of the Commission of the European Communities; Count Rene Boël, a director of Solvay; Baron Daniel Janssen, director of the Société Générale de Banque; and Max Nokin, Governor and CEO of the Société Générale de Belgique, had agreed to join. Hans Magnus and his wife Tove were there to meet us and get us settled. Hans was the European coordinator for Up with People. It was definitely the beginning of an exciting two years. Up with People made a great impact on Belgium and Europe under the leadership of Hans Magnus.

For Jenny and Katie it was challenging. Betty entered Katie in a Catholic nursery school, and each morning the large arms of the mother superior would reach out to engulf her. Katie, who didn't speak French, was frightened each day. She had extracted a promise from her mother not to leave until she was seated and could wave to her out of the window. One day, however, when we went to pick her up, the mother superior nervously announced to Betty that Katie had just walked away! Fortunately for all of us, we spotted her red stocking hat and matching red jacket marching along the sidewalk two blocks from the school. Katie was then five years old. Jenny, at seven, entered the international school where English was spoken.

Lucky for me Betty was fluent in French. I had studied French in prep school but I was a complete failure at trying to understand or speak it. However, Betty and I seemed to make our way. Quite a few of our new Belgian friends said to us, "You are different from others we have met from your country. Somehow you have an international presence and understanding." The word seemed to have gone through Belgian society, and soon we were being invited to many parties and making lasting friendships. Europeans are different from Americans: they don't ask you what you do. They are much more interested in who you are and what you're really like. If you make a friend there it becomes a lifetime friendship.

Hans and Tove, who was fluent in French, had already become friends with a dynamic young couple named Chantal and Géry de Limelette. Géry came from one of the well-known families of Belgium and Chantal was Swiss. Betty and I became their friends also. They went all out to introduce us to their circle of friends. Both of them knew of my love of shooting and hunting, and one day Géry arrived with three of his friends and knocked on the door. They said, "Come with us, we're taking you out to test your marksmanship." So off we went to the trap and skeet facility, and I was loaned a double-barrel 12-gauge shotgun while these four men in their blue suits evaluated my prowess. Fortunately, I shot quite well, and they were impressed, saying, "Now let's go to your house and see what you have to wear." They immediately turned it all down and said, "We've got to get you some knickers, a loden jacket, proper green shirt and tie, and colorful socks with tassels." We went to the gun shop where I was properly attired. Even Betty was impressed when I arrived back at the apartment and showed what I had bought. It was some time before I was invited on a shoot but I was ready!

Our host, Jean Wittouck, was more cautious about my skills as a marksman, and it wasn't until our second year there that he had the courage to invite me on one of his shoots. He made up for all of that with introductions to dinner parties and cocktail parties that he arranged in our honor. On one such occasion, I was honored to be introduced to Jean Rey, a very distinguished gentleman and colleague of Johnny's on the board. He told me he was proud to be on our Belgian board. Jean Rey gave me some great advice, "If you're trying to bring people and cultures together, always have a round table. If you do this everyone feels equal." I've never forgotten it.

As a member of the Belgian board Jean Rey opened many doors. One such connection he made was with Patrick Hillery, an Irishman who was Vice President of the European Commission. He became a good friend and was keen to have Up with People perform in his country to reach the young people there. When he finished his stint in Brussels, he returned to Ireland where he became the sixth president of the Republic of Ireland. Soon after that President Hillery arranged an official invitation with sponsorship for Up with People to tour Ireland in 1977. Neither Hans nor myself was free to attend the opening event but fortunately Jean Wittouck, as Chairman of the Board in Belgium, volunteered to go. We notified President Hillery, and he was delighted. Jean, from all reports, did a great job in representing Up with People on the highest level and urging the young people of Ireland to participate. Paul Colwell recollects: *Between 1974 and 1989, Up with People casts made multiple visits to the Republic of Ireland and Northern Ireland at a time when the North was beset by sectarian violence. In 1977, I had a call from author and journalist Derek Gill, who had seen a special report on TV about Northern Ireland's children growing up in the midst of bitter conflict. He had an idea for a song. Ralph, Herb, and I followed up on it and wrote "Give the Children Back their Childhood." It started with the lines "Give the children back their childhood / Let the children run and play / Don't make them fight your battles / They're the ones who always seem to pay." The song could apply to children of conflict everywhere.*

Hans and I worked closely with Jean Wittouck and became convinced that he was the right man at the right time to establish Up with People in Europe. As we learned more about him personally, he related this story one evening: During World War II, a German general and his staff had taken over Jean's house when Germany occupied Belgium. Jean had been arrested but kept as a prisoner in his own home. On one occasion the general decided to do away with him. The general had Jean hanged by his hands from the top railing of the circular staircase and verbally abused. The general waited for Jean's strength to give out and for him to drop to his death on the marble floor. At the last minute, the children's Swiss nurse, who also lived in the house, came rushing out saying, "You cannot do this! I am from a neutral country. I demand you let this man go free." Miraculously, the passion of this Swiss nurse stopped the Germans and they helped Jean down. We could all feel the emotion in Jean's voice as he recounted this experience. He ended by saying, "I decided then, even though my mother was Austrian and I grew up speaking German, I would never speak it again as long as I lived." However, Jean and his daughter Beatrice joined me in Munich for the 1972 Olympics. The first evening there he invited Hans, Beatrice, and me to accompany him to the Vier Jahreszeiten Restaurant, which had been one of his favorites in his youth. When we appeared at the door the manager miraculously recognized Jean and came forward, shaking his hand vigorously and welcoming him in German, and Jean answered speaking German! It was a moving moment.

Already the news of Up with People had gone out across Europe, and two invitations had come from Yugoslavia and Poland. We accepted and waited for them to tell us when they would like us to come. We had three casts on the road and a fourth developing. Hans and I were excited with the possibilities, feeling completely free and dreaming wild.

Another outstanding personality had joined our Belgium board, Yannick Boes, head of the Cristal Alken Brewery. He was married to a wonderful woman named Veva, whose father had been a teacher for King Baudouin in his younger years. Yannick telephoned Hans and said, "I have heard from the palace how impressed our king and queen were when Up with People performed for them in their arboretum in 1969. I think they might enjoy meeting the founder, Blanton Belk." Hans fully agreed, and the request went to the colonel in charge of the king's schedule. Word came back to Yannick that an appointment was set for an audience in the Royal Palace of Brussels.

The colonel met me at the door and ushered me through a number of rooms to the reception room. When King Baudouin entered, I immediately stood up and said, "Your Majesty, it is a great privilege to meet you. I have heard so much about you from the people of Belgium." He said in reply,

"I'm very impressed with what you're creating with Up with People and these young people. I am delighted to meet you personally. Both the queen and I were so taken not only with their performance but with them and their characters. We talked to many of them, and it was obvious to us that this experience was maturing them in every way." I thanked him for his words, and he added, "The queen and I are in touch with a number of our Belgian young people, and we're urging them to attend your performances and to talk with your international students."

There was a pause in our conversation when coffee and pastries were passed around, and I had a chance to observe his features. I said to myself, what a totally alive personality, trim and direct, he looks you in the eye and listens intently. What a father to young and old in Belgium! As we parted the king said, "You have a sacred responsibility for these young people, and I applaud you and I will help wherever I can. Blessings on you to all the young people traveling in your program. We will meet again." When the colonel escorted me out, I thought to myself, it's almost a spiritual experience to be with a man so committed to his people and his country! This was the beginning of a sincere friendship that lasted the rest of his life.

I called Yannick and Veva to report on the visit, and they were thrilled it had gone so well. When I thanked them for arranging the audience Veva said, "Since King Baudouin and Queen Fabiola have no children they have made all the children of Belgium their own. That has to be one of the reasons that they so resonate with you and what you're trying to do for young people everywhere." When I reported to Jean he said, "I knew it would go well. Get Hans and Tove and bring Betty and join me at my house for drinks and dinner tomorrow night. I want to hear all about it."

People connecting people seemed to be an important key in the development of Up with People. When I left Tucson, a friend and lawyer for Up with People named Anthony Terry said to me, "If you ever go to Spain be in touch with my cousins, the de Terrys, who run a sherry bodega. The don of the family is Fernando. I think the two of you would hit it off in a big way since he's a sportsman, loves hunting and shooting."

I tucked that in my quiver, not realizing how quickly this connection would be made. One of our three casts were now on the road in the northern part of Italy in the Po Valley near the city of Bologna with its communist city government. The advance team was having problems with getting host families in that area. The Roman Catholic Church had become a great supporter and wanted to help. They asked a priest named Father José de Sobrino, a Spaniard who had a family radio program, to assure the people in the north that the young people in the cast were of good character. After Father de Sobrino mentioned this on the radio, families started to open up their homes. In fact, in one small village more families arrived looking for students than we had cast members. The cast director had a great idea and worked it all out by sending one student per home instead of two.

When the cast went to Genoa, I went with them. Betty stayed in Brussels taking care of the girls. I was entertained by one of the great ship owners in that port city. He had been to the show with his wife and family and was enthusiastic about our leadership program. He invited me to lunch at his headquarters with several of his officers. Before we even got into conversation he said, "You gave all of us a demonstration of the science of action. You met a need created by the demonstrating students of the 1960s and later on, you worked out your philosophy. My congratulations, and I offer a toast to you personally, and to your staff and students. May Up with People thrive and prosper and spread in the years to come. I salute you and thank you for coming to Italy."

Father de Sobrino was a tremendous help in Italy and, eventually, in his home country of Spain. We were with a cast in the northern Italian city of Brescia. He introduced me to a colonel who was the commander of a battalion of Alpini troops preparing for military exercises in the Alps. They were a fine-tuned outfit and impressive with their trademark mountain laurel in their caps. When the colonel informed me that they would be staging at 7:00 a.m. in the large lobby of our hotel the next morning, I volunteered for the cast to come up with a short performance to give them a special sendoff. It was a challenge but the cast responded, and they were all there bright and shiny at 6:30 the next morning. We had, however, forgotten to inform the Zanotti family who owned the hotel, so they could alert their guests. The hotel had previously been a convent, and the large lobby was surrounded on four sides with rooms and suites that went up six floors. When the band struck up at 7:00 a.m. and the cast rushed in from all corners of the square to take their places, the noise was enough to wake the dead. When the lights came on and doors were flung open, people were thinking some alarm was being sounded to evacuate. No doubt many of them were terribly upset at being awakened in this way. Being Italians and always ready for fun, however, they grabbed their bathrobes and gathered on their balconies, looking down to see what was happening in the lobby. Not only were they looking at the colorfully costumed cast but they were impressed to see the lobby packed with Alpini troops. I am happy to say that at the end of 20 minutes, when the cast finished their final number, the troops jumped to their feet. There was a rousing ovation, and even many of those surrounding us from the balconies were applauding. Many of the cast were still half asleep when they arrived, but at the end they were totally awake and mingling enthusiastically with the troops. It was something that they would not soon forget.

When I returned to Brussels there was a phone call awaiting me from one Fernando de Terry from Spain. When I picked up the call this gentleman in perfect English said, "My cousin Father de Sobrino has informed me that you are a sportsman and love shooting. I was wondering whether you would consider accepting my invitation to come to Spain for a red-legged partridge shoot over the holiday period? It is an annual event in which our extended family is included." I was excited to accept since the dates fit our plans. The Magnus family had invited us to have Christmas in Norway, and Jenny and Katie were greatly looking forward to a holiday with snow. I would go to Spain before that and return home to join Betty and the girls for the trip to Norway.

How I got to Spain is a bit of a convoluted story. Before I left the US, I had been in San Carlos, México, for much needed R&R in October 1972. The manager of the marina there was a former PT boat squadron commander in the British Royal Navy, and when he heard I was going to Spain he told me to look up an old friend of his named Rudolfo "Rudi"

Bay, who owned a large charter airline named Spantax out of Spain. So when I informed Rudi of my invitation from Fernando de Terry, he said, "Be my guest. I'll send you a voucher for a flight from Brussels to Majorca, and from there you can rent a car and drive the short distance to Puerto de Santa Maria," which was my destination.

All I needed now was to find a gun since all of mine were a long way away in Tucson. Here again friends came to my aid. Beatrice Lunt asked her cousin to loan me a matched pair of 20-gauge shotguns. The trip went well, and I arrived in the de Terry's small town of Puerto de Santa Maria in Andalusia. I was introduced at a large family gathering that included his three sons. The graciousness and hospitality extended to me as an American was outstanding. One could tell right away that Fernando was an impressive figure. I certainly didn't realize at that moment that this meeting would lead to a lifetime friendship with Fernando and the de Terry family. During that visit I learned he was the owner of one of the largest sherry bodegas in Andalusia and also a well-known breeder of Andalusian horses.

I was nervous the next morning when I learned I would be one of eight guns that would shoot that day. However, I'm relieved and happy to say that I shot quite well and stuck religiously to the etiquette of never shooting a low bird and never poaching a bird headed for a neighbor. There were three drives during the morning with riders on the Andalusian horses on each end of the drive. They had white flags waving in the sunlight to move the partridges. Quite a few of the more experienced partridges did 180-degree turns and flew back over the walking beaters. When it was all over Fernando gave me a hearty handshake and said, "You must come again and next time bring your wife. In the meantime, here are two brace of partridges—four birds for you to take back for your Christmas dinner." I was happy with this introduction to shooting in Spain. Betty was shocked to open my suitcase and find the four birds nestled among my socks!

As I flew back to Brussels I thought about how my life was coming together. For many years in MRA I was too busy "changing the world" to live in a well-rounded way. Now I was realizing how much I had missed this important part of my life. My father had trained me well so that my love of hunting could be the entrée to meeting many interesting people.

Christmas in Norway in 1972 was a delight. Katie was determined to learn ice-skating. Falling down in no way seemed to deter her. Betty remembers a hair-raising but exhilarating trip down the mountain with Hans holding her up as she tried skiing. Hans's father and mother, Konrad and Dora, were good friends, and they seemed happy that the Belk family had bonded with Hans and Tove and their children. Jenny and Katie were thrilled with the tiny lighted Christmas candles, helping to decorate the trees, and all the small things that made a Norwegian Christmas so special. Of course, the Norwegian traditional holiday drink, *gløgg*, added greatly to the Christmas spirit. Hans's younger sister Katrina made a big hit with our two girls, and they were delighted when we invited her to join us the following year as an au pair in Belgium. She later accompanied us back to Tucson in 1973. Before leaving Norway I had a nice chat with Konrad and a chance to thank him for all Hans was doing in the development of Up with People and as a partner with me. I added that he and Dora could be most proud of him, and that if I had ever had a son, I would hope he would be like Hans. Very good memories of our time in Norway! After spending these months in 1972 and, again in 1973, we felt like international citizens.

Ten years later, Yannick and Veva Boes arranged for a performance of Up with People in their hometown of Hasselt in the Limburg province of northern Belgium. This coincided with an international board of directors meeting in Brussels. Word had also come to Yannick that Their Majesties King Baudouin and Queen Fabiola would accept his invitation to be the guests of honor. We heard from Her Royal Highness Princess Margriet of the Netherlands and her husband, Pieter van Vollenhoven, that they too would attend. The November 11, 1983, board meeting was held that morning in the Wittouck home in Brussels with invited guests including members of the Belgium board. It was a full house including Admiral Wally Schirra, an astronaut who was there representing Captain Gene Cernan. Jean's daughter Beatrice and her sister Eliane hosted a wonderful luncheon.

By mid-afternoon we were all on a bus heading to the town of Hasselt, where over 6,000 people had gathered in Yannick's brewery, which had been transformed into a giant theater. Yannick told the board there were 500 kegs of beer holding up the stage, and after all the singing and dancing, it would be years before the beer would settle down. When Their Majesties King Baudouin and Queen Fabiola entered, the whole audience rose as one, and after welcoming them, Yannick ushered them to their seats. Then he went on the stage and introduced the show. I was honored to be seated on the queen's right and Her Royal Highness Princess Margriet of the Netherlands was seated next to His Majesty King Baudouin. When the cast sang the special song "Pays de Coeur/Hartelijk Land"—written for Up with People's tour of Belgium by Ralph and Paul Colwell, Chantal de Limelette, and Herb Allen—the queen was visibly moved. She said to me, "What a great tribute."

Earlier in 1980, to commemorate Belgium's 150th anniversary, Up With People performed throughout the nation accompanied by the Belgian National Orchestra. In the words of the songwriter Paul Colwell, *We wanted to especially honor Belgium and the many people who had supported us through the years. Playing on the French phrase, "homme de coeur" (person of heart), we changed it to "pays de coeur" (country of heart). The song pays tribute to the beauty, culture, and the spirit of this country at the heart of Europe, and to its "joy and warmth to which we always return."* At intermission, the king's military attaché informed Yannick that the king would like to receive the board of directors and congratulate them on their service. We were all ushered up to the boardroom of the brewery. Yannick asked me to present the board, one by one. It was a memorable day.

There were several other occasions when I had the honor of meeting with King Baudouin but one stands out. That was the *Fêtes 40-60* celebrating 40 years of his reign and 60 years of his life. The king initiated a formal invitation for Up with People to participate and perform on Belgian national day, July 21, 1991. The invitation also included Betty and me as well as members of our board of directors. So there we were standing in the lobby of the theater at the Atomium made famous at the 1958 Brussels World Expo. Some of the Belgian board members of Up with People were with us—Yannick and Veva Boes, Beatrice Lunt, and John Goossens.

As we stood there, we heard loud applause outside when Their Majesties King Baudouin and Queen Fabiola got out of their car and were walking to the theater. Betty and I welcomed them as they came in. We followed the king and queen down to the front row and the show started. It went straight through for an hour without an intermission. Their majesties were clapping along and seemed delighted with the show. At the end of the performance they stood up and led the crowd in a standing ovation. At that point the cast poured off the stage and gathered around the king and queen. Then the king said to me, "I would like you to escort us back to our car." By that time the crowds outside had increased and they were lining the pathway waiting for the king and queen to come out. About halfway down the path, King Baudouin stopped abruptly and turned to me and the crowd went silent. He said, "The queen and I have a message for you and all those involved with Up with People around the world. Please tell them to give more than they think they can give without any fear because they are the true voice of spirit and hope for the world." The crowd was silent and the king said to me again, "Did you get that?" and he repeated it. I did get it and it is indelibly printed on my mind. When we said goodbye he said, "Thank you for coming, your young people have made my day." This was the last time I would see King Baudouin because he died two years later while on holiday in Spain.

22

First Americans/First Nation

"In a Sacred Manner I Live"
In a sacred manner I live,
To the heavens I gaze

My father had great respect for the original inhabitants of the United States—
the First Americans. We all grew up in this country with the movies and
stories of the Indians and cowboys in which the cowboys were always the
good guys and the Indians were the bad guys. It was a terrible stereotype.

One of the First Americans I met was named Ernst, the chief of the
Pamunkey Tribe in the Tidewater area of Virginia. When I was eight years
old, my father took me hunting with Ernst one morning in a marsh. My
father was watching a flock of mallards that were circling our decoys. They
were gliding in and landing among Ernst's live mallard decoys, which were
tethered out front—a practice that was outlawed two years later. That was
the first and last time I ever saw my father let ducks land among our decoys.
He said with a whisper, "Pick out that big male greenhead mallard, a little
to the right of the group. Aim for his head with your shotgun." I did as he
told me and it was successful. My father killed two more when they took
off, and Ernst quickly shoved his boat out of the reeds and paddled out
to pick them up. When he entered the blind, as he presented me with the
greenhead mallard, my first duck, I saw the nobility in his smiling face. He
said, "Good shot, you hit it in the head." He became a friend who hunted
with us until I went off to the US Navy when I turned 18.

I learned a lot from my father. He neither looked down nor looked up
to First Americans; he looked at them eye to eye as equal human beings. I

saw the way it had built trust between him and Ernst over the years. The next person of First Americans descent I got to know closely was a man named Bill Keeler, the CEO of Phillips Petroleum in Bartlesville, Oklahoma. I think Bill made history when as a Cherokee he attained that position at Phillips. My secretary at that time was Barbara Bluejacket of Shawnee descent. Her father, Bill Bluejacket, was a good friend of Bill Keeler and helped me connect with him. The chairman of the board at Phillips was Boots Adams, who was married to Bill Keeler's sister. Once when I was visiting Bill Keeler on his ranch he said to me, "As a Cherokee, at least once a week, I have to get out of all this metal and concrete of my office building and get on my horse and ride across my ranch." Bill liked what we were trying to do with young people in Sing-Out/Up with People, and he sponsored us in Bartlesville and other cities in Oklahoma. He telephoned me one day and said that the US government had requested that he represent his people at a conference of indigenous peoples in Quito, Ecuador. He asked me to come along as a guest on his plane, so I went. Some years later after he retired, he became chief of the Cherokee Nation. When I saw him next, his hair had grown out past his shoulders and he had traded his blue suits for native attire. He had gone back to his roots, and he stood tall.

These earlier experiences had prompted me to urge John Sayre and Rusty Wailes to do their best to get a delegation of First Americans/First Nation youth to the first gathering at Mackinac Island in 1964. By the end of the summer, about 200 First Americans/First Nation students had experienced Mackinac. In 1965, 350 First Americans/First Nation came including representatives of the 15 out of the 19 Pueblos outside of Santa Fe, New Mexico. The Pueblo delegations were led by Governor Abel Sanchez of the San Ildefonso Pueblo.

Governor Sanchez, representing the delegation, invited Sing-Out '65 to visit on September 12, 1965, when Sing-Out Express stopped in Santa Fe on their way across the country. Their show was a great success. The high point for some of the students was staying in the homes of the Pueblo families. It was never to be forgotten, both by the students and the Pueblo families. The event was successful and many young people from the area came forward wanting to travel with the cast. I asked a friend and staff member Don Saul and his wife, Maya, to move there.

They were wholeheartedly welcomed and maintained constant contact with the Pueblo community outside of Santa Fe. At this time, any students that wanted to travel had to have written permission from their family and the government of their tribe. Our coordinating center was established in Santa Fe in 1966. As a result many of the young people in the community took part in Sing-Out and later Up with People.

There was and is such a synergy between Up with People and the First Americans culture. In fact, what was happening with them and Up with People in Santa Fe expanded to many of the other tribes across the United States and Canada. Don and Maya had such a big job on their hands that I invited another couple and their family to join the Sauls. A good friend from Peru, Esteban Daranyi welcomed the opportunity to come to the States with his family and help with the development of Up with People. Esteban and his wife, Ines, were fluent in Spanish and English, and they fit right in. They were most sensitive in building close friendships with the Pueblo People. One of their new friends was the great pottery maker Maria Martinez, known for her exquisite work with black pottery. Maria and her husband, Julian, and their son, Popovi Da, were a host family when the students came to the San Ildefonso Pueblo. When I went to visit them, Popovi Da presented me with a silver letter opener engraved with my initials, which I treasure.

During the Bicentennial Year Celebration, Up with People was invited to be the guest of 15 Southwestern tribes in 17 communities, both in Arizona and New Mexico. Peter MacDonald, chairman of the Navajo Nation Tribal Council, sent the first invitation saying, "On behalf of the Navajo People, I invite your group to our land. I know that you will enrich our lives and make us more aware of the many opportunities that we have in this great country of ours."[1] Mrs. MacDonald, in the tradition of Navajo hospitality, returned to her native town of Tuba City, Arizona, from her residence in Window Rock to welcome the cast. They treated the cast to a delicious meal of Navajo mutton stew and fried bread. The cast performed in the Tuba City High School theater, one of the most modern facilities in the state. Some people may know that many tribes including the Navajo have a separate nation within the United States. They have their own incorporated municipalities and police departments, and their own elected government. Window Rock, the capital city of the Navajo Nation, welcomed Up with People for the third time in two years. Dr. Kenneth Ross, superintendent of schools, arranged for 1,000 students from six high schools in the Window Rock area to be bussed in for an afternoon performance. The Navajo students from the first song to the last stood and stomped at the end demanding more encores.

Earlier at staging in August of 1975, Preston Keevama of the San Juan Pueblo and Ramos Sanchez from the San Ildefonso Pueblo came to speak. They wanted to prepare those who would be living and performing in the Laguna and San Juan Pueblos outside of Santa Fe. Both Mr. Keevama and Mr. Sanchez supported Up with People in spirit and action since its inception. Three of Mr. Keevama's daughters had traveled in a cast, including Kateri, who was in a cast that performed before her own people. Both men expressed their hopes for Up with People in the framework of their own traditions. Mr. Sanchez urged us to go on our tour with dignity and pride and learn to respect other people for their beliefs. He believed that Up with People could help young people develop positive character and leadership in this country. Mr. Keevama spoke of his traditions and Up with People on a global level. He correlated the tradition of love, hope, and prayers through song to the Up with People medium of music. He underlined the need for us to strike for a purpose greater than ourselves." He talked of "a rededication of virtues" and called on the group to go into their tour "possessed with understanding, not hate, for peace in the world."[2]

The governor of the San Juan Pueblo, Tony Trujillo, invited me to say a few words before the show. I had a chance to underline for the elders and the young people the impact that young First Americans in the cast have had on the world. I thanked the elders and governors for their trust in us and for allowing their young students and often their own sons and daughters to travel with Up with People. I said that, "We're proud of what they have given us and the world. The [First Americans] taught us two things: how to live with nature, and how to live with our neighbors. We need what you can give. If we give to each other, maybe America can learn something."

The cultural impact of the occasion did not go unnoticed. The British Broadcasting Corporation happened to be filming life in the pueblos and decided to include the presentations in the Pueblos and segments of our show in their documentary.

One fact that shows how Up with People won the respect and trust of both elders and governors of the tribes is that more than 130 young First Americans and First Nation students from at least 29 tribes were able to travel and represent their people. They made a unique contribution.

23

Moon Rider: Captain USN Eugene Cernan

"Moon Rider"
I see the world without any borders,
Without any fighting, without any fear...

I first noticed Captain Eugene "Gene" Cernan when I was invited to the Kennedy Space Center at the launching of Apollo 11 in July 1969. I was the guest of Tom Paine, the National Aeronautics and Space Administration (NASA) administrator, along with, among others, Ambassador Sargent Shriver. I noticed an astronaut with a crowd of press around him and asked my host, "Who is that?" Tom replied, "That's Captain Gene Cernan. He's been chosen for the upcoming flight that will circle the Moon and lay the groundwork for the first Moon shot." I was struck by how trim and fit Cernan looked, and he seemed to bristle with energy as he stood in the middle of the press corps. I said to myself, I'd like to meet him someday.

That day came just about a year later when I was invited by Langhorne Washburn, director of the US Travel Service for the Department of Commerce, to be part of a government delegation to Japan to encourage tourism. Mr. Washburn had seen an Up with People performance and his son had traveled with a cast for two years. By coincidence, around the same time, Up with People had been invited to perform at Expo '70 in Osaka for a month beginning on May 15. When I arrived to join his party in San Francisco for our flight to Japan, I was surprised and delighted when he introduced me to Captain and Mrs. Gene Cernan. When I shook hands with Captain Cernan I had no idea that it was the beginning of an enduring friendship. We were both Navy men, and Gene and I laughed when I told him that my official serial number in my navy days during World War II was much lower than his. His wife, Barbara, was charming and she struck me as a perfect partner. They were definitely a power couple, outgoing and completely themselves. Gene was impressive as the spokesman for the delegation.

Our accommodations had been arranged at the Imperial Hotel in Tokyo. The second day there, the manager of the hotel, after conferring with Mr. Washburn, asked that the cast of Up with People perform for his guests in the giant lobby. It was a bold move because guests were constantly moving in and out. Suddenly, this dynamic group burst into the lobby and brought the hotel to a standstill. Barbara and Gene were with me, and they were so excited at the end of the performance that they led a standing ovation. The hotel manager said later that something like this had never happened in the lobby of the Imperial Hotel. He added, "Even those who could not get to the front desk to pick up their keys were happy once they got over the initial shock."

When we informed the manager that Captain Cernan and his wife would like to thank the cast, he put a large suite at our disposal. It was probably the first time a top gun aviator had chatted with student activists from the 1960s. It was a freewheeling, no-holds-barred conversation about their unhappiness with the war in Vietnam and their eagerness to participate in the civil rights struggle. Gene Cernan was masterful and encouraged them to speak their minds while he listened intently. Without a doubt, his willingness to listen and give them a chance to express themselves completely won the day. They also responded to his convictions that not everything that was happening in Vietnam or elsewhere was to his liking but that he had sworn an oath to do everything in his power to preserve freedom. He said, "That freedom extends to all of you. You can freely express the things that you're not happy about. More importantly, the freedom I experienced in the lobby as I watched your demonstration was the freedom that we all cherish, to build the kind of world that we all dream about." He ended by saying, "I salute all of you with gratitude." They gave him an instant standing ovation. During the whole time in Japan

Gene did his best to include me and, as the old saying goes, "If you really want to get to know a person, travel together." That was certainly true for the two of us on this trip.

On our flight back to the United States, Gene had a word with the captain, and I was moved up to sit next to him and his wife in first class. We talked so much about our lives and our dreams that at one point, Barbara said, "Listening to the two of you I think you've both told enough lies and covered enough dreams—so now go to sleep." The gentleman next to us had passed out from drinking too many cocktails, and when we were disembarking for customs he only made it because Gene and I were supporting him. Then the question came up, what to do with him. He was standing there and sleeping at the same time! Gene came up with a brilliant idea. Anyone who landed in Honolulu at that time may recall that it was a long walk from the airplane to customs but your baggage was put on a conveyor belt that stretched all the way to the airport. Gene put a baggage tag on our friend and we laid him out on the conveyor belt. We tipped a porter to walk beside him to be sure he got up when he reached the customs area. It seemed to work to perfection because after the layover a more sober man appeared in the plane. Barbara did not seem at all as happy with our part in the joke as we were. It probably led to pillow talk that night but I never knew!

Sometime later I flew to Houston to ask Captain Cernan to join Up with People's Board of Directors. He seemed excited with the prospect, saying he'd like to do so but he had to check first with NASA. He would be in touch when word came.

That summer of 1970, Betty and I invited Gene and Barbara to come for a little R&R at our place in México. There was never a dull moment when they were around, and of course Gene won the fishing tournament, catching the biggest sailfish on light tackle and was awarded the Captain Eddie Rickenbacker Trophy. One morning after breakfast Gene said to us, "I would appreciate it, Blanton, if you would drive me out to the Empalme Valley on the other side of Guaymas so I can have a look at our old Guaymas Tracking Station in Empalme." Gene had been tracked from this station during his walk in space in June 1966. An hour later we arrived at the desolate tracking station, and Gene said to me, "If you don't mind I'd like to walk up there alone. I'd like to stand and remind myself of the experience of stepping out of my spacecraft over this spot and walking some 30,000 miles twice around the Earth." I saw him standing there looking at the skies, and when he came back to the car, you could tell it was an emotional experience. He said, "I had a near death experience on that spacewalk. When I tried to get back into the spacecraft my spacesuit had become so enlarged I couldn't get through the porthole. Fortunately, my arms had grown very strong through all the calisthenics I had been doing for my spacewalk and that saved me. With a superhuman effort I was able to inch by inch work my way through the small porthole. I felt absolutely spent when I finally entered. Months later I was informed that Tom Stafford, my partner and pilot of the spacecraft, had been given strictly private orders. After a certain number of minutes in the attempt to reenter, if it proved to be unsuccessful, the orders were to cut me free." Gene then turned to me with a big smile and said, "Luck was with me and I'm still here and it's high time we hurried home to one of your margaritas!"

Sometime after this an excited Gene telephoned to say, "Hang on to your hat! I've been chosen to be the commander of the next flight to the Moon." All of this coincided with our summer staging for the new casts of Up with People, which that year took place at the University of Arizona in Tucson. Gene knew we were in staging and he called to let me know that he would be flying a military jet from Houston to the sand dune area west of Yuma, Arizona. He wanted to stop in and say hello to the students. The military at Davis-Monthan Air Force Base here was alerted. When I arrived I was permitted to pick up Gene. He was an impressive sight when he climbed out of his military jet. He wore a gold flight suit with "NASA" embossed over the left top pocket and "Captain Eugene Cernan" over the other pocket. He even had a white scarf. He was the embodiment of Captain America! When he hopped in the car he said, "Let's move it! I've only got a certain amount of time and I want to use it with the students." When he walked in, 1,000 students from many countries gave him a long standing ovation. In fact, it went on so long that Gene said, "What should I do?" and I said, "It's already a success. You could just say 'thank you' and wave goodbye." Instead, he stayed and inspired them with his convictions and passion and answered all their questions. Of course, it started with them covering the question, "How do you go to the bathroom in space?" He said, "That is always the first question, and the answer is very simple. There are only two ways!" There was another long ovation at the end. As he walked out, he shook as many hands and hugged as many girls as possible—even for an astronaut!

The launch of Apollo 17 was scheduled for December 10, 1972, and an invitation arrived from Gene to attend the liftoff. It was scheduled as the first night shot. I flew in from Belgium, where we were living at the time, to be there. When I arrived in Cape Kennedy, I was delighted to find friend and board member Ralph Hart there. The next day, after Ralph and I had finished breakfast, he said, "Why don't we drive across the causeway and try to see Gene before he takes off tonight." It seemed like a wild thought but we took off in Ralph's car knowing there would be heavy security. We arrived at a checkpoint in the middle of the causeway and an armed guard came to inspect our car. It's hard to believe but the guard said, "Mr. Hart, what are you doing here?" I learned later that Ralph had often had this same gentleman do security work at some of his parties in West Palm Beach, Florida. Ralph told him of our friendship with Captain Cernan and that we hoped to pay our respects on his upcoming trip. The guard had an incredulous look on his face but said, "I'll call over there." We waited quite a while and finally a message came back, "Let them come," so away we went! We were met by security and taken to a large room that was divided by a plexiglass wall, some six to eight inches thick. In a short time, Gene appeared on the other side in a golf shirt and a pair of slacks, looking for all the world like a man getting ready to play a game of golf. We thanked him for letting us in. He said, "I'm glad to see you. I was just getting ready to go into space." He then took a pointer and turned to the back wall where there was a map of the Moon's surface. He took the pointer and said, "We'll land there." And he did! Apollo 17, the last lunar mission, hit the bullseye, right on target.

That night Ralph and I stood with several thousand invited guests and were riveted by the sheer power of the rocket when it blasted off. We both said a silent prayer for a safe journey there and home again. No one could've been more prepared to captain this flight than Gene, I thought to myself as I pondered the power and extraordinary bravery of both the men in the rocket and the people who sent them there. If only men and women had grown up as much in character as in technology perhaps, we should have faith that this could still happen.

There was hardly an Up with People board member who was more faithful than Gene. We had an official invitation from President José López Portillo of México to come personally and bring a cast to celebrate his wife's birthday in 1977. It would be at Los Pinos, the White House of México. Catalina Quinn Colwell was coordinating Up with People's participation in this event. She was the daughter of movie star Anthony Quinn and had invited her father to come. México claimed Quinn as their own. I flew down with Betty and Gene. It was a wonderful Mexican fiesta with hundreds of candles illuminating the bountiful food and a group of mariachis circulating between the tables. We were lucky Americans to be included. While dessert was being served, President Portillo paid a special tribute to his wife, Carmen. Then, to her surprise, he called on Up with People to perform. They burst in singing and dancing. His wife was delighted and called for an encore. At that point, President Portillo asked me to introduce Gene. He surprised us all by producing a Mexican flag that he had carried on his trip to the Moon. Everyone was on their feet as he presented this to Señora Portillo, and she reciprocated with a big kiss and hug. There was much applause.

We thought this was to be the main surprise of the evening but Anthony Quinn—who at this point might have been feeling a little upstaged by the astronaut—added to the surprise. He stood up and asked Señora Portillo to dance to music from *Zorba the Greek* with him. He offered her his hand, and she accepted. Everyone stood up as the band accompanied them with their dance. Anthony sat down with a big smile. It was truly an unforgettable evening, and it was almost daylight when we finally made it back to our hotel.

The next night the cast gave a benefit performance for Fonapas, the Mexican National Fund for Social Activities, under the auspices of Señora Portillo. In the audience that night were 48 members of the cabinet and their families, and a great representation of Mexican business leaders. It was very well received.

Even though Up with People is officially incorporated as an apolitical and nonsectarian organization, we have been received multiple times at the Vatican. In April 1984, we were officially invited to have the cast perform on the steps of St. Peter's following a Papal Audience and afterward to be received by the Holy Father. Gene flew to Rome to attend this occasion. Betty and I were there with other members of our board. The Vatican had thoughtfully arranged seats in front of the reserved section. There were 50,000 in attendance, and when the cast sang in Italian "What Color is God's Skin?" and "Up with People," the audience sang with them. They had learned the songs in their schools, youth groups, scout troops, and churches. It was a perfect Rome day with bright sunshine.

When Gene was presented to Pope John Paul II, he leaned over in the Catholic tradition to kiss the pope's ring. Halfway down, the pope stopped him saying, "No, no Captain, we don't have time for that. Tell me, what did you see from the Moon!" Gene stood up straight and was boggled for a moment but he recovered. He said that when he was on the Moon, it felt like he was sitting on the front porch of God and that the Almighty was looking down on all the peoples of the Earth. Then he added, "When I was looking the other way, I could only see the black and blue of infinite space." We all were watching the pope's reaction as Gene ended by saying, "No one can have the experience I had without believing that there is an infinite power greater than man that made it all possible." Pope John Paul II seemed visibly moved by Gene's convictions and offered him his blessing. Standing next to Gene were Manuel and Marie-Therese Arango. Watching them, one could see that they were also moved by this brief conversation. During the days we spent together in Rome, there was clear bonding between Gene and Manuel.

Some months later Manuel telephoned to say he had invited Gene for a little R&R on his boat in the Sea of Cortez in México. Manuel was sending his plane to pick us up in Tucson and added that Gene would fly his plane from Houston to Tucson. Two days before our scheduled pickup, Manuel called and said, "You won't believe this but Gene has just called me with the news that he's fallen off his horse and broken his leg. He can't come to México." Then, Manuel went on with a good bit of humor, "Can you believe that a man that got safely to the Moon and back would fall off his own horse?" However, he added, "I'm sending the plane for you, and we'll celebrate nonetheless." His jet arrived with two pilots and the stewardess to pick me up in Tucson. I felt for Gene and how sorry he must be that he ever got on that horse! It was a great weekend, and I was even able to use my fishing expertise to help Manuel catch his first marlin—a nice 200-pound blue. It's always fun with Manuel, and this was no exception. After the weekend I was once again flown alone on his plane and I was feeling quite important until Betty picked me up and said, "Thank goodness you're back, the trash cans are overloaded since we missed last week!" Welcome home, Belk!

Forty years after the Apollo 17 mission, Gene decided to plan a party, along with Neil Armstrong, first man on the Moon, to mark the occasion. Sadly, Neil Armstrong died before the plans could take shape, but Gene felt his best tribute to Neil was to go forward with the celebration. It turned out to be a most fitting tribute to the pioneers of space and the 40th anniversary of the Apollo 17 trip to the Moon. Betty and I were invited. The event was hosted by the National Museum of Naval Aviation in Pensacola, Florida, where many of the astronauts had gone through training. We were welcomed by Captain Bob Rasmussen, a former Blue Angel, the Navy's flight demonstration squadron, and the current director of the museum. He took us immediately to see Gene, who was having a drink in the bar with some of his buddies. He welcomed us warmly and said that we would be staying with him and his wife, Jan, at one of the guesthouses. He also said how happy he was that a small group of students from Up with People had come to perform. He turned to his fellow astronauts and introduced me as the founder of Up with People, saying he had proudly served on the board of directors for many years.

He escorted us along with Captain Rasmussen to a guesthouse. In the car he said to me, "I want you to say a word about my participation in Up with People." This was a challenge I had not anticipated. Here we were with eight of the original astronauts, the men who pioneered the space program, including the first man to orbit Earth in 1962, Senator John Glenn. It was not a lot of time to prepare but I was determined for Gene's sake to give it my best shot.

That first night, Friday, December 14, 2012, Gene hosted a private reception at which the newest exhibit, the Apollo Lunar Excursion Module (LEM), was unveiled. A dinner followed to honor these pioneers of space. When the master of ceremonies invited me to say a word about Gene, I started by describing taking him to meet 1,000 college-age students from many countries at the Up with People staging. He always challenged all of them to reach for their own star. I also described his meeting with Pope John Paul II in Rome. I noted how he was a role model to more than 22,000 alumni from over 130 countries and spoke of his willingness to travel to special events for the program all over the world.

Saturday opened with a panel on the near catastrophic flight of Apollo 13 as told by the astronauts themselves—Commander James Lovell, the Apollo 13 lunar module pilot, and Captain Fred W. Haise. The audience was spellbound as they described successfully bringing the spacecraft home after an oxygen tank explosion crippled the Apollo 13 command module.

A highlight for Betty and me was the luncheon at which Senator Glenn and Gene spoke together. John Glenn described how as he broke through into space, a mouse came floating up from under his seat and hovered in front of him. He reached out and took it in his heavily gloved hand. He held it out to all of us saying, "Here it is. When I found out later that my friend Gemini astronaut Alan Shepard had put it there, I debated whether I would end his next spaceflight by reporting this to NASA headquarters." But he added, "I just couldn't do it."

The final evening was called a "Salute to the Pioneers of Space." It was a much larger event and many more people had been invited. The LEM replica was on display during this fundraising dinner in Hangar Bay One and the Blue Angels Atrium. The program featured recollections by Mercury, Gemini, and Apollo astronauts. There was a touching tribute to Neil Armstrong including a performance by Up with People. The small cast sang in Gene's honor the Up with People song he had inspired, "Moon Rider." It was the first time that most of these astronauts had heard it, and they all came to their feet cheering at the end of it.

Paul Colwell reflects, *Those original astronauts gave songwriters and poets a lot to write about. They were the first in human history to give us a view of Earth as a single entity spinning in the blackness. While each astronaut had his own individual description of the lunar experience, it was Gene Cernan, the last man on the Moon, who summed it up best. His observations were profound and a challenge to a world in conflict. They had such eloquence and depth, it was a daunting prospect to do them justice in a song. It took us five years. In 1977, I was at an event with Gene and the Belks at Los Pinos in México City, and it reminded me that we had unfinished business. Ralph, Herb, and I got to work. Surprisingly the song practically wrote itself. With Gene's words and a little of our own poetic license it was done. When my wife, Catalina, heard that the title was "Gene's Song," she felt strongly that it was too weak, not heroic enough. She suggested " Moon Rider." And so it was!*

In January 2017, I was sitting in my home watching the evening news when suddenly there was a newsflash across the bottom of the screen saying that astronaut Gene Cernan, the last man to set foot on the Moon, had died at the age of 82. I was privileged to have been his friend for almost 50 years. I had visited with him only a few weeks before at his home in Houston to say goodbye. As a distinguished member of our international Board of Directors, we had traveled the world together. He was a cowboy at heart who loved his ranch and horses in the hill country of Texas. He had started out as a fighter pilot jock who relished a good party with his pals. Gene had reached far beyond himself to become a global statesman, and his faith had sustained him. It always seemed to me that he had two great missions in life. The first, to be one of the astronauts who was chosen for the Moon shot. The other mission that seemed to drive him, however, was best summed up in his own words to me: "I have had an experience that only a few in the world have had, and I have an urgent responsibility to pass that experience on to people everywhere."

On January 25, 2017, the last man to walk on the Moon was laid to rest on a hilltop that he had chosen in the state cemetery in Austin, Texas. It was a full military tribute with a 21-gun salute, a flyover, and an honor guard. At the request of his daughter, Tracy Cernan Woolsey, Reed Thompson and 20 Up with People alumni sang the song Gene had inspired, "Moon Rider." Those words will be part of his legacy forever:

The painter tries to paint it, the poet tries to say it
The philosopher tries to convey the meaning to your mind.
But here I am—a quarter million miles away
One human being—one human seeing it for the first time.
I can see the white of snow-capped mountains
The blues and turquoise of the oceans blend.
Australia and Asia coming round the corner
And I can't tell where one country starts and the other one ends

The sun is setting on the Pacific
They're just getting up in Rome.
I don't see the lights of my city
All I can see is home.

I saw the world without any borders
Without any fighting, without any fear.
So Captain, give the order
We're going to cross the next frontier.

I know this view won't last forever
Soon I'll be back to reality.
But isn't it the way we perceive things
That makes them what they will be?

24

Bicentennial Year and Super Bowls

"Two Hundred Years and Just a Baby"
Someday she's going to be quite a lady...

In March 1975, I had two telephone calls that lifted Up with People to a new level. They came about a week apart. My wonderful executive assistant, Ola Cook Henry, picked up the first call, saying to me, "The president of the Lilly Endowment, Eugene Beesley, wants to speak to you." I had met Dr. Landrum Bolling, the vice president of the endowment, but I had never met Mr. Beesley. He came in strong and clear saying his management committee had been meeting and debating what contribution the endowment could make to America during its Bicentennial Year Celebration. "We have $1 million to produce an attractive program," he explained. Then he went on to say, "Since time is short. If you can come up with an exciting program during the next 48 hours, the $1 million dollars is yours."

We loved challenges, and here was a good one. The whole staff pulled together to come up with a plan. Mr. Beesley was on the phone 48 hours later. I put him on the speakerphone and introduced our staff. They outlined their plan to divide our three large casts into nine or ten smaller casts. They would travel and perform across America from California to New York and from Canada to the Mexican border. The casts would go all out to reach as many people as possible with a message: "We are many but we are one" here in America as we celebrate our 200th birthday. They would reach out to service clubs, schools, colleges, prisons, churches, drug rehabilitation centers, and city halls. The staff's enthusiasm seemed to reach Mr. Beesley, and he peppered them with questions. With each question the staff seemed to hit the mark, and he became more and more enthusiastic. He finally said to me, "Mr. Belk, you've got a deal. We are proud to be a participant with Up with People in this gift to America on her 200th birthday!" This big challenge brought the whole organization together.

Things just magically happen when such a culture is in place, so I shouldn't have been surprised when less than a month later, NFL commissioner Pete Rozelle called and invited Up with People to perform in Super Bowl X. Pete underlined that it would give us a global audience. He hoped I would agree, and naturally I said yes. When I thanked him he said, "No, I thank you for giving us this opportunity to salute our country on America's birthday." Then he added, "If you would like to meet Don Weiss and Jim Steeg, who will be coordinating the Super Bowl, you can arrange that with my secretary." I did that, and as they were meeting in New Orleans, I flew there for a wonderful first visit with Pete and Carrie Rozelle. Pete and I hit it off right away, telling lies to each other about the marlin and sailfish we had each landed. Carrie was charming and enthusiastic that we had accepted having Up with People perform the halftime show. Pete introduced me to Don Weiss, Director of Public Relations and Jim Steeg. All of this laid the groundwork for Up with People to perform in an unprecedented four half-time shows at Super Bowls X (1976), XIV (1980), XVI (1982), and XX (1986).

When I asked my close friend Ralph Colwell, our Vice President for Television Production, what his reactions were to producing a half-time show for the Super Bowl, he wrote me this report: *By 1975, 10 years after the start of Sing-Out/Up with People, we knew that what we were doing had struck a deep chord with huge numbers of the public all over the world. It was like a grassroots movement with three casts, soon to be four.*

When Pete Rozelle invited us to do the halftime show, we were faced with the unnerving challenge of taking what we were doing to a whole new level—performing on national TV for millions of people at one time. I was the Vice President of Up with People Television Production at the time. This was a rather terrifying gut check to see if we could produce a powerful event on that kind of stage and do it well. If we could pull it off, it would propel the

Up with People program to a new level of public awareness. If we stumbled, it could have been disastrous. Were we ready for prime time?

Fortunately, we were blessed with a talented production team including Director of Choreography Lynne Morris, Technical Director Steve Rokowski, Music Director Herb Allen, and a staff of writers that included my brother Paul Colwell and David Mackay, renowned record producer for EMI in London.

We realized that we had the opportunity to do something totally different for Super Bowl halftime shows from the usual marching bands and kitschy floats. Lynne Morris had choreographed shows on Broadway but immediately knew this was a different animal. Undaunted, she devised a revolutionary concept of how 450 young performers could use the whole field as their stage. They would sing and dance in dazzling formations with a huge stage midfield for musicians and soloists. It was a format that has been replicated in various forms in Super Bowls every year since then, from Michael Jackson to Jennifer Lopez and Shakira. Steve Rokowski designed the stage. He introduced live concert sound on the field for the first time at a Super Bowl, moving huge speakers on and off the field.

The night before the game was torture for me worrying about all the things that could go wrong. Rokowski and the tech crew were given just two minutes to get everything on the field at the end of the first half of the game—which they did. Our young cast members, though eager and well-rehearsed, were not professional performers. The band and all the singers were to perform live. There was too much that could break down. By the time the show ended with the cast singing 'America the Beautiful' in honor of America's Bicentennial Year we all had a huge sense of relief. We were sure that the NFL would be pleased with what we had done. Up with People had created something new and enduring for all the world to see.

It is impossible to describe the metamorphosis that had taken place with our production team from a year earlier when Pete Rozelle's bombshell landed in our midst. Ralph Colwell's crew knew from the beginning they had to produce something absolutely spectacular. Paul Colwell, a brilliant wordsmith, had produced a song for the celebration entitled "200 Years and Just a Baby." Steve Rokowski was shocked when he realized that the movable stage they had built inside the warehouse was too large to get through the doors. They had to take it down in sections and put it back together in the stadium. Tom Sullivan was to sing the national anthem but was rattled when Pete Rozelle welcomed him saying, "We're so glad you're here, Tom. In a few minutes you'll be singing to millions of people, don't screw up." As Pete walked away, Tom said to me, "I was scared before—now I'm petrified!"

It was the first time a halftime show would be done live—nothing prerecorded. Steve Rokowski described the challenge: *We had to fit everything into a 14-minute slot. We had exactly two and a half minutes at the start to put the entire cast and stages in place and set up a sound system. The speakers had to be powerful enough to reach people at the top of the stadium.*

The Orange Bowl in Miami was packed. The two superstar quarterbacks, the Steelers' Terry Bradshaw and the Cowboys' Roger Staubach, stood waiting for the anthem to start. Tom Sullivan said later, "There I was a bundle of nerves. The announcer said, 'We proudly present our National Anthem sung by Tom Sullivan and the cast of Up with People.' When I hit the high C at the end, the crowd just seemed to explode." The audience was still cheering and shouting "Bravo! Bravo!" when he left the field.[1] TV announcer Brent Musburger turned to his co-host, Phyllis George, and said, "I don't believe I have ever heard the anthem sung better, that was so strong." Herb Allen, Up with People's musical director and composer, had created the arrangement for Tom, and that arrangement was copied many times thereafter.

By the time Betty and I made it back to our hotel lobby after the game, to our surprise there stood Don Weiss. He gave us both bear hugs and said, "It was a great success. Congratulations to you and all your outstanding young people." He also brought greetings and thanks from Pete and Carrie Rozelle, who according to Don were greatly relieved and excited with the halftime performance and Tom's moving rendition of the anthem.

The next night in New York City, Johnny Carson started *The Tonight Show* by saying, "Did you see that halftime performance at the Super Bowl in Miami with those students from Up with People? Their rousing tribute to America on her 200th birthday and the singing of our national anthem by artist Tom Sullivan gives you hope for our future!"[2]

As a prelude to the Super Bowl Floridian, Frances Wolfson, a member of Up with People's Board of Directors, hosted a wonderful dinner cruise for fellow board members, spouses, and friends on Biscayne Bay. After the game and performance, all of our board of directors in attendance sent high praise to Ralph Colwell, Herb Allen, Lynne Morris, and Steve Rokowski, who had pushed and inspired the entire crew to achieve the impossible. The board members gave special thanks to the 450 young men and women who had done so much to make it such a memorable experience for all of us and the country.

Without a doubt it marked the beginning of a new chapter in Up with People's development. Later Don Weiss told us that our appearance at the Super Bowl X halftime had ushered in a whole new phase in halftime shows. An approach that would become the norm going forward.

The whole Bicentennial Year Celebration was a milestone year for Up with People. The Super Bowl publicity gave us a big boost for the nine casts who were performing and doing community service in 771 American and 68 European cities. The Lilly Endowment tracked the casts' progress, and they estimated that from the first performances in September 1975 to the culmination in 1976, we reached 3.9 million people live and millions more through television.[3]

25

Board of Directors

"We Are Many, We Are One"
We all dance to a different drum

One of the great hostesses of Tucson was Bazy Tankersley, the niece of the famous Colonel Robert McCormick, owner and publisher of the *Chicago Tribune*. She was cosmopolitan, international, and one of the top breeders of Arabian horses in the country, constantly giving back to the people in the city and the state. Bazy was one of a kind, and when she died she was sorely missed. Although she never was actually involved in Up with People she remained a strong backer of all Betty and I reached out for in the world. Bazy said to me one day, "Blanton, you are the envy of the nonprofit world with your international board of directors! How did you meet such fascinating people and capture them for your board?" This is the story!

The tale behind each board member is different and quite fascinating. It's important to know that I met them because I wanted to meet them. I was excited about what had been created in Up with People, and I wanted to share that passion with as many people as possible. At the beginning, all of these board members had seen an Up with People show; some had hosted cast members in their homes, and some had children who spent a year with the program. All of them wanted to keep the program vital and growing. It was definitely not a name-only board. Members were involved in every aspect of the company, from finances and strategy to student recruitment, host families, show production, press and media, and future planning.

The proof of their commitment was evident when we faced our first internal crisis, which involved our co-founder and executive vice president,

Don Birdsall. He had been left in charge in the early 1970s when I moved to Belgium at the request of Jean Wittouck. Up with People was rapidly growing in Europe at that time, and Jean wanted us to make the most of the many opportunities that were quickly arising there. Some of our board members and staff were not satisfied with Don's management skills and his lifestyle during that time. It came to the attention of N. W. "Dick" Freeman at a board meeting in Tucson. He was CEO of Tenneco and chairman of our Finance Committee, so he called a Finance Committee meeting on his ranch outside of Houston on Sunday, January 25, 1976. Deane Johnson, senior partner of O'Melveny and Myers, Nella Barkley, past president of the Association of Junior Leagues International, and I were on this committee and flew in for an informal meeting. At the recent Tucson board meeting, Dick had listened to the complaints about Don from our senior staff. He kept saying, "He just doesn't fit." Deane and Nella said they felt the same. Dick asked me what I thought, and I paid tribute to all Don had done for me and the program and how closely we worked together at the beginning. I also noted that things had not been the same since the death of Don's wife, Sue. I definitely felt the time was now to make a change.

The next morning, Dick called the committee meeting to order. Nella spoke first, saying she and Deane had come up with the following recommendations: Don Birdsall would still remain as vice president but no longer be executive vice president, and his salary would be adjusted accordingly. I was directed to tell Don personally of the decision. I found this very difficult to do since we had been so close in the creation of Up with People. However, I wholeheartedly agreed with their decision and thanked them for their heartfelt concern for the future of our program.

Back in Tucson on January 27, after briefing the staff, I went to see Don. I informed him that the Finance Committee had directed me to inform him of their recommended changes. Don said nothing but I could tell he was very angry when he got up and walked out of the room. Jack Hipps was appointed the new chief operating officer, and I underlined that I wanted the move to take place right away. Shortly afterward, Don agreed to the board's recommendation.[1]

Two weeks later, James "Jim" T. Morris of the Lilly Endowment came to Tucson and invited me to breakfast at the Skyline Country Club. He was in town to monitor our Bicentennial Year program that the Lilly Endowment was financing. More than that he came with a proposal that was a bombshell! He had been contacted by a man who called himself one of our biggest local donors. He would give Up with People $1.5 million dollars over the next three years if we would keep Don Birdsall in his position as executive vice president. I was shocked and didn't reply. Then Jim Morris said, "Wouldn't it be worth keeping Birdsall on for the next three years just to get this million and a half?" I made no comment but the shock on my face must have spoken to him.

As soon as I could get away, I got in my car and headed to the office. I met with Peter Voevodsky, Up with People's lawyer, and briefed him on my conversation with Morris. Peter was as shocked as I had been. We telephoned Dick Freeman and made an appointment as soon as he could see us, which was 10 days later in Houston. When we walked into his office, he said, "I could tell from your voice that you uncovered something urgent. So cut to the chase and give me the news." He listened carefully, but when we reported to him about the conversation with Morris and the $1.5 million, he kept saying, "I can't believe the crookedness involved in such a proposal." Then he turned to us and said, "Take the first plane and confront Jim Morris. This cooks Birdsall's goose! He has broken all the rules of a nonprofit by dealing in such a way with one of our main contributors and sponsors, without permission from you, as the CEO or the board of directors. Do this immediately!"

Four days later in Indianapolis, Peter and I lunched with Jim Morris at his country club. Morris was agitated and asked, "Was I set up on that phone call from the Tucson donor?" He added, "I haven't talked to Birdsall on the phone since the Super Bowl." Peter said, "His lawyer is quoting you as having talked to Birdsall several times on the phone." Peter then added, "Of course, Jim, if it gets to a lawsuit, which they have threatened, you would be called as a witness. If they don't subpoena you, Jim, I would have to do so."

With that thought, Morris said he wanted to get his lawyer into the conversation. We then returned to Morris's office to wait until his lawyer arrived. Peter described the whole situation so that the lawyer was fully briefed. It was done very well and achieved its purpose of not causing undue excitement or giving any impression that our management didn't have the situation completely under control. Jim Morris was one shaken individual when Peter and I said goodbye.

As we flew back to Tucson, I found myself thinking about Don. We were both veterans of World War II and had worked together in MRA. I had been the best man at his wedding to Sue Manning, whose family had built Manning's Inc., the coffee and food company in California. They were impressive as a couple, and Don was at his best during those years.

When my sister Barbara and her husband Jim Tinsley heard of our crisis with Don Birdsall they dropped everything and flew to Tucson. They were a great help and support. Jim recalls, "You just put on your double breasted blazer and went in to confront Don with the decision of the Executive Committee." We have always been grateful for their heartfelt backing.

Two days after arriving back in Tucson, all of our senior staff gathered in my office, and Peter came in and introduced Don's lawyer, Charlie McCarty. Charlie was very professional in saying he had no intention of interviewing any of the staff. He only wanted an answer to his question: "Are you for Birdsall or for Belk?" They were all for Belk. Charlie thanked them all and came over and shook my hand. It was sad that the situation with Don had so deteriorated, but even with this, our board was very fair and equitable in Don's termination. They paid tribute to his contribution to the development of the program. I knew I could count on the board to do what was right, in this and in all circumstances.

Over time we had so many people volunteering to be on the board, James "Jim" McDonald, president of General Motors, offered to help select applicants. He told the board his criteria was not whether they had a recognized name or lots of money but whether they had our mission in their hearts. Wherever we went with board meetings in the United States, México, Europe, and Japan, board members reached out to involve their contemporaries. It was a fun group to be around, and they seemed to be completely enjoying themselves whenever we met.

Amazing as it seems this diverse group seemed to balance each other. Great Olympian Jesse Owens, competing and joking with astronaut Captain Gene Cernan, both who had a way of keeping each other grounded and sticking to the point. From Asia there was Naoko Mitsui Shirane, a member of the renowned Mitsui family of Japan. And Dr. Shoichiro Toyoda, Chairman of the Board of the Toyota Motor Company, opposite Jim McDonald, seen walking around together in the parking lot in Tucson comparing the brand names on cars and keeping score, Toyota versus General Motors. Next, Pieter van Vollenhoven, husband of Her Royal Highness Princess Margriet of the Netherlands, would always say, "The bloody foreigner has something to say." Waiting for his turn was his neighbor from Belgium John Goossens, president and CEO of Alcatel Bell. Then, Larry F. Lunt of Connecticut who was the grandson of Jean Wittouck, chairman of our first European board. Larry, a philanthropist and environmentalist, is head of Armonia LLC. From México was Manuel Arango, entrepreneur, philanthropist, and environmentalist, who sat across from Jim Boswell, head of J. G. Boswell, one of the nation's largest farming empires. Representing the Midwest was Wesley Dixon, president of G. D. Searle and Company of Chicago. Wes's special interest was in maintaining and raising the quality of Up with People's show production. Jerry Jarrett was the CEO and Chairman of AmeriTrust Company in Cleveland. Martha and Jerry Jarrett were always on the lookout for inner-city students who should have the experience of Up with People. The Texas group always came on strongly. There was Thomas "Tom" Cruikshank, former chairman and CEO of Halliburton from Dallas, sitting next to Dan Cook, former senior partner of Goldman Sachs. Robert "Bob" Marbut from San Antonio was intrigued in March 1987 by two alumni, John Parker and Forrest "Duffy" Bledsoe who made a proposal to the Board that was exciting and far-reaching. Their proposal was to found an international alumni association. They described the purposes: "to support and strengthen the goals of Up with People, present and future; to establish mutually beneficial communication between Up with People and its alumni; to build and strengthen and network among the alumni of Up with People; and to provide a framework through which alumni can participate in the purposes and activities of Up with People."

An Ad Hoc Committee of 130 interested alumni was formed and made a presentation at the next Board of Directors meeting. At that meeting Bob Marbut was asked by the Board to meet with the Ad Hoc Committee leaders to work out the final details. The charter signing ceremony in June 1988 resulted in an enthusiastic thumbs up by all! The Up with People International Alumni Association has been monumental in supporting the mission of Up with People—so many students who applied to the program, so many alumni sponsorships in their cities and towns, so many host families offered and many heartfelt contributions made. Dick Freeman of Houston, chairman of Tenneco Company, who served with Nella Barkley from Charleston, South Carolina. Carrie Rozelle of New York served on the board. Dr. Henry Koffler, president of the University of Arizona, said, "I have traveled the world with this program, and I have observed firsthand the global educational experience and their efforts to build bridges of understanding in this troubled and divided world."

Some may ask why I wanted such a board of directors. I think what Tom Cruikshank said to me is important: "People, foundations, and large corporations will study your board of directors when they make decisions about investing in your program." That is definitely one reason for a 501(c)(3) nonprofit corporation. Another strong reason is the parents of the over 22,000 alumni from 138 countries who help fund their children to travel and have this experience. I knew they would feel more secure about the program when they studied the board of directors.

For me personally, when someone new agreed to serve on our board, it was just the beginning. My passion was to see that they had a maximum experience. It would perhaps not only educate them about the program but give them new international friendships. So, for example, one time we came up with the idea of having a board meeting in Europe that would take us from Stuttgart to Bonn and Düsseldorf in Germany and to Amsterdam in the Netherlands from May 11–13, 1992. We would end in our European headquarters in Brussels, Belgium. When the leaders in these countries were shown the international list of board members, every door seemed to open. It was a wonderful time for all of our board members and especially our newest member, Dr. Toyoda, and the Japan delegation.

Germany had been a key country in the development of Up with People since 1966, when Sing-Out/Up with People toured the country as the guests of the German government. So here we were in May 1992 with an international group of 60 consisting of board members, guests, and staff. It was an important time to be there, less than two years after the reunification of East and West Germany. Our host in Stuttgart was Dr. Hans L. Merkle, chairman of Robert Bosch GMBH. He and Jim McDonald of General Motors were longtime friends and associates. Dr. Merkle had also played a significant role in establishing Dr. Konrad Adenauer as the first chancellor of West Germany. At a black-tie dinner for the board, he introduced dignitaries from Stuttgart and asked Mayor Manfred Rommel to say a short word. The mayor turned out to be the son of the famous World War II "Desert Fox," Field Marshal Erwin Rommel.

Early the next morning we departed by private bus to Bonn, which then was the capital of West Germany. That evening our hosts, Chancellor and Mrs. Helmut Kohl, welcomed us at a dinner party in their residence. It was a memorable event, and the chancellor's wife, Hannelore, personally seated all the tables. Betty and I were honored to be seated with Chancellor Kohl at his table where he had two interpreters to interpret from German to Japanese for Dr. Toyoda and another to interpret German into English for others. Chancellor Kohl was an imposing figure at six foot four and a gregarious personality. After he welcomed us and sat down, he addressed Dr. Toyoda saying, "I'm sure you know that I have the best wine cellar possibly in Bonn but I've had a very rough day with my cabinet and I'm going to have a German beer." Dr. Toyoda, in true Japanese fashion, said, "I will have a beer, also!" He also enjoyed joking with Jim McDonald and Dr. Toyoda about which of them produced the best cars. At the end of this back and forth, he very quietly said, "I think our German Mercedes and BMWs will give any of you a run for your money."

Toward the end of the meal he got quite serious and told us of his private meeting with the Soviet Union's General Secretary, Mikhail Gorbachev. Chancellor Kohl then described how he and Mikhail Gorbachev had had a long private dinner right where we were sitting. Prime Minister Margaret Thatcher had alerted him that Gorbachev was a Russian that he could trust. After dinner they had gone out and sat on a bench on the lawn facing the Rhine River. He said, "We talked long and deeply about the situation in the world and about our own families, and we learned that each of us had relatives injured or killed during the Second World War." Gorbachev's father was injured at the Battle of Kursk, and Kohl lost an elder brother in Westphalia. The chancellor went on to say, "Something happened between us, and a bonding took place." Later, when the Soviet troops surrounding Berlin went on alert, it looked as if they might attempt to occupy and claim the city. Chancellor Kohl had a long talk on the phone with General Secretary Gorbachev discussing this problem. At the end of the conversation, Gorbachev asked Kohl for help. He said, "We're facing a freezing bitter cold winter and thousands of my people have no shoes, can you help?" The Chancellor took this to heart and went to work with shoe manufacturers all over Germany, and they sent thousands pair of shoes in all sizes to Moscow for distribution.[2] The Soviet troops never made their move on Berlin thanks to the friendship and trust that had been built between the two leaders.

We were all pondering this story when Dr. Toyoda said to the chancellor, "I admire your diplomacy. Perhaps you could give me some good advice. As you probably know the Chinese are slowly claiming our islands in the East China Sea. What would you advise me?" Kohl thought for a moment and then said, "My advice for what it's worth is that I would build automobile factories quickly in the People's Republic of China if I was in your position."

At that point I had the opportunity to thank Chancellor and Mrs. Kohl for their hospitality, and they responded, saying, "The thanks goes to Up with People for bringing such a prestigious group of people to our country." Chancellor Kohl urged us to do all we could to help with the reunification of East and West Germany, commenting, "It has now taken place officially, but there is still much fear and mistrust that needs to be overcome. Hopefully, your young people can help with this." I assured him we had taken it to heart. In 1989, when the Berlin Wall fell, our Up with People students were there singing and celebrating with people from the East and the West. At that time, the cast had reported to me, "Our return to Germany was an emotional one. Just two weeks earlier we had visited the barren border that divided the people of the East and the West, and now the people were able to walk freely amongst each other. For our cast, this was one of those moments when humanity brought tears of joy because people forgot about their stripes and hammers, suns, crescents and stars, and stood shoulder to shoulder in friendship."[3] At around the same time, a small part of the cast went to Berlin to witness the wall coming down. They chiseled off a piece of the Berlin Wall, part of which they gave to me for the Up with People Archive.

In Bonn the next night, 2,000 people filled the famous Beethovenhalle on the Rhine River. The occasion was a benefit show for Hannelore Kohl's charity to help students who had suffered brain damage from car accidents. All of us attended with many German government officials. On stage, Mrs. Kohl welcomed everyone and said, "We have a very distinguished guest with us, Captain Gene Cernan, the last man on the Moon, and I'm going to ask him to come up and introduce the evening." When Gene arrived on the stage there was loud applause and to everyone's surprise, Mrs. Kohl said, "I've always wanted to kiss a Moon man, and I think I will right now." She turned and gave Gene a kiss on the lips and a hug. Gene turned quite red in the face, and there was even louder applause. The evening was a success, and everyone was invited for ice cream, which had been provided for the evening. Gene and I were invited to scoop ice cream along with Chancellor Kohl and US Ambassador Robert Kimmitt. It was people diplomacy at its best, and everyone was filled with praise for the performance and the ice cream.

The next morning after a bus trip to Düsseldorf our board gathered in the boardroom of the corporate headquarters of Henkel KG and Company for a special meeting. A luncheon was hosted by the chairman of Henkel. On that occasion we had a chance to thank Hans Magnus, the president of Up with People Europe, and Thomas Reinecke, head of our operations in Germany and son of the late Ernst Reinecke. Their planning and execution of our visit in Germany had been perfect. Following the meeting and luncheon, we went by bus to the Bonn residence of Ambassador Kimmitt for a reception. The next morning we left by bus for a three-hour ride to Amsterdam.

When we arrived in Amsterdam everything was arranged, and once we had checked into the Amsterdam Hilton, we boarded a boat for a tour of the city and lunch aboard. In the early evening, we walked from the hotel to the ABN AMRO Bank. Dinner was in the boardroom, hosted by its chairman, Jaap Rost-Onnes. His guests of honor were Her Royal Highness Princess Margriet and Pieter van Vollenhoven.

We traveled to Brussels for our final days and again experienced superb European hospitality. After completing our board meeting, we were entertained for dinner by Beatrice Lunt, which was always a treat, and John Goossens. At the dinner party at John's home, he thanked the board for what he felt they had done by building stronger links among Japan, the United States, and Europe. John thanked the board for their volunteer service to Up with People. It had been an historic three days with the minds of Europe and Asia thinking and planning together for the future of our young people in Up with People. We had achieved my goal for the Board that they make international friendships. The board members whose schedules prevented them from making this particular trip but who made a great contribution to the program were: Sue Anschutz-Rodgers, chairman and president of the Anschutz Family Foundation; Sharon Magness Blake, the president of the Thunder Foundation; Peter Coors, the Coors Ambassador; John Fuller, owner and founder of Fuller Western Real Estate; and A. Barry Hirschfeld, former president of A. B. Hirschfeld Press.

All of the board members were a band of friends on a common mission and had an impact on everyone especially us. A huge thank you from Betty and me.

26

México and Up with People

"El Puente"
Grandes y pequenos, con todos sus sueños
Atravesando un puente

México was important to us personally, but it also played a significant part in our lives with Up with People. Not only could we entertain board members at our place in San Carlos; we also found great support in México for our work. Without a doubt Up with People/Viva la Gente had become a household word in México through our tours of the cast, home stays in 20,000 families, and with TV coverage.

One September in the early 1970s, we were 12 to 15 miles offshore from San Carlos Marina in the Sea of Cortez trolling for billfish, dorado, and tuna. We had come out to get the early morning bite, and we already had several nice dorado in the ice chest. The Humboldt Current with its deep blue waters was still with us. We had been scanning the surface with binoculars hoping that we could locate feeding tuna. Suddenly my boat radio started crackling. I heard a voice saying, "La Palomita, La Palomita, San Carlos Marina calling, come back." So I did just that saying, "La Palomita here, Mr. Belk speaking." Quite a nervous young man's voice replied, "Mr. Belk, the former president of México Miguel Alemán Valdés is here in the office looking for you and wants to speak to you."

There was a slight pause, and then a strong voice came through saying, "Blanton Belk is that you? Miguel Alemán Valdés here, over." Quickly we were speaking to one another as if we were in the same room. He said that he had come to Guaymas on business and he remembered that we had a house and kept a boat in San Carlos nearby. He had been driven out to the marina hoping to see us. I offered to come in immediately so we could talk, but he said his schedule was just too tight. He had a government airplane waiting to fly him back to México City from the Guaymas airport. I told him how honored I felt that he had taken the time to be in touch and thanked him once again for all the wonderful support he had given introducing Viva la Gente to his country. Viva la Gente is Up with People's brand in Spanish. He said he had a most successful visit in Guaymas and San Carlos, and he was especially impressed with the San Carlos Marina. He assured me the next time he came he would give me fair warning and accept my invitation for a day of fishing. We made plans to meet soon in México City.

I first met Miguel Alemán Valdés at the end of the 1960s. He had seen one of our earliest performances and wanted to be involved. He had a giant personality. Even after leaving the presidency of México after six years, he wanted to continue working for his country. The government created a position for him as president of the National Tourism Council. They couldn't have chosen a better man. Furthermore, it was as if he was sent at the right time to help establish Up with People in México. Ever since his first meeting with the cast, he was determined that this program would grow and flourish in México. He insisted that every time a cast came to his country he would have the privilege of welcoming and briefing them. He said to me after one such meeting, that every time he met Up with People he felt a greening in his spirit.

On October 25, 1969, the headline in México City's largest paper, *Excelsior*, was "Brilliant Reception for 120 Young People from 22 Countries."[1] This appeared after the cast arrived to start a six-week tour under the auspices of the National Tourism Council. Each student was presented with a sombrero, a gift from our sponsors. The press and TV cameras met the plane, and the cast did a short presentation right on the tarmac.

The audience of 4,500 that came to the premiere performance in the Olympic Arena sang with the cast for two encores after the show. As the cast left the stage, a mariachi band came on stage singing and dancing. The entire audience stayed to join in the celebration. Up with People was called back on stage, and the audience and the mariachis again sang our theme song, "Viva la Gente." Miguel Alemán Valdés spoke to the cast at the end of the performance and said, "What you are singing and doing in so many countries, and now in ours, is a message that is not only important for the youth of México, but is of vital value for the people and the future of the world.... It is the only way they can react to such a supreme demonstration of the highest goals of humanity."[2]

Naturally, living by the sea in México, the next thing I wanted was a new boat to take advantage of the fishing. Research brought me to boatbuilders Jule Marshall and Myrna Elliott, who had a company called Californian Yachts in San Diego. They had a 29-foot fishing yacht that caught my attention. With the help of Betty's mother we bought one, called it *La Paloma*, and trailered it to Tucson and eventually to San Carlos. We became friends, and Myrna later introduced me to her brother, who was on the staff of the Mexican First Lady Señora Carmen de López Portillo.

In early December 1976, shortly after the inauguration of President José Lopéz Portillo, his wife, Señora Portillo, invited me to come to México and meet with her and her staff. I was met at the airport in México City by a dynamic young businessman and close associate of Señora Portillo. His name was Andres Holzer, and he was to become a good friend of mine. He took me at breakneck speed in his sporty car through the streets of México City to our lunch with the first lady. Her other guests were Miguel Alemán Velasco, son of the former president of México, and Alejandro Quintero Iñiguez from Televisa. At that lunch we made plans for the visit of Up with People/Viva la Gente to give a benefit performance for Fonapas at the beautiful Teatro de la Ciudad de México on February 11, 1977.

About this same time, I was given an introduction to Manuel Arango. It was a most fortuitous occasion. In May 1976, I was invited to speak to the board of directors of Jewel Companies, a supermarket chain in Illinois. Wes Christopherson was Chairman and CEO. When we were saying our goodbyes, Wes took me aside to thank me for coming but then he added, "I heard you mention that you're planning to go to México. One of our board members is from México but unfortunately couldn't be here this evening. I'll write you a letter of introduction. Please look him up. He'll be turned on by what you're doing!" This of course was Manuel Arango. Personal connections and friendships have been one of the best things that happened to me personally and for Up with People.

Remembering Wes's suggestion that I meet Manuel Arango, I made an appointment to see him a day after my December meeting with the first lady. I met him in his office and told him of the upcoming visit of Up with People/Viva la Gente. He immediately offered to entertain the board of directors and some of his friends from México City for an informal luncheon at his country home, Xochitl, on February 12. Manuel and I hit it off immediately. We quickly formed a friendship. I was struck from the beginning with this man's dynamism, vision, and alertness to all that was happening around him.

A few days earlier, Betty and I had flown down with Captain Gene Cernan to be a part of a three-week tour of México City sponsored by Televisa, which included an appearance with the cast and myself. It was a popular nightly show called *24 Horas*, hosted by Jacobo Zabludovsky. They told us that it would reach over 22 million households and was carried by Spanish-speaking stations throughout North and South America. It included a performance by the cast and a personal interview with me. Manuel Arango responded to my invitation to attend the performance at Teatro de la Ciudad de México. What an outstanding beginning for their three-week tour! The following day, the Arangos delighted us with a beautiful paella luncheon. It was an informal enough occasion where the Up with People Board of Directors who had just flown in could meet the Arangos and their friends and get a taste of Mexican hospitality.

Less than a month later, Manuel Arango and his brothers arranged for the cast to do a series of performances for the employees of their company, Bodega Aurrera. When I heard of this initiative, I thought, "Here's a man who would be a wonderful addition to our board of directors." When I first asked him he turned me down, but I approached him again several years later and he agreed. At the December 1983 board meeting, there was unanimous approval for his selection to the board. Betty and I were delighted when Manuel and his wife, Marie-Therese, were able to join us in Rome in April 1984.

Our host in Rome was the publisher of *Il Tempo*, Gianni Letta. When he learned that Gene Cernan, was coming as part of our board of directors, he went into overdrive. He laid on wonderful events for our board members and students. Fortunately, some years previously, I had become friends with Roberto Wirth, the owner of Hotel Hassler at the top of the Spanish Steps. Roberto is a great Roman personality. He's deaf and is an active advocate for the deaf community both in Italy and the United States. He has a strong friendship with the United States since he studied at Gallaudet University and Cornell University. He also introduced me to one of the great drinks of Italy, *sambuca*.

By the time Manuel and Marie-Therese arrived in Rome for a Papal Audience with John Paul II, we had quite a delegation. There was the cast of 140 from some 20 countries and 18 board members, spouses, and friends from North America and Europe. Our PR person was Rebecca Garcia from Guadalajara, México. She was a charming young woman fluent in Italian. The cast did a wonderful job performing. When the Mass was over, a cardinal escorted Pope John Paul II down the line of cast members. He greeted many of them in their own language. When he got to the young man who was dressed in Polish national dress, the pope embraced him and thanked him in Polish. The cast members around him have sworn that he spoke back to the pope in Polish, but he actually was an English-speaking Arizonan! Then Pope John Paul II came to greet our board, spouses, and friends. Manuel and Marie-Therese Arango stood next to Gene Cernan in line and were moved by the exchange between the pope and Gene when he asked Gene what he had seen in space.

That evening, *Il Tempo* hosted a celebration dinner with board members, friends, and cast. Gianni was at his best introducing everyone. The next morning the mayor of Rome had arranged for schoolchildren to be bussed to a large amphitheater in the middle of Rome to experience Up with People. The cast and the young audience became one, with everyone singing and dancing in the aisles. Some even climbed onto the stage! *Il Tempo* gave it great coverage, and it was an event we will long remember.

In 1988, I invited Manuel to join me on April 23 at a special performance of the cast in the bullring at Monumental Plaza de Toros México. He accepted and brought his two young daughters, Manuela and Paula. The next day he sent me a handwritten note complimenting us and saying the young crowd, including his daughters, had called for encores.

For Up with People's 50th Anniversary, the celebration for Latin America was in México City in April 2016. Manuel and Marie-Therese gave a beautiful dinner party at Hacienda de los Morales. Our friend Eduard Malayan, the Russian ambassador to México, gave a reception. Eduard, jokingly said to me, "You wanted to celebrate in Russia and your wish has been granted. This reception will be at the Russian Embassy which is designated Russia." The cast, as well as friends from México and abroad, came to honor the occasion.

What a hospitable country México has been to us personally and to Up with People/Viva la Gente. Casts have toured México 82 times since 1966. The first show in México was in the Palacio de Bellas Artes in México City where youth full of enthusiasm applauded each song in the program. Sing-Out '66 videotaped a half-hour TV special to be shown on Christmas night. They departed México City for Laredo, Texas, and, then on to Santa Fe, New Mexico for Christmas. Since 1966, there have been more than 650 Mexican students in Up with People. Our international students find the exceptional hospitality of the families who host them to be most moving. To date, thousands of Mexican families have opened their homes to host Up with People students.

Betty and I often talk about how lucky we are to have a neighbor like México. We have many, many lifelong friends there.

27

People's Republic of China

"Wǒ Men De Yǒu Yi Shēn Yòu Cháng"
May our friendship be as deep and long
As the Yangtze River

In 1965, in speaking to the first cast of Sing-Out/Up with People and to every cast after that for the next 23 years, I would ask the question, "Would you like to go to China and the Soviet Union?" There would be a thunderous response, and I would say, "Come with us. We'll find a way to link your generation with the youth of the world and we'll find a way to go to China and the Soviet Union."

How in the world did we ever get to these countries? As far as China was concerned, Señora Amalia S. de Cárdenas, the widow of a former president of México, maintained a great friendship with China. Señora Cárdenas had seen the show in February 1977 as a guest of First Lady Carmen López Portillo. She was very enthusiastic about it and arranged an appointment for José Rios, our Vice President for Latin America to meet the first secretary at the embassy of the People's Republic of China in México. José agreed and accepted the appointment. It was clear that Señora Cárdenas had made a very good introduction for Up with People.

The negotiations went on for several months with many meetings, both at the embassy and with Señora Cárdenas, José Rios and I went to México and met Senora Cárdenas at her home on January 27, 1978. Even though we met her at tea time, we had little time to drink tea listening to her enthusiasm about the show and her eagerness to have us go to the People's Republic of China (PRC). She proceeded to tell us of her long friendship with the people of China. José was often on the phone to me. He underlined that his Chinese hosts were grilling him on the background of all of our board members and staff. After many weeks of this intense work, I had a telephone call from the counselor of the PRC Embassy in México City. In perfect English he said that everything José had told them had been proven to be absolutely true. He continued, "When we checked the organization out, we found that you do not belong to the US State Department, CIA, FBI, or big industry. You will be receiving an official invitation for Up with People to come to the PRC. And we would like you to arrive in Peking on May Day." José was the man to handle these delicate negotiations. Three cheers for José Rios!

While these negotiations were going on I flew to Burbank, California, to visit Jim Boswell and brief him what was developing on the PRC. I didn't even telephone. When I walked in he gave his usual cordial greeting. Mr. Boswell, the CEO of J. G. Boswell Company, was on our board. "What the hell brought you unannounced to Los Angeles?" When I told him about the invitation he was quite excited and said immediately, "Ros and I will go with you and I'll fund this trip. Give me the exact dates because I'll be at a board meeting of General Electric in London and we will fly over the Pole and join up with you in Tokyo."

Another challenge from the Chinese was a request that we have a large group of Mexican students in the total group of 35. At that point, we had five casts operating in the world. We tried to be as fair as possible, picking one or more representatives from each cast including nine from México.

The whole staff gathered to get the news firsthand from José, Chief Operating Officer Jack Hipps, and Vice President of Scheduling and Promotion Steve Woods, all who had been involved in meetings with the Chinese. There were big challenges ahead: translating the songs into Mandarin, booking the transportation, and paring down the equipment to be transported. In Paul Colwell's words, *When we received the official invitation to visit the PRC, Herb and I met with a Chinese student at the University of Arizona. We composed a song in Mandarin with the theme of friendship—"May our friendship be as deep and long as the Yangtze River." Much to our relief it worked and throughout the tour it proved to be the icebreaker with audiences, most of whom were seeing an international performing group for the first time.* The Department of East Asia Studies at the University of Arizona was a big help in preparing our students. Everybody bought in, and there was a flurry of activity.

When I informed Punch Sulzberger, publisher of *The New York Times* and a member of our International Advisory Board, he immediately said, "I have a very good friend who is the president of the *Asahi Shimbun* [a Japanese newspaper]. Since you're stopping in Tokyo, I'll send him a letter of introduction." Then he added, "There is one other person with whom you should be in touch. Art Cooper is the publisher of the *Family Weekly* that is inserted Sundays in most of the major newspapers." He gave me the publisher's phone number saying, "I'll alert him."

In late April 1978, Betty and I flew early to Tokyo, but before leaving I spoke to the publisher of *Family Weekly*. When Art Cooper heard about our invitation to the PRC, he said immediately, "Get a good picture and short story and get it to me and I'll see what we can do." When I got to Tokyo I telephoned Mr. Seiki Watanabe, the president of the *Asahi Shimbun*. His secretary said, "Oh yes, the president has received a letter from Mr. Sulzberger and he wonders whether Mr. Belk could come by." We had a cordial visit, and when we said that we would like to offer a small private invitational show for their own benefit, they were very interested. We decided to do it in their own auditorium upon our return from China. They would invite their people from TV Asahi. Then we went up to see the auditorium with the cultural project people. We made arrangements for an hour-long show at 6:30 p.m. on May 27. They said that half the audience would be their people, and they would do an article to promote the show.

Our first view of the PRC was somewhere near Shanghai—that was the pattern you had to fly at the time. It took four and a half hours to fly to Peking from Tokyo. We looked out of the window and could see the mainland looking very much like the patchwork farmland of Arizona. Jim Boswell, our agribusiness friend, could spot the irrigation from the air and even flooded fields.

On May 3, we landed at Peking Airport. It struck us immediately that everything was very quiet as compared to other major airports. We got out of the plane and walked about 400 yards in bright sunlight to the terminal. The facade was totally dominated by huge portraits of Mao Zedong flanked by Deng Xiaoping and Hua Guofeng, with Mao's picture claiming the center of the building. As we walked along, two young Americans in our delegation, Reed Thompson and Michael Knowles, took me aside and said, "Mr. Belk, we owe you an apology. Every time you made the comment, 'Stick with us we will take you to the PRC,' the two of us would lead the snickering and say that would never happen. But here we are and thank you for getting us here."

We were met by four members of the Chinese People's Association for Friendship with Foreign Countries. Everyone turned in their passports. Since the baggage was coming out slowly we were invited into the lounge of the airport. We all sat on benches while Mr. Chang, the leader of the delegation, sat across from a few of us and welcomed us very informally.

After the technicalities were over, we were taken by bus to the Peking Hotel. We were located on the 11th floor. We looked down on Tiananmen Square. On either side of the square were four large movable portraits of Karl Marx, Friedrich Engels, Vladimir Lenin, and Joseph Stalin. Mao's portrait was on top of all the large buildings around Tiananmen Square.

The streets were active at 5:30 in the morning. You could see people sweeping the streets and sweeping the sand under the trees along the streets—all dirt being cleaned up. Bicycles were starting to move along the broad avenues but few buses. I could see three coming down the long boulevard. It was very smoggy. Now the joggers had appeared up and down the streets. Coming on the left was a whole platoon of Chinese soldiers jogging. The avenues leading to Tiananmen Square were so big that the bicycles looked like ants crawling along down below and in the distance. I saw cast members Jean Pol Warkin and Michael Knowles walking out of the hotel going down toward the square together. Our hosts allowed us to go out as long as we were two together. I came in after jogging with Paul Colwell in the square and it was a sight to see everybody exercising from the old people to the young. People were playing badminton on the boulevards. They stretched lines between trees and set up badminton games. I saw one old woman, gray haired with a crutch, doing exercises, her body gyrating. It was very quiet. There was very little talking. Paul went ahead and I came back later, feeling perfectly at home by myself. Once when Paul and I were jogging along a street, a bus driver honked as he made a right turn in front of us and waved at us with a big smile. This country boggled our minds. I had so many different feelings and emotions, thoughts, and impressions. On the first day our guide had taken us to the Great Wall and afterward to the Tombs of the Ming Dynasty.

With no notice we were told we were to put on the whole show in the Central Conservatory of Music. Originally we heard we would only have 35 minutes to perform. We sat around and sweated it out, worked all night and morning to redefine our show and cut it down to the allotted time. That morning they announced that they wanted us to do the show just as we had sent it to them in the original rundown. They told us all the song lyrics had been mimeographed and circulated and studied, so we had to do it just as we had sent to them. So, then we were back to the original version of the show. The organizers wanted an introduction in Mandarin to every song, explaining what the song meant, even the world medley. So the show would have a different pace that would be more acceptable to them. We came to realize how important this was to the Chinese. For the first time since 1949 music and songs from the Western Hemisphere were being sung by an international group of students. It was going to be heard and studied. They took it very seriously.

The Up with People show at the Central Conservatory of Music was an experience. We were treated to a most impressive display of talent and virtuosity, both vocal and instrumental, Western classical as well as Chinese traditional and modern music. The student performers were selected from high schools and colleges all over the country. The youngest were two girls, 13 and 14, who played piano and violin with astonishing brilliance. There were tenors, sopranos, and a basso profundo who gave a stirring rendition of "Ol' Man River" in English. There were songs and compositions with revolutionary and patriotic themes by contemporary Chinese composers. During all of this I quietly motioned to Betty to look at our students who were slowing sinking down into their chairs. I said under my breath, "I wonder if our presentation is really going to fly."

Our students sat there entranced and, with the realization that they were next, somewhat intimidated. The difference was that very few in our group had studied music formally. They were students of many fields who used music as a means of communication.

At this prestigious institution the audience was about to witness a style of performing they had never seen before. It was certainly less formal and freer in expression than what they were accustomed to. So we just didn't know how it would go over. After a slow start to the show, the first real response was to Stephanie Cruz singing "El Puente" (The Bridge). They liked her and the Conservatory director turned to José Rios and said, "Now, what music courses is she studying?" This showed that they hadn't yet understood and could not quite comprehend what we were doing.

At this point the show began to move and connected with the audience; the whole world medley was very well received. Each song was introduced by our interpreter, Mr. Chin. When the cast did the conga line, the audience all started clapping along. The cast didn't try to pick up anybody out of the audience—they weren't sure how that would go over—so the cast just danced through the audience, who loved it. There was great clapping and applauding. Perhaps the high point of our show was the unveiling of a brand-new song written especially for the tour and, of course translated into Mandarin. It was called "Friendship Deep and Long." The theme was one of friendship between peoples, and the refrain referenced the Yangtze River. Even though our soloists Stephanie Cruz and Sandy Forsman as well as the cast had worked hard to perfect their pronunciation, Mandarin is an elusive and subtle language. To make sure it was understood we wrote the lyrics in Mandarin on poster boards that were displayed on the side of the stage. They applauded after nearly every line, and by the second time around were singing the refrain with us.

This was at the first of several joint performances. These occasions were remarkable cultural exchanges. As far as our part went, it was not really a performance. It was 24 young people of different races and backgrounds from nine countries. They communicated a feeling that probably music can best convey—saying that we are on this Earth together. Our futures are intertwined. We want to learn how to live together with people everywhere. It is that intangible element that supersedes politics and power. It is between people.

Some days later at a banquet, Professor Wu Tsu-Chiang, vice director of the conservatory and a noted composer, presented an out-of-print book of folk songs to Paul Colwell, writer of "Friendship Deep and Long" as a symbol of their gratitude. Also at the banquet was the Mexican Ambassador to the PRC, Omar Martinez, who said to me, "It is an amazing feat that Up with People was invited to perform at the Central Conservatory of Music in Peking. ...My congratulations."[1]

For the whole trip, the organizers were very professional in moving our party around. They had box lunches and orange soda and beer on the bus. Every person had a job, everybody had an aim. As tourists it was necessary to listen to their propaganda, but at the same time it was important to know why you were there and what you wanted to achieve.

At every point our guides tried to educate us about the virtues of communism, and it was clear they had a completely different set of principles and values. It is definitely a country that makes you think in a very new way what you are living for and what you believe in and what you want out of life. In 1978, it challenged us on everything.

Everything about our tour was prearranged. When we arrived at the hotel, we were just handed a little card; there was not even a name on it, just a room number. There was no registration, no signing of anything. You were given a room equipped with everything you needed including a large thermos of boiling water and tea so you could make your own. On the way out, you hung your key on a little board at the end of the hall. There was a man at a desk who was in charge of the floor, handled the laundry, and protected the rooms. That was it.

One day we went to a handicrafts exhibition that displayed arts and crafts from all over the PRC. This was the first year that it had been allowed since 1966, when the "Gang of Four" closed down all creativity. The artwork we saw was absolutely exquisite. There were jade carvings, porcelain, woodwork, paintings, tapestries, baskets, and lacquer work. Betty was thrilled to see everything and that art was again flourishing in the PRC.

The current leadership of the PRC had urged its people to keep an open mind about new forms of art and music and take whatever was profitable to bring forth new cultural expressions, Chinese or international. Our presence was an example of that philosophy.

Two of the guests on this trip were Herbert Hutner, an investment banker, and his wife, Julie, from Holmby Hills, California. Herb was the father-in-law of Steve Colwell. After the first few days, Herb said to me, "I just can't tell you what it means to be here. Nobody can describe this to you. You have to come and experience the feelings of this country. You have to be here in person to realize what is represented in the PRC. I can't help but feel that what you are doing in Up with People is going to be more important. I think this trip of young people is a foot in the door. It is going to do more in the long range for the relationship between America and the PRC than all the money, all the diplomatic relationships that have ever taken place. Someday they are going to ask you to take the first few young Chinese into Up with People, and when you've done that, you'll have conquered the world."

I talked to Jim Boswell and he said, "I just want to congratulate you, the work that you have done already. The way the young people have handled themselves is just amazing and the effect it is having. You have got to give high marks to these kids. You haven't had time to explain a lot to them, but they are sensitive, they are feeling their way along, they are absolutely open with everybody, and they are being pummeled with questions about Up with People from our guides and they have just done extremely well."

At the big Trade Crafts Fair, the cast started handing out yellow buttons that said "Up with People" in Mandarin, and they literally caused a near crush when the Chinese started giving them their Communist Party pins.

On the last morning we went to the Central Institute for National

Minorities, the top university for ethnic minorities in the PRC. There are 55 minorities whose people represent almost 9 percent of the total population of the PRC, but the land area they have covers 60 percent of the total land area of the country. The students received us marvelously; they danced and sang for us, and we danced and sang for them. We did it for the first time in national costumes—everyone who had a national costume wore one—and it was a tremendous hit. When I left, the head of the Institute said to me, "I hope your organization, Up with People, becomes very big in the world."

It was an interesting and informative trip through six cities in China. We saw some of the fine art of China and, also, the handicrafts. Our hosts gave us tour of farmlands and a tea commune. At a silk factory, they took us to see the silk worms feeding on mulberry leaves and fertilizing the fish in the pond. Also, we were impressed with how the Chinese people cared for their parks that were always manicured. In Hangchow, we were given a boat ride on West Lake. It is a beautiful resort town. We flew to Kweilin by plane, landing for lunch at the birthplace of Mao Tse-tung. It gave time for the rainstorms in Kweilin to abate so we could enjoy that beautiful city with its famous caves. Then we left Kweilin for Canton. During the time in Canton we visited the Canton Trade Fair. To end this memorable trip to the PRC, our Chinese hosts offered a beautiful final banquet. It was complete with a parade of waiters carrying domed silver platters. The fare for that night was suckling pig. The whole dinner was a true feast and a fitting farewell, and the toasts went on and on until late. Several hours after the banquet in Canton Betty and I had just gone to bed with the mosquito netting draped around us. There was a knock on the door. A waiter stood there with one of the domed silver platters. When I took off the cover, there were tails of two pigs with a message: A late night snack, Jim Boswell.

After this memorable trip we put together a report and I would like to quote a passage, "The most impressive aspect of the visit, as far as our Chinese hosts were concerned, was the lifestyle, spirit and discipline of the Up with People students. The Chinese commented on their enthusiasm and eagerness to learn…their [friendliness] with everybody regardless of who they were. The Chinese have a very high moral lifestyle and were impressed with the way our young people worked and lived together, and especially by the fact that students from nine nations got along so well."[2]

The train pulled out from Canton to Hong Kong on May 23. We were met by representatives of Jardine, Matheson & Co., the foremost trading company, which acted as agents for firms all over the world. The head or *tai-pan* of Jardine, Matheson at that time was David Newbigging, a close friend of Jim Boswell and his agent in the PRC. The shock of arriving in Hong Kong was enormous. The contrast between the PRC and Hong Kong was startling. After a spartan three weeks in the PRC, we received luxurious treatment in Hong Kong. After a beautiful steak banquet, the cast a chance to debrief after not being able to comment frankly while in the PRC.

We flew to Tokyo for the final leg of our journey and for the promised show at *Asahi Shimbun*. On May 27, the cast performed in the auditorium of the newspaper before 600 employees as well as alumni and friends. The audience loved it so much that they wouldn't leave.

After a memorable three weeks—never to be forgotten—we left for home.

In December 1985, we returned to the PRC with a full cast after seven years away. The changes since 1978 were immense. Cars had replaced bicycles as the predominant vehicles on the streets, including lots of Japanese cars and quite a few Mercedes. The telephone in my hotel room now had a dialing system to the other rooms, as well as to the town and overseas, which had not been there before. In 1978, you had to go to a central telephone booth to handle calls. There was much change taking place.

Since we started again in Peking—now usually called Beijing—I went to the US Embassy and met with the chargé d'affaires, Dowell Johnson; Ambassador Winston Lord was out of the country. Joining him in the meeting was the man in charge of the Cultural and Economic Affairs Section for the US Embassy. They wanted to know all about our program. Mr. Johnson had been working on the China Desk in the State Department since 1960. He said, "I think it is a very proper time for you to be here, and I think the Chinese will have interest in young Chinese traveling with you. The problem will be financing them." He went on to say that there were probably 6,000 Chinese studying in American universities at that time. Mr. Johnson wanted to know how we recruited, where our 10,000 alumni had gone in life, and so on. He asked, "Have a lot of them gone into politics? Have any gone into industry? Education, etc.?" He asked about the criteria we were looking for in young people and how we auditioned them. He was sorry he couldn't get to the show, and it seemed to me there was a growing respect from the State Department for what we were doing. It made me consider whether there was some way we could adapt our program to what the Chinese wanted for their young students with regard to an experience in America and other countries.

Before we left Tucson a friend wanted me to meet his son, Frank Hawke, who was living in Beijing. I called Frank and he invited Betty and me to dinner with his fiancée, a charming Chinese girl named Sue. Her father was the deputy military commander for the Beijing area and the political commissar. We had a Mongolian hot meal, which was delicious, and a very interesting evening. Frank was most knowledgeable about China. He came from Stanford University as a graduate student to study Chinese and remained to teach economics. He felt, as did Sue, that our translation of our name "Up with People" was political and needed some fine-tuning.

On December 3, we again visited the Central Institute for National Minorities, the top university for ethnic minorities in the PRC. It was a tremendous experience. We were greeted at the school by the president and a long line of students. The building was like a bomb shelter basement, but it was highly decorated with tables of food. The students were all in ethnic costumes, and it was very colorful. They did the usual Chinese custom of performing for us exquisitely. Up with People responded with a 45-minute excerpt from our show *Beat of the Future*. It was the first performance in costume for our cast. The atmosphere was electric; we loved their dances, and they loved our expression of song and dance.

A few days later, in a fierce wind and snowstorm, we filmed the cast at the Great Wall, rehearsing for the Super Bowl XX halftime performance, which took place in the Superdome in New Orleans on January 26, 1986.

This sequence was included in the halftime program broadcast by NBC Worldwide.

A highlight for us was meeting again our friend Wang Chinchen, who as deputy director for the Chinese People's Association for Friendship with Foreign Countries, had hosted the first visit of Up with People to the PRC in 1978. Mr. Wang, now vice president of the association, told us how optimistic he was about the future of Up with People in bringing East and West together. He said, "Your visit in 1978 laid the groundwork of friendship which has brought you back to the PRC seven years later."[3]

In 1978, one man was a visionary and our sole sponsor. Seven years later our trip was sponsored by corporations, companies, and foundations: General Motors, General Electric, Halliburton, the H. J. Heinz Company Foundation, and Laurance S. Rockefeller and other individual contributors. In the PRC, the tour was made possible with the assistance and cooperation of the Ministry of Culture, All-China Youth Federation, China Association for the Advancement of International Friendship, the China Youth Travel Service, and the Panda Associates for Cultural Exchange (Canada).

We have been happy to welcome Chinese students to Up with People. The first Chinese student traveled in 1987. Since then, 60 Chinese students have traveled. Two of these students have written books in Chinese about their experiences that have served as recruiting tools for other Chinese students. The translated title of Siyi Zhu's book is *Unbelievable: A Chinese Girl's Study Abroad Around the World*. The English title of Lyra Yuchen Li's book is *Volunteer Work Around the World*.

28

Soviet Union and Eastern Europe

"Hearts Still Beating"
The heart's still beating, the fire's still burning
We may be feeling
That the wind is turning

From the very beginning of Up with People I felt that we should reach out to the young people in the Soviet Union. I had made a pledge to the first cast that we would do our utmost to connect with the students of that country. It was a daunting challenge but I had a passion to see it happen and my enthusiasm seemed to inspire others along the way. In 1985, Mikhail Gorbachev had initiated the Soviet policies of *glasnost* and *perestroika*. These new policies of openness made it possible for Up with People to visit the Soviet Union and Eastern Europe. Eight casts over the next four years had the opportunity and the excitement of fulfilling this mission.

Shortly after arriving in Los Angeles in 1965, I had the great fortune to meet Barron Hilton, CEO and Chairman of the Hilton Hotel Corporation and Chairman of the Conrad N. Hilton Foundation. Barron, as well as being a superb businessman, was a skilled entrepreneur and was inspired by the thought of Up with People building a link with the youth of the Soviet Union. "If this could happen, he said to me one day, it would augur well for these young people to lay a foundation for peace between the United States and the Soviet Union. We need to build some kind of friendships with young people for the future." He responded to that concept and helped to fund our first tour of the Soviet Union in 1988. Our long-awaited dream was finally realized.

Several other personalities played a key role in us fulfilling this dream. The first was a friend of Jim Boswell, Dr. Frederick "Fred" Starr. His Louisiana Repertory Jazz Ensemble of New Orleans was to be the entertainment at one of Boswell's Fourth of July parties in Ketchum, Idaho. The Boswell's had invited Betty and me to be part of the festivities, which gave us a chance to get to know Dr. Starr. He is an expert on Russian and Eurasian affairs and was, at that point, president of Oberlin College. Fred became enthused about our idea of Up with People building a link with the Russian youth. He accepted an invitation from Jim Boswell to come to an Up with People board meeting in Tucson, which gave him the opportunity to meet the staff and learn about the program. Later, he introduced us to key Russian personalities.

Another important link was Bob Magee, Senior Executive Vice President of Occidental International Corp. based in Washington, DC. I had been a friend of Bob and he telephoned me one day saying, "I've been thinking about our last conversation. You described your desire to take Up with People to the Soviet Union and I think I might be helpful." This led me to fly to Washington, DC, in late February 1985 for a delightful introductory luncheon with Eduard Malayan, the Counselor for Bilateral and Cultural Affairs at the Soviet Embassy. Eduard was quite enthusiastic about what we were doing with the young people and my desire to link up with Soviet youth. In May, I issued him an invitation to fly to Tucson that August for the upcoming summer staging with the new casts and asked him to speak about the Soviet Union. Phil Gregory from the US State Department called me with Mr. Malayan's arrival and departure dates. He also told me that Tucson was an open city in a closed area, which meant that Mr. Malayan could not leave the city limits. This was disappointing since we lived just outside the city limits and we had hoped to have him at our home and to show him more of Arizona. I also had a telephone call from the FBI agency in Tucson saying they had been made aware that Mr. Malayan was coming for a visit. They requested an appointment with me the afternoon of his arrival. When I met Agents Fred Coward and George Siao they were cordial but firm and said again that you cannot take Mr.

Malayan out of the city limits. Therefore, the dinner at your home must be canceled as well as the trip to view the Grand Canyon. Agent Coward also informed me confidentially that the FBI was very concerned about why he had accepted the invitation to come to Tucson.[1] They wondered whether he wanted to defect. They wanted us to report each evening about what we learned. We met him at the airport and took him right away to the Arizona Inn. He had to be up early to speak to the casts at 8:30 the following morning. Eduard was very well received by the students and there were lots of questions. Each night when we drove Eduard from different events back to the Arizona Inn a car followed us. On the final night, another car pulled out of a side alley and followed the car following us. Eduard, who observed everything happening around him turned to me and said, "Don't worry I know who that is." We never learned who that was, but Soviet security was also keeping an eye on his visit.

That final evening I joined him for drinks at the Arizona Inn bar. It wasn't very crowded but sitting at the bar were three very out-of-place personalities dressed for tennis with rackets leaning up against the bar. I immediately recognized the FBI agents who had paid me a visit. Eduard didn't say a word until he leaned over me and in a whisper said, "There they sit at the bar!" We were thoroughly enjoying ourselves reliving all we had experienced in the last three days. Eduard was especially happy that Betty and I had hosted him the night before at the Mountain Oyster Club. He said, "Mountain oysters are one of the delicacies in my province of Georgia but they come from sheep. I hadn't had any for a long time." At Eduard's request I handed him a sealed envelope with a letter to Mikhail Gorbachev asking for his assistance in facilitating Up with People's visit to the Soviet Union. Eduard reached under his chair and took out a beautifully wrapped bottle of Russian vodka. He insisted I have a look at it and on the inside of the bottle was painted the skyline of the city of Moscow—a treasure. I was hardly back home that evening when my phone rang. It was a call from FBI Agent Coward who wanted to know what the whole gift exchange was about. Also, I told them that at no time did Eduard mention defection. For the record, that was the last I heard from the FBI.

Highest tribute must be given to Hans Magnus who shared this dream with me that Up with People would eventually go to the Soviet Union. Hans reported back after the first meeting in Moscow when he and Steve Woods met the officials of SPUTNIK for the first time. The director opened the meeting saying, "Welcome to the department for all not-yet-socialist countries!" Hans admitted that at first he was a little taken aback but soon good relationships developed. He became friends with a dynamic young Russian named Sergey Yastrebkov who worked for SPUTNIK, the travel/exchange bureau of Komsomol, the political youth organization. After making it exceeding clear with them that Up with People was a nonprofit corporation, a totally apolitical and non-sectarian program, an invitation to sponsor us was forthcoming.[2] Then the work began.

Hans Magnus was the architect and leader of our first Soviet tour in June 1988. In his report to the Up with People Board of Directors he wrote, "On June 7th we crossed the border from Finland into the Soviet Union. The cast was very quiet as they entered the Soviet Union for the first time. We all realized that we had two weeks ahead of us that could be very significant though we had little idea of what to expect."[3]

The cast of 110 from 15 countries and 35 US states performed in three cities—Leningrad, Kallin, and Moscow—to enthusiastic audiences. From the very first song, the public participated, applauded, listened, and were absorbed through the entire show. Songs like "Can We Sing a Song of Peace?" and "What Color is God's Skin?" were translated into Russian. They were projected on a screen above the stage and received tremendous applause. At intermission, Hans reported that Sergey Yastrebkov said "I am extremely relieved and pleased. Your show speaks from the heart. It is about human emotion."[4]

The final city on the Soviet tour was Moscow. Hans Magnus reported with great excitement, "This has been an incredible experience from beginning to end." The last two shows at the Olympic Arena in Moscow were outstanding with 26,000 people attending. He said that, "Up with People had presented something that the Russians had never experienced. People say this is right, we agree with what you are saying—we agree with it. It's what we feel, it's what we mean. Russians are really marvelous people. All of our prejudices were challenged. We could not have been in the Soviet Union at a better time."[5] After further meetings with SPUTNIK, an agreement was reached for a return visit the following year. Up with People also achieved a breakthrough in our exchanges with the Soviet Union as many young people from that region would participate in our program within two years.

In June 1989, a cast of 140 representing 17 countries made a successful three-week tour of Ukraine. This was made possible in large part by a grant from the Conrad N. Hilton Foundation.

Dr. Fred Starr turned out to be a great help in introducing us to Mikhail Ulyanov, a famous actor and head of the Union of Theatre Workers for the Russian Federated Republic. Before I left the US for a planned trip to Moscow in December 1989, Ralph Colwell and I had a meeting in Chicago with Mr. Ulyanov. He was a very powerful figure. Through his interpreter, he said, "I have heard about your organization from producer Eduard Smolny." Ralph and I had entertained Mr. Smolny in Tucson. Mr. Ulyanov was also a friend of Eduard Malayan and had heard about Up with People from him, too. I told Mr. Ulyanov that President and Mrs. George H. W. Bush had been invited to be honorary patrons of the 25th Silver Anniversary Celebration in Denver in the summer of 1990. Then, we talked about the possibility of inviting General Secretary and Mrs. Gorbachev to also be patrons for this event. I offered to give Mr. Ulyanov a letter to that effect if he could get it to them. Then he said, "Our young people in the Soviet Union have blinders." He held up his hands, like blinders, and said, "This is the way they see things. We promised them a world we imagined, but it wasn't reality. Now they have to face reality. You are giving youth a broad vision of the world."[6]

From Chicago, I flew to Brussels to meet Hans and together we flew to Oslo, Norway, and spent the night. We were in Moscow the next day, December 7. It was snowing and dark when we arrived. The terminal was crowded but very quiet. We went through customs and the official stared at me a long time while checking my passport picture, but otherwise we had no problems.

We met Sergey Yastrebkov, the assistant to the director of SPUTNIK, our sponsoring organization in both 1988 and 1989. Hans had been working with him and Aleksandr Demeshko, his colleague. We ended up in a very big limousine, the type normally only used for government people. We took off and went halfway into town stopping at the apartment of an artist friend who lived there with his wife, a prima ballerina, their daughter, and his mother-in-law. He had been a lead drummer in a popular rock band. They had prepared a table full of food—caviar, smoked salmon, cabbages, meats, black bread, rye bread, and a lot of vodka.

Then Sergey and Aleksandr took us to the Budapest Hotel, adjacent to Red Square. It looked dreary. The room was nice, small, with a bed and a bathroom connected to each room. When I came in it was freezing cold because it was snowing outside and the window was open. I finally got the window closed.

The next day Sergey and Aleksandr took us to the Pushkin State Museum of Fine Arts where we were received by the director and had a brief tour. Next, we went through the Kremlin complex and St. Basil's Cathedral. Our group got stopped going into Red Square because the Central Committee of the Communist Party of the Soviet Union was meeting. Sergey showed his identification card so we were able to go through the Square to our meeting. Next, we had a press conference about Up with People. However, Hans and I couldn't get any real direction about what was going to happen. There were about 50 people there—representatives from Tass, Izvestia, Pravda, Komsomol, and two state TV stations. Also, there were official representatives of all the cities where Up with People had been in 1988 and 1989. They had come to meet Hans and me and go over a list of potential students who had expressed a desire to participate with Up with People. Later, about 100 students took part in this exchange.

Then we met Mikhail Kiryluk, the producer of the one-hour Lenfilm video called "Hello! Privyet, Ukraine!" It was the story of Up with People's tour in Ukraine earlier that year. At the end of the film there was applause, led by the Ukrainian group, because the film covered the great songs of Ukraine. To our surprise, my friend Eduard Malayan came into the room.

Eduard had become a great friend and totally supported the work of Up with People. Although we don't know what role he played for certain, our good relations with the Soviet Union were always assured. I got up and said, "This is my friend." The TV crew filmed him as we were talking. That evening Mr. Kiryluk, our host, gave a dinner party and Eduard stayed for dinner and gave me a toast. Mr. Kiryluk also gave me a gift for Ralph Colwell, in thanks for his collaboration on "Hello! Privyet, Ukraine."

The next day we had a meeting with Mikhail Ulyanov, who I had first met in Chicago. He came out of a Central Committee session and asked us to come over to his theater where he had a beautiful big office. Mr. Ulyanov said, "What interested me in Up with People was hearing of your aims, values, and purposes. I subscribe to what you are trying to do for young people."[7]

Our hosts took us on a drive an hour and a half out of Moscow the following day which I greatly enjoyed. Seeing the villages was interesting, and we passed large forests with big signs warning people to avoid moose. We went to an ancient monastery and were impressed with the colors, particularly in the onion domes, beautiful blues and yellows. The splashes of color reminded me of what you see in México, which surprised me. I had never connected that with the Soviet Union. The restaurant where we were scheduled to eat was closed for repairs, so we went to the central party headquarters in a little town. They prepared a private room with a table full of food, starting with caviar and smoked salmon. The Russians were superb hosts. I returned home on December 10 thrilled with what I had seen and done.

It was a remarkable effort to have six casts impacting the Soviet Union and Eastern Europe during 1990 and 1991 and gave all of our students a chance to experience life behind the Iron Curtain. In March 1990, two casts went to cities in Poland, Russia, and Estonia. It was notable that it marked the first time that students were able to live with host families in those countries probably because of improved conditions there. In Leningrad, the students were treated like royalty. They experienced the rich culture of the arts and visited the music conservatory where the composer Pyotr

Ilyich Tchaikovsky began his studies. The cast interacted with international friendship groups and children from government-funded orphanages. After seeing the Up with People show in Leningrad, Rolan Bykov, the head of the All-Union Children's Center for Cinematography and Television said, "The most critical problem facing the Soviet Union is not the issue of the republics or the economy, but what to do with our youth. That is why Up with People is so important to us."[8] One Soviet host said, "Perestroika means that you are here with us in our home this evening and no one will question us about it."[9]

In late March, 15 Ukrainian youth had joined the cast for a day in Tallinn, Estonia, the capital. I heard a description of a memorable event there at one of their rehearsals that captivated the spirit that we hoped to get across. In the words of Bill Welsh, Director of Music Services, "We sat in a big circle with one of our students in between each of the Ukrainian students. It was literally half-West and half-East. They were repeating the words of the Up with People songs in unison to learn them. The most incredible moment came as the group read the words to the song, "Face to Face"—"The world is not the same now, it is wiser, and it's older, with enemies becoming hard to find...We're different people who have come together in this time and place, and now we're standing face to face."[10]

One of the most unforgettable moments of that tour came during a visit to Tallinn. It is a beautiful and historic city on the Baltic Coast. It coincided with the Estonian Parliament declaring its intention to negotiate independence from the Soviet Union. Patriotic feeling was running high. On opening night, a sellout audience of 4,200 crowded into the hall for Up with People's performance. The show ended with a parade of international flags and the cast and spectators joined in singing in an Estonian song considered to be a national hymn. As an Estonian flag was carried to center stage the audience stood as one, cheering wildly—and they continued cheering through four encores.[11]

The other cast went to Poland at the end of March. They performed at the Gdansk Lenin Shipyard where Solidarity, a Polish labor union, was born. Many of the cast members were housed with union members. A representative of Solidarity spoke and said, "The work done by you today is difficult to describe. It is the work of the human heart."[12] So many said you must come back. The greatest need is to give hope, ideals, and a purpose to the young people. Without that, nothing will work."

In April 1991, a cast toured Czechoslovakia for the first time. They started their seven-city tour in Ostrava and ended in Prague where they were received by Mayor Kořán. In describing their visit a newspaper wrote, "When Up with People was on stage performing, it was as if they put their heart on the palm of their hand and gave it to us."[13] A second cast visited Russia that June and July, ending in Moscow. In the town of Viska, the mayor thanked the cast for "opening the eyes and ears of our young people to the world outside the Soviet Union." A TV crew followed the cast through much of the tour with the intent of making a documentary. One of the directors said, "The Up with People program was important for its expression of hope and [a] call for young people not to be indifferent."[14] In September, a third cast visited two cities in Estonia. The cast had a memorable visit as they witnessed the restoration of Estonian independence. To finish the year, a fourth cast went to Poland in November and December of 1991. Their show in Warsaw was broadcast on national TV. As President of Up with People Europe Hans Magnus's commitment to the opening of these many countries for Up with People was extraordinary. I feel these tours of the Soviet Union and Eastern Europe occurred at a time in history that will be noted for building understanding between the East and West.

29

Up with People's 25th Silver Anniversary Celebration and the Move to Denver

"The Day the People Came Together"
The day the people came together.
A day that changed the world forever.

In October 1988, I was invited to Denver, Colorado, for the 60th birthday celebration of John Fuller, founder and chairman of Fuller Real Estate and a member of the Up with People Board of Directors. It turned out to be a fortuitous moment for Up with People. When I informed John and his guests that we were searching for a city to host our 25th Silver Anniversary Celebration in 1990, there was considerable excitement. John said, "If all of you will help, I will chair the committee and let's put in our invitation for Denver." That conversation led to our Silver Anniversary Celebration when 5,600 alumni, board members, and guests from 38 countries and all 50 states descended on Denver. Denver was selected from among 36 cities worldwide. Our Celebration also coincided with the opening of the new Convention Center in Denver, and we were billed as the feature event.

The 25th Silver Anniversary Celebration was unique and the excitement was felt everywhere. This was typified by the opening ceremony, hosted by NASA astronaut and Board Member Captain Gene Cernan, who said in his opening remarks, "I don't think I've been this high since I went to the Moon."[1] Cast 1990E and the Colwell Brothers set the stage for a special video salute by the Honorary Chairman, President George H. W. Bush. He observed, "In this time of historic change throughout the world, we must continue to reach out to people across political and geographic boundaries…. Your members have helped to build better understanding among nations not only through their outstanding musical performances but also through public service and educational activities in their host communities. On behalf of all Americans, I commend you and all the generous volunteers and sponsors who support your efforts. Each of you has demonstrated clearly how one individual can make a difference."[2]

Guests of honor Her Royal Highness Princess Margriet with her husband, Pieter van Vollenhoven, were superb ambassadors from the Netherlands. Pieter not only attended as a board member but came with his jazz group, De Gevleugelde Vrienden. They were met with enthusiastic applause when they performed during the opening ceremony. Princess Margriet and Pieter made a big impression on Denver and Colorado by attending all the receptions. They were hosted by Governor and Mrs. Roy Romer, Mayor and Mrs. Federico Peña, and many others. Everyone spoke of their warmth and graciousness in meeting the public.

There was a long standing ovation from the attendees when the first cast of Sing-Out '65/Up with People was introduced. They made their way to the stage to be welcomed by Captain Cernan. Two gold medal Olympians who had played such an important part in the beginning of Up with People, John Sayre and Rusty Wailes, were also introduced. Thomasine Hill, a former Miss Indian America and early cast member, introduced her father, John Hill, a former chief of the Crow Nation. After lighting his peace pipe, he gave his blessing to the occasion. He also presented me with a fully feathered headdress.

On the evening of July 25, there was a black-tie dinner hosted by John and Jeannie Fuller. They emceed the evening event with much of Denver's leadership in attendance. A high point for me personally was when Lieve Martens, wife of the prime minister of Belgium, invited me to the stage where she presented me with the Order of Leopold, the highest honor bestowed on foreign citizens on behalf of His Majesty King Baudouin of Belgium. She paid great tribute to what Up with People had done for her country and underlined the important contribution it had made in allowing so many Walloons and Flemish students to travel and bond together. I was moved and honored.

Christine DeVita, president of the Reader's Digest Foundation, flew in from New York City to present a $1 million check in honor of DeWitt Wallace's conviction about Up with People. Another highlight was the introduction of Gina Hemphill Tillman, member of Cast 1983E and the granddaughter of Jesse Owens. She had come to accept the Founder's Award on his behalf, presented posthumously. It honored his selfless contribution to the development of Up with People, his actions at the Munich Olympic Games, and his lifelong commitment to the inner-city kids of America. She underlined how much Jesse's participation in the Up with People program meant, especially during his last years when he was dying of cancer.

In February 1985, I was introduced to Eduard Malayan by Bob McGee. Mr. Malayan joined us for the 25th Anniversary Silver Celebration in1990. He welcomed the Ukrainian dance troupe who performed for an enthusiastic audience. They had been invited to join a future cast during Up with People's visit to the Ukrainian Republic of the Soviet Union in 1989.

A special moment for Betty and me came when Ken Ashby invited the international board of directors of Up with People and their spouses on stage to be recognized. Ken Ashby along with John Parker and Steve Schmader were the superb architects of the special events for the 25th Silver Anniversary Celebration. As I looked at the board I thought what a gift Up with People has been given—these men and women leading so many giant enterprises had come from all backgrounds and countries to serve on the board without remuneration. They loved the students and the mission of Up with People. For many of the alumni and guests this was the first time they had seen the entire board of directors and realized there was much more to Up with People than just the show. Ken continued by paying tribute to what these board members and their spouses had done worldwide for Up with People.

Another important guest was Dr. Shoichiro Toyoda, Chairman of the Board of Toyota Motor Company. Accompanying him was his most charming wife, Hiroko, and 10 of his staff members. Mrs. Toyoda was a cousin of Naoko Mitsui Shirane who was on our board of directors. Dr. Toyoda was an impressive figure. I had met him several years earlier through Taro Kimura, a leading TV newscaster in Japan. Crown Prince Naruhito had announced a visit to the Toyota Automobile Museum in late July 1990. Dr. Toyoda felt compelled to be there to welcome him. However, Akio Morita, Chairman of the Board of the Sony Corporation and a friend, telephoned him, "I heard of the cancellation. You made a commitment to go to Denver and you must stick to that. Your top officers can welcome the crown prince!" So thank you, Mr. Morita! They were a wonderful Japanese group and they involved themselves in all of the activities. During the Celebration, Jim McDonald, President and Chief Operating Officer of General Motors, Tom Cruikshank, CEO of Halliburton, and I asked for a private meeting with Dr. Toyoda. At that meeting, we officially invited him to join our international board of directors and he accepted. He was concerned about future generations. This was the only board he had agreed to serve on outside of Japan.

I was delighted that two of my sisters, Lillian Belk Youell and Jane Belk Moncure, had flown in from Norfolk, Virginia, and Burlington, North Carolina, respectively for the Celebration. My older sister, Lil, was brilliant—the valedictorian of her prep school and then her university class. She was an officer in the Daughters of the American Revolution and the Daughters of the Confederacy, and had her own column in the Norfolk newspaper. Her husband Mac Youell had been a colonel in the US Marines and ended up a captain in the US Navy, and both of their sons had attended Virginia Military Institute. Lil had always been my mentor, particularly when it came to education. She was always pushing me to return to college and finish the couple of courses I still needed for my BA. I kept telling her someday in the future—I'm too busy right now! My middle sister, Jane, was a well-known author of children's books with more than 30 million of her books in print. She was married to a university dean at Elon College, and they had one son who was the joy of their life! Barbara, my youngest sister was unable to attend. I've always been close to Barbara and her doctor husband, Jim, who live in Virginia and North Carolina. They have a son and daughter. My sisters always treated me as if I was in short pants. At one point in our 25th Silver Anniversary board meeting, when Lil felt I had not followed Robert's Rules of Order, she stopped the proceedings to correct me. That fortunately brought forth much laughter.

Betty and I were thrilled with the Celebration and so happy that so many of our friends from when we lived in Europe in 1972 and 1973 could attend. There was Beatrice Lunt; John Goossens; Chantal de Limelette and her husband, Géry; Fred and Etta Loudon; and many more. Board Member and President of Up with People Europe, Hans Magnus and his wife, Tove, did a superior job in heading such a prestigious delegation.

Tremendous momentum was created during this Celebration, and the city of Denver got a new look at the full dimension of the program.

Betty and I personally were overwhelmed with the response from the alumni. So many of them stopped us and thanked us for the experience: it redirected my life, or I found my potential and my career, or I became part of the global village with all the friendships and host families we lived in—thank you! Betty and I were as moved as they were.

Without a doubt it was much more than a reunion; it was a launching pad for the next 25 years, and I was honored to be asked to give some final remarks. I said, "Looking back and looking ahead 25 years—a quarter of a century of indelible experiences and memories. Chancellor Konrad Adenauer in his office in Bonn saying, 'Drugs may do away with a generation. There must be a positive alternative. Stand on your own. Make your program available for youth everywhere.' It feels like yesterday that President Eisenhower phoned me saying, 'You must incorporate, make it available for the world. Freedom is a precious ingredient and only self-responsibility and inner discipline will hold it together. You are trying to put in those ingredients.' Jesse Owens, who all his life kept faith with his inner-city kids, believed Up with People could touch them, inspire them, and help them to reach further and reach higher. My friend DeWitt Wallace of the *Reader's Digest*, who was a big supporter of Up with People, told me, 'This is a great educational program. I want you to incorporate and be independent.'

"We owe these men a debt of gratitude. They pushed at the right moment. They saw what could be. They were visionaries. To build a worldwide network of friends, a global structure for action, has been the passion of my life.

"Up with People is a dream of what could be, but it is a fire. It has been molded, shaped, and energized with the fire, a fire this time—a fire that it remain free, a fire that will be available for all, a fire that did not become political or a movement, a fire that reaches for perfection at all times, a fire to include everyone who has it in their heart and spirit to encourage understanding and build toward that ideal of freedom and democracy.

"Up with People—a golden passport for all who touch it and spend a year in the program. Nothing of value is built easily. Sacrifice, commitment, failure, pain, disappointment, and successes have all been factors along the way, but never deterring from a passion to build something that can affect the world. A task bigger than yourself where you use everything— your strengths and your weaknesses. The reach is longer than your arm. It's an unknown way. It's an untried road. But vitality and creativity are there if you live at that point. The real story of the next 25 years is what you do with this experience in your communities, cities, countries, and the world. Godspeed to all of you!"[3]

The momentum from the 25th Silver Anniversary Celebration carried us forward for the next few years, and our new Board Member Dr. Shoichiro Toyoda did much in establishing us in Japan. An outcome from the very successful 25th Silver Anniversary Celebration arrived promptly. The official invitation came from Governor Roy Romer and a leading group of Denver industrialists inviting Up with People to move its world headquarters to Denver. John Fuller had alerted the board that this might occur. This was much sooner than expected. The board was somewhat divided. Many, especially our board members from Europe and Japan, loved coming to Tucson for the weather and the friendly atmosphere. Others raised the fact that we had a large pool of host families in Tucson.

Others favoring Denver, made the point that there were at least 17 major foundations and multiple corporate headquarters there. Next, the question arose about the winter weather in Denver and no proper airport—so it went back and forth, pro and con. Ultimately, it was unanimously decided that Don Weiss, the executive director of the National Football League, would be in charge of reviewing and determining such a move. Don, in his wisdom, recommended that we invite representatives from Denver and Tucson to attend a special board meeting in Washington, DC, on October 15, 1991. This was also unanimously approved, and invitations were submitted to both cities.

In the midst of this, Jim Boswell, who was chairman of our Executive Committee, was conferring with Jim McDonald of General Motors about who would succeed me as CEO of the company. Both of these men had become close personal friends, and we had hunted and fished together in many different places. Jim Boswell came to me and proposed that I physically remove myself from the company. They would find me a new office, including one for my longtime executive assistant, Ola Cook Henry. The hope by doing this was to give the board some idea of the leadership that might come forward. Mr. Boswell also announced this decision to the staff. I was happy to go along with this since I also was concerned that we get an inspiring leader who was eager to take on such a worldwide operation. I voiced to Mr. Boswell whether the timing was right with so much uncertainty at that point. I suggested that we put it up to the whole board, which didn't happen. I do know that much later, when the decision was made to remove me, both John Fuller and Peter Coors said to me, "We think it would have been wiser if you had remained CEO with your visionary skills during the relocation."

Don Weiss was outstanding in the way he handled the meeting of our relocation in Washington, DC. Both Tucson and Denver came with large delegations and tempting offers. Janet Marcus, a City Council member from Tucson, spoke of how the city would help financially to build a new headquarters. Don Diamond, the largest developer in Tucson, offered a piece of land for such a building. The whole delegation was strong and paid tribute to what Up with People had already meant to the city of Tucson and state of Arizona. They were determined to keep the headquarters there. The board questioned them about nonstop flights in and out of Tucson, and unfortunately they could only answer that they were working on it. John Fuller, leading the Denver delegation, hopped right on the airline transportation problem. He announced that the city had already allocated funds to build one of the biggest airports in the country. That was definitely a tipping point. Don graciously thanked both delegations, and the board gave them a standing ovation. Don Diamond, a personal friend, said to me later, "Blanton, you just don't have the horses there with the vision to take on this company. During the last 25 years everyone knew you were the hot hand on what you envisioned. All of us wanted to have a part. I didn't see that element in your staff."

When I moved out of the office, I also resigned from the board of directors. Both Bob Marbut and Jerry Jarrett were concerned and went to Jim Boswell saying, "You ought to give him some title so he can still attend board meetings if he chooses." So I was bestowed with the title of chairman emeritus.

One day, Don Weiss came to visit me in my office saying he was getting more and more frustrated not knowing what Jim Boswell was going to do. It was known that he owned a large piece of land that he was developing as a high-tech center. Don felt strongly that we needed a piece of that land if we were going to build a new headquarters in Denver. Jim Boswell remained silent "in 10 languages," and as hard as Don tried, Jim remained that way.

I stayed in close touch with Jim Boswell and Jim McDonald, and they informed me that the choice for the next CEO was between Steve Woods and Dale Penny. So the big day came and the board and staff gathered in our headquarters in Tucson. The board had met earlier that day privately to hear from Jim Boswell and Jim McDonald on the choice of new leadership. They also heard from Don Weiss on the choice of the future location. The board had unanimously approved the recommendations that Steve Woods become CEO and Dale Penny, president. They also unanimously approved Don Weiss's committee's recommendation to move Up with People to Denver.

I was asked to speak first to the staff who were standing by in our meeting room and inform them of the new leadership. When we walked into the room there was excitement and some concern. I introduced Steve and Dale with their new titles. Don Weiss was brief and to the point. The board had unanimously agreed with the committee's decision that Up with People headquarters move from Tucson to Denver. He ended his remarks by saying, "I think this move could be compared to the National Football League's decision to move its headquarters from Cleveland to New York City." He paid great tribute to Jim Boswell and his decision to donate acreage and $2 million for a new headquarters. Jim immediately resigned from the board to avoid any possible conflict of interest. Jim MacLennan, Senior Vice President and Chief Operating Officer, was thanked for his leadership and asked to head up and coordinate the move of the staff to Denver. Subsequently, he was asked to be the liaison with the architects and contractors of the new headquarters, and he did that well. The Up with People headquarters remained in Tucson until the summer of 1993.[4]

The question of raising the funds for the move and the building fell on my shoulders, and I went to work. With the help of John Fuller we visited Governor Romer, who was aware of the decision to move to Denver. He underlined how excited he was for Up with People and the city of Denver. When we showed him the rough drawings of the new headquarters building he said, "You need somebody who will put together a business committee to help raise funds." He asked his secretary to get Peter Coors on the phone. The two of them were good friends. Peter agreed to put such a committee together and offered that the Coors Brewing Company would kick it off with a pledge. They would definitely raise the money to cover the moving of Up with People and its staff.[5]

Back in my office in Tucson I put together a letter to Wesley and Sue Dixon. Over the years, Betty and I had become their close friends and often visited them in their home in Lake Forest, Illinois. We had hunted together in the United States, México, and Europe. I think it's fair to say that Sue was, perhaps, a little better shot than Wes. Both of them were wonderful people, and we had much fun together. My letter outlined some of our vision for the future and considered this move to Denver to be the kickoff for the next 25 years of Up with People. Their response was an invitation to come and talk with them at their ranch in Elko, Nevada. It is a beautiful spread in the foothills where Sue raised her Arabian horses. During my visit, I only saw the part that you could see from their gravel roads since the rugged part with wild game required horseback or hiking. I told them that someday I hoped to come back and cover that part of the property. When we passed a nice body of water next to the river, Sue questioned me about whether I thought it would be possible to turn that spot into a duck shooting area. She asked what kind of plantings would attract the birds. I described my experience with Smartweed and Japanese millet in my duck club in the deserts of Arizona. We returned to the ranch house and chatted about my proposal for our vision for the future with the move to Denver. They both said how much they were committed to help. At this point they wanted to match the $2 million that Jim and Ros Boswell had given. I gave them my profound thanks for their commitment and told them, "I would make it a challenge grant and would keep them posted." I also took the occasion to tell them personally what their friendship over the years had meant to Betty and me and their wholehearted commitment to the development of Up with People. The challenge grant was more than matched by board members and spouses Ralph and Laura Hart, Dan and Gail Cook, Dr. Shoichiro Toyoda, Jim and Betty McDonald, and Jerry and Martha Jarrett. On September 10, 1992, Colorado Governor Roy Romer welcomed Up with People at the groundbreaking ceremony for the new international headquarters. It was a festive occasion attended by many leading Coloradans including Peter Coors, representing the Colorado Leadership Committee and the Colorado business community. Also welcoming Up with People were Dr. Bruce Ekstrand, Vice Chancellor for Academic Affairs at the University of Colorado, and Robert Schulze, the mayor of Broomfield, where the headquarters was to be located. There was a performance by an Up with People cast.[6]

Ten months later, the Up with People International Center was dedicated as part of a three-day board of directors' meeting. The night before the public dedication over 1,000 friends and supporters attended the Black Tie Gala fundraiser hosted by Governor Romer and Peter Coors. The next morning 3,000 people attended the official opening of the new headquarters on July 23, 1993.[7] It was a great beginning!

30

Our Life in México

"Cielito Lindo"
Ay, ay, ay, ay, Canta y no llores

Betty and I came to Tucson in 1957, and our daughters, Jenny and Katie, were born here in 1965 and 1967, went to school here, and both graduated from the University of Arizona. We built Up with People from here. Tucson is home. Living in Tucson, being in the desert, I found myself homesick for the ocean. The nearest one was the Sea of Cortez, and we discovered the resort town of San Carlos in Sonora, México. For the past 58 years, we have experienced México as our Shangri-La. When most of our friends in Tucson went to California for their holidays, we went south to México and were welcomed with a warm heart by that country. When we crossed the border, we would relax. We felt at home because of the many close friendships we had developed with the Mexican people. We used our home there to entertain friends from around the world, as did our children with their friends.

San Carlos is 310 miles from our home in Tucson on a four-lane highway. If it's not too crowded at the border, we can drive it in six hours. The town looks out over the beautiful Sea of Cortez. San Carlos is a perfect area for a hunter and fisherman like me, but what about Betty and our two daughters? For them, and for all of our friends, there are beautiful pristine beaches and swimming in the warm waters, snorkeling and diving in the many coves and rocky points. It is a spectacular country where for many miles the mountains come straight down to the sea. At certain times of the year the fishing can be extraordinary. In the winter, it is possible to drive inland to the agricultural Empalme Valley and hunt white-winged doves feeding in the maize fields.

Fortunately for all of us, Betty's mother, Kay Wilkes, also fell in love with San Carlos. She built a lovely house in 1967 on a hill overlooking the Sea of Cortez with enough rooms for the family. We spent many happy hours with Jenny, Katie, and our friends traveling the coastline and exploring the coves and beaches.

Being a Navy man who operated a small boat during World War II and who loves the sea and big-game fishing, I just had to have a good fishing boat. I chose a 26-foot boat called a Fish Machine and I named it *La Palomita*. It had a diesel engine and was fully equipped for offshore fishing with long-range capability. It had outriggers, radio, microwave oven, rods and reels, and what Betty calls my sporting goods store of colorful trolling lures of all sizes and shapes!

Every year Betty and I had the pleasure of entertaining our very good friends from Japan, Dr. Toyotane and Mrs. Sohma. Dr. Sohma was a professor at Chulalongkorn University in Bangkok, Thailand, and devoted his life to building bridges between those two countries, working especially with young people. He had been decorated by the royal family of Thailand for his efforts. He had also been involved with the founding of Up with People in Japan and Thailand. Over the years he remained a passionate fisherman and came every year to fish with us in the Sea of Cortez. He would say, "I have come to the Belk Fishing School to learn more about how one catches big fish." Toyo and Tokiko would appear each morning dressed completely in white, with Tokiko even wearing white gloves, as was customary in Japan. Toyo was one of the most serious fishermen I've ever met. He would sit in a chair on the deck every day, all day, watching the four or five lures bouncing in the waves behind the boat. He was always the first to see the fin of a marlin or sailfish appear in the spread. If there was a strike from a tuna or dorado, he would have already seen it and was the first to grab the rod.

We often fished the International Billfish Tournament that is run yearly out of San Carlos during the month of July. We were fishing such a tournament with our team aboard the *La Palomita*—Up with People friends John Parker, Steve Woods, Hugh Soest, my nephew Russell Wilkes, Toyo, and myself. It was the first day, and about 35 boats had left the harbor at 8:00 a.m., all going to their favorite spots. I decided to go due south, and we had run some 15 to 18 miles when we hit blue water, a sign of the Humboldt current. Suddenly, we scattered a big school of flying fish that took off in every direction and we put the lures out. Immediately, the line in the starboard outrigger popped out with a bang, and we had a hook up. The rod was buckling and the reel was zinging. I ran up the ladder to the wheel, and at that point a very large marlin jumped and jumped again heading right up our wake. Marlin have been known to jump into boats, so I hit the throttles and turned abruptly starboard, just as the large marlin jumped past us. We could tell it was a good fish, well over 500 pounds. The rod and reel that the fish was hooked on was a light tackle 28-pound test line, which needed some skill to handle. At that point John Parker was in the fighting chair, holding on for dear life while the marlin was heading south at top speed. It was just before 1:00 p.m., and we reported into tournament headquarters that we had a hook up on quite a large fish. Betty, of course, was hearing all this on the citizens' band radio in our house and following the fight step by step.

The fish went deep then, and I was backing down when we hit a critical moment. All the line came off the small reel, so the metal was exposed. We all held our breath, but John did a good job of slowly lifting the rod and gaining some line. It was creeping up on two hours now, and we were more than five miles from where the strike had occurred, still heading south. I told Steve to put on the heavy gloves so he could handle the 300-pound leader if the fish did surface. I said, "If you see the leader you'll know the fish is 15 to 20 feet down. Take the leader in your gloves and while I'm backing down, see if you can slowly move the fish toward the surface where we might have a chance of landing it." We did get over the fish, and we could see it, magnificent with its iridescent blue color shimmering in the water. It was a picture of power.

Steve, using all his might, had lifted the marlin about two feet when it yanked the leader out of his hands and headed for the bottom once again. During the next four hours this sequence happened three more times with the same results. It was a much bigger fish than we had estimated. Toyo was pouring cold water over John's head to keep him from dehydrating, and we were urging him to keep drinking water. It had been seven hours since the hook up, and the sun was going down on the horizon with a brilliant sunset. When darkness came I asked Steve to go into the cabin and bring out a searchlight that fitted on the flying bridge. It lit up the whole deck as well as the water around the stern of the boat.

We were now some 30 miles from port, and I was silently worrying that I only had a single engine. What would happen if we lost power? Still, I was too busy backing down and keeping the angle of the line in sight so that we didn't back over it in the darkness. I did notice lightning and black clouds were somewhere in the area where the Yaqui River runs into the Sea of Cortez. As nighttime descended on us, the storm seemed to be growing in intensity, but I put that thought aside since there was no wind in our area. How wrong I was! In 30 to 40 minutes we were in the middle of a chubasco, a suddenly occurring, localized storm capable of very high winds, rain, lightning, and thunder. It hit with a fury! All at once the wind and rain were howling around us and the sea became turbulent. Without warning, lightning was hitting the sea around us and bouncing across in front of the bow and behind the stern.

By that time, John had fought the fish for eight and a half hours, and he had been noble in his commitment. During the next half hour, the storm intensified 100 percent and the wind was howling to the point I had to take down the Bimini top on the flying bridge before it was ripped off. I yelled to the crew who were now in the cabin, "Everybody in life preservers," and Steve said, "Oh shit, this is serious!" And it was—but still we fought the fish. Now the winds were directly on my stern so as I backed up, the waves were crashing on the stern and pouring water into the boat. The bilge pumps were pumping it out but at any moment we might have a big wave swamp the stern and the bilge pumps would not be able to keep up. I thought to myself, we can't fight this fish much longer.

Suddenly more strong bolts of lightning hit the water all around us with a simultaneous clash of thunder. The waves were getting bigger and bigger, and the rain was so hard it was stinging our faces. I said to John, "I'm very sorry but we have no choice but to get out of here. I'm asking you to tighten the drag on the reel all the way. Hold tight as I go forward and we'll pop the line." John had a stunned and incredulous look on his face as if to say, "You gotta be kidding me. I fought this fish for nine hours and I'm not quitting now." We had no alternative. I was captain of the boat and felt responsible for everyone aboard, so I put the boat in gear and we slowly started moving forward. John tightened the drag on the reel and it wasn't long before the line stretched tight and popped. He reeled in what was left and sat there not moving while we were crashing through the very heavy seas, some of which were now breaking over the sides and stern of the boat simultaneously.

The lightning, wind, and rain was all over us and seemed to be gaining in intensity and our bilge pumps could not keep up. The water was pouring in from all sides. I thought to myself that about five to 10 minutes was all we could sustain. Then Toyo, who was standing on the ladder to the flying bridge, grabbed me by the leg and yelled, "I see the lighthouse." I turned back to him and desperately yelled, "Where?" He pointed 90 degrees from where I was heading. Even though I was following the compass, the wind and tides were moving us out to sea. I corrected my heading, turning 90 degrees to starboard, and within 20 minutes we were out of the storm into calmer waters. I'm sure everyone aboard said a private prayer of thanks.

I opened up the full throttle in calm water and an hour and a half later we rounded the point and entered the harbor. Even though it was nearly midnight I asked the guys to hand me up the siren I kept on a heavy battery in case of an emergency. I decided this was a moment to use it, and when I turned the siren on to full volume, lights went on all over the mountainside. The word went out that we were safely in port. Betty was the most relieved woman in México when we walked into the house still dripping and disheveled—but home! As we were saying good night, Parker said to me, "Thanks for your seamanship, you brought us safely home."

Years later during a fishing tournament, Katie was fighting what would have been the first-prize fish—a beautiful, large sailfish. She had successfully brought it to the stern of the *La Palomita II*. One of my friends on the boat said, "Hold it there before we release it so we can get photographs." Of course, the wily sailfish swam under the boat and cut the line on the spinning prop and was gone. Katie was terribly disappointed but felt better when we said in jest, "Let's keelhaul the photographer!"

Many times our dearest friends from Belgium, Larry and Beatrice Lunt Wittouck, would accompany us to San Carlos. They also had a winter home in Tucson. Both of them loved going offshore in the *La Palomita II* and experiencing ocean life. There were schools of porpoise racing with the boat and riding the bow wave and then jumping in all directions. In the wake sometimes there were acres of them. Then there were whales moving in schools and occasionally one would breach completely out of the water and make an enormous splash. The wonderful sea turtles would float on the surface, often identified by a seagull perched on their backs. There were days when the giant manta rays were migrating. Other times the young manta rays, numbering 30 or 40 would be somersaulting in and out of the water. Occasionally a hammerhead shark appeared or a marlin or sailfish would jump, grabbing our attention. Sometimes our eyes would focus on a frigate bird with a wingspan of six feet hovering over a school of fish. Then we'd head for one of our favorite coves for Betty's lunch, which was nearly always a rolled up tortilla with green chilies, ground beef, and cheese steaming hot from the boat's microwave. In the midst of this Larry just had to dive overboard and swim the short distance to shore and look for rocks and shells. One time he found several large rocks he wanted to bring aboard and take back to his yard in Tucson. I hooked a long line to an inner-tube with a net in the bottom to hold the rocks. On the return trip, however, the rocks became too heavy for the inner-tube and the whole shebang went to the bottom with Larry desperately trying to avert such a tragedy. He was sad but I backed the boat close to him, cut off the engines, and one by one, in four feet of water, Larry retrieved the rocks. He placed them on the swim step on the stern of the boat where they stayed as we made our way back to shore. When I heard Larry say, "I see another big rock I need to get," I knew it was time to lift anchor and move on! The sun was going down in the west, a gorgeous sunset was emerging, and it was time for drinks. Fortunately for everyone I had all the ingredients and the recipe for my famous margaritas. So home we went to hot showers and a change of clothes.

In 1983, I was at our board of directors meeting in Amsterdam when Pieter van Vollenhoven, sitting across the dinner table, said in a loud voice to his wife, Her Royal Highness Princess Margriet, "Margriet, we're going to México. Betty has just invited us so I can go scuba diving!" I thought to myself, good grief, how will we entertain this royal couple in our small house and with our small boat? They did come, and everything worked out. My close friend and attorney Peter Voevodsky and his wife Reyn loaned Princess Margriet and Pieter their beautiful house overlooking the water. When the governor of Sonora learned that they were coming, he quickly sent his roadbuilding crew to patch the bumpy dirt road that led to the Voevodsky's house. Unfortunately, the heavy blading equipment to smooth out the road broke through the water pipes going to the homes along the road. As the water was spraying in all directions, the locals dubbed it "San Carlos Springs."

Pieter had great scuba diving in the clear waters, and both of them loved my boat, *La Palomita II*. The seas were flat and the weather was perfect, and the four of us greatly enjoyed ourselves. Pieter kept saying, "Don't pay any attention to the larger boat that's following us with our four Dutch bodyguards."

Even though we did our best to keep it a private visit, the news seeped out that the princess and her husband were in town. One very hot day Betty and the princess came in from shopping, and the princess said, "I would like to go for a swim in the pool at the country club." Betty had to inform her that we didn't belong to the San Carlos Country Club and that it would be against the rules to go swimming there. At that, the princess replied, "I love to break rules, let's go!" So there they were floating around and cooling off when suddenly the manager's wife came steaming out, full of fire and brimstone to have them removed. However, the moment she saw Betty, she realized who the other person was and said in a most sweet voice, "I've come to welcome you. Would you like iced tea?" Her Royal Highness and Betty were still laughing about their escapade when I came to pick them up. Their visit was a memorable time for all of us.

Some other Dutch friends that came to visit us in México were Fred and Etta Loudon. Fred was a member of the Dutch board of Up with People. He and I had much in common—we were both sportsmen, dog lovers, hunters, and fishermen. Their visit was perfection—the fish were plentiful, the seas were beautiful, and Freddie caught a marlin, a sailfish, a large dorado, and a tuna. We released the marlin and the sailfish but had many wonderful seafood dinners with the dorado and tuna.

The Loudons came a second time to visit us in México. It was during the winter, and we were going to hunt the Mexican white-winged dove. We had wonderful days together. The weather was perfect: in the seventies, sunny, with little wind. The Loudons gloried in it since they had come out of a frozen winter. Sometimes when the seas were right, we would go fishing in the morning and then drive up to the maize fields in the afternoon. My friend Ernesto Zaragoza from Guaymas, who owned the fields, would bring a young man to accompany us who would always know the fields where the white-wing doves were feeding.

It was a laid-back, completely restful kind of hunting. Nobody was in a hurry and we could set our own pace. We took reclining chairs, and Betty brought tortillas and sausages and ample amounts of salsa. Then we would find space in the shade under the large mesquite trees. We would set up camp with our portable picnic table, reclining chairs, a cooler with ice and cold Mexican beer and water—lots of water. That made a five-star lunch. Then it was time for a siesta. We would stretch out in our reclining chairs and relax and sleep until the birds started flying again around 3:00 p.m. By that time both Freddie and I would go back to the maize fields. I always carried my binoculars since the doves would change their flight pattern. I scanned the mesquite *bosque* that circled the field. Then we would position ourselves with the sun at our backs and the challenge would begin. Sometimes there were large flights numbering 50 to 60 birds. I can tell you they are tricky to shoot, but we shot well enough to get birds for dinner. As the sun was going down our young man would breast out the doves, wash them, and put them in plastic bags in the cooler. They were iced for the hour drive back to San Carlos. Later, they made a delicious meal wrapped in bacon and fresh chilis and roasted over a fire.

Betty and I had the wonderful experience of watching our daughters, Jenny and Katie, grow up and mature in México. Then to watch their children, our grandchildren, Chameli, Surina, Tommy, and Teo, do the same. How lucky we are as parents to have two wonderful daughters who have in turn raised, with their husbands, such outstanding grandchildren. They all love our Mexican getaway as much as we do. Oh, lucky us!

When we first arrived in San Carlos in 1965, there was a marina that was anything but modern. Eleven years later, rumors went around that a young couple had bought the marina. When I checked into the marina office that year, a bearded young man said, "Where have you been? You're the commodore of the yacht club here, and I've been looking for you. I guess you've heard that Tere and I have just acquired this marina." So began a friendship with Ed and Tere Grossman. They have marvelously led us, counseled us, advised us, and been our best and most loyal friends in San Carlos. They are two very talented, attractive people out to pursue their dream of creating a five-star marina in San Carlos. Ed, an American who was raised in México, was slight of build but with not an ounce of fat—a scuba diver who piloted his own plane and an avid golfer. He had recently retired as the CEO of Laboratorios Grossman. After his grandfather won the lottery in México, the family debated investing in ice cream or pharmaceuticals, and they chose the latter, building a very successful company. Tere, a beautiful, savvy woman, is a power in her own right. She had discovered the world as a stewardess on Canadian Pacific Airlines and had worked in the Vatican, spoke English, Italian, and French as well as her native Spanish. Tere was brilliant as a businesswoman and helped create a successful marina. Later she was appointed by the Mexican government to be in charge of all the marinas of México.

They are definitely a power couple who worked tirelessly to bring a run-down marina up to the highest standards. I remember five years earlier rolling barrels of gasoline down the wooden dock with Peter Voevodsky to fill our boats' gas tanks. That was all transformed when Ed made a deal with Pemex, the Mexican oil giant, to establish first-class service in the marina. It was Eddie's entrepreneurship and his engineering ability behind the whole development. It was also their long-range planning that led them to buy a piece of raw land nobody thought was worth anything and develop it into one of the best dry-storage areas on the Sea of Cortez. It now has hundreds of sailboats and powerboats enclosed and protected with 24-hour guards. At one point the Mexican government offered Tere the job of minister of tourism for the country. Since this meant moving to México City she declined. It was fortunate for us because she, Ed and their daughters, Heidi and Kiki, have continued the family tradition of managing the marina. All of us owe the Grossmans a great vote of thanks for their hard work and commitment to bringing their dreams to fruition. We have been their benefactors, and we salute them and cheer them on.

Betty and I, along with thousands of Americans, have enjoyed the warm hospitality of México. It is a place where we can bring our fishing boats, scuba diving boats, and sailboats and launch them in the pristine waters of the sea and vacation with our families.

I was pondering what there is about México that feeds our spirits so well. Part of it, I think, is that México is not a frenetic country. They are more easygoing and take life as it comes. Mexicans laugh and joke more than Americans do. They celebrate on all occasions, and if there isn't an occasion, they create one. If you break down on the highway, they'll stop and help you. There is also a certain mystique in México. For example, I was very uptight one day trying to locate a painter for our house, and one of my Mexican friends said to me, "Just relax, you'll run into him." By golly, after several hours I ran into him at the grocery store—it just happens. I know all this sounds contrary to the view and press in America, but this is what Betty and I and our two daughters have discovered after all these years of friendship with México. It is why over the past 51 years, so many Mexican families have hosted students from Up with People, from the very wealthy to the very poor, and the experiences these students have had has left an indelible mark on their lives.

Perhaps it is true that people who live in fear build walls and those who love liberty and freedom build bridges.

31

Friendships

"These Are My People"
This is where I belong
They're always in my heart, I am never alone

When we first came to Tucson, I was 32, Betty was 28, and we had been married for three years. My younger sister Barbara and her husband, Jim Tinsley, had moved here in 1955. Jim was an ophthalmologist. They introduced us to their friends Tom and Anne Via. Tom was a fellow Virginian.

Several years later, when we returned to Tucson to make it our home, we reconnected with Tom and Anne and hit it off big time. At that point Tom was a planning consultant for John Murphy, a visionary who in the early years of Tucson had bought a vast amount of foothills acreage in the Catalina Mountains. Anne, who was originally from Wichita, Kansas, had made a wealth of friends and always knew what was happening in town. We were at home with each other immediately. It was a complete bonding, and the Vias took us on and introduced us to their many friends. Tom was a high-spirited man whom everybody liked. He treated us as family and he would come whistling up to our door at any time. His voice would then echo through the house saying, "What's happening here?" Later on, he did the same thing quite often at the Up with People offices on Campbell Avenue. The staff was always blindsided when he appeared. He paid no attention to protocol and would march in, speaking to each of them and then come into my office without knocking. This was just Tom, and it didn't bother me at all, but it sometimes upset those I was conferring with. It didn't upset him though, and he would just sit down and join in.

After Up with People started, three of Tom and Anne's four daughters traveled with the program for a year. Anytime Up with People's Board of Directors was in town, which was quite often, Anne, along with another close friend Reyn Voevodsky, were always on hand to help Betty prepare dinner for the board. Tom was a soulmate and a great support during the early pioneering days of Up with People. If I was down, he would pick me up, and if I was struggling for where the next pot of money would come from, he always had a new idea.

Tom and Anne joined us on a trip to San Carlos just after we had acquired a small house there at the San Carlos Country Club. Since I had my secret recipe for making margaritas, I won Tom over from being a bourbon drinker, at least while he was in México. So there he was, sitting in the living room with his feet up, sipping on his second margarita, when he suddenly said, "Betty, this place needs a porch—a screened-in porch like we have down South." So he built us one—and built it before he realized he had bypassed all the official permits necessary to do such a thing. That didn't bother him. He said, "I would rather do what needs to be done and ask for forgiveness if I am wrong, rather than wait on permits!" For all the years we had that place, we greatly enjoyed the screened-in porch.

Tom loved fishing! We could never really tell whether it was the catching of the fish or the eating of the fish that most interested him. He enjoyed going out early in the morning and late in the afternoon when the reef fish would come in feeding on the schooling mullet. I taught him how to use a spinning rod, and he became passionate about it. I had an inflatable rubber boat with a 2.5-horsepower motor, and we would slip along the shoreline until we found a diving pelican. Then we would cast our spinning rods. Once Tom moved too quickly, shifting sides. Of course, the air in the inflatable shifted with him, and I was dumped overboard just as I was getting a strike from a nice fish. Tom just kept on fishing while I climbed back aboard. We were catching cabrilla, pargo, mackerel, and sometimes corvina. All of these are top table fare. Later, when we were filleting the fish, you got a true picture of Tom. He had been raised in the middle of the Depression and nothing was ever wasted or thrown out. When we picked and cleaned ducks in the winter, he always saved the hearts and gizzards. When cleaning fish, he would take time with his sharp knife and cut out what he called the cheek filet from its head.

Then there was offshore trolling for the big fish. This was all new for Tom, and he found out quickly he got seasick. In fact, he got seasick while we were still idling out of the harbor! However, he was not to be slowed down and he pioneered using ear patches and pills until he found the right mixture and, thank heavens, they worked.

One day in 1979, I went to John Murphy's office, where Tom worked, because he said he had an idea for me. An agent showed me a map of the Foothills Estates and told me there was one lot available. He thought Betty and I should buy it and build a home there. Fortunately, it was near the Via home, and it fitted us perfectly at that moment as we were looking for a place. Tom, when he heard of the project, naturally got involved, and Betty and I were delighted. His one stipulation was that Betty would be the contractor and work closely with him in the architectural design and planning, and that she did in spades. That home on East Cerrado Los Palitos was ours for the next 20 years. It was the site of many happy gatherings with friends and family.

One day, a small notice appeared in the *Arizona Daily Star*, hardly noticeable, but I saw it immediately. It said, "A chance to build your own duck club," with a telephone number and address. I jumped on it like a rainbow trout on a floating grasshopper. Betty said that I hardly put my boots on before I was away in a cloud of dust. The 70-mile drive from my house to the Buenos Aires Ranch, the address in the notice, flew by. There I met the wildlife manager George Vensel. George was later to say to Betty that Blanton gave him a check for a $100 down payment before we even spoke. I told Betty that was not accurate; I had already said "good afternoon" to him. The 120,000-acre ranch sits on the Mexican border with rolling hills and fields of sacaton grass with two large bodies of water for waterfowl and a beautiful habitat for quail—a sportsman's paradise! I got Tom involved, and we established the Buenos Aires (BA) Duck Club. I also enlisted Peter Voevodsky as a charter member, and this led to 10 great years when we undoubtedly had the best duck and quail hunting in Arizona.

George Vensel became a lifelong friend, and he did extra service in keeping the dam in shape after floods and notifying us when any large migration of waterfowl hit the ponds. He showed us the best spots for the quail. George also gave us our own entrance. He designated a place to camp under a large mesquite tree with shady limbs next to one of the lakes where we could keep our duck boats. As a couple of Southern boys, Tom and I felt we were walking in high cotton. We had many memorable shoots, often ending with our families joining us from Tucson for a cookout and picnic.

When I think of Tom, one shoot stands out. He had a friend from Virginia named Franklin, who basically was a quail hunter. I had placed them in a duck blind on the far side of the lake. By daylight there was a freak snowstorm and rainstorm at the same time, the wind was blowing, and the temperature was dropping. However, the ducks were flying, and I could hear quite a bit of shooting. An hour after daylight I saw white handkerchiefs being whipped back and forth above their duck blind. So I took my dog, Duke, and motored across and found two very wet hunters who were ready to come in and try to build a fire. Tom had already waded out and put his decoys in a big sack. As quickly as they could, they got in the boat with their guns, lunch boxes, and bag of decoys. I said, "Stay put in the bow right behind where Duke is sitting." We started across the lake but by that time the wind was whipping and the whitecaps were appearing. My little outboard, which had not run properly all season, suddenly came up on plane and the icy spray was dousing us.

The first sign of anything serious was when the bag of decoys floated by, followed by a big black dog swimming and Franklin screaming, "We're going down and I can't swim!" It was too late. The bow was underwater, and at full throttle we hit the bottom at about four feet and the engine cut off. Franklin was still screaming that he couldn't swim, and I said to him, pretty upset, "Stand up, Franklin, we're on the bottom!" We dragged the boat with the guns to the shore, and I sent Tom ahead with Franklin to walk to the campsite. We learned later that Peter Voevodsky and one of the officers from Up with People, Steve Woods, were in another blind watching and restraining themselves from laughing. At one point, Steve said to Peter, "Please don't laugh or make any noise or I'll lose my job." Fortunately, the storm stopped, the wind died down, and the sun came out. When Tom got to the campsite, he said, "Betty, we've had a little accident, and Blanton needs some time alone!"

Sadly for all of us, these halcyon days at Buenos Aires came to an end when the government bought the ranch in February 1985 with the aim of saving the Mexican masked bobwhite quail.[1] Thus we had to find new territory, and George Vensel once again came to our rescue and pointed us to his in-laws' ranch on the San Pedro River in Cochise County, Arizona. Tom lived long enough to help us lease a piece of wetlands and start with the purchase of 25 acres, which is now our Sandhill Farm LLC, with 1,000 deeded acres. Tom's last shoot there was in October, when we had unusually heavy rains and Stockton's Draw was running full force. Tom, at that point, had been diagnosed with prostate cancer, and unfortunately it had metastasized. Still, I didn't realize at the time that it would be our last shoot together. It was October 1987. Tom was determined to go, so we went down with Miguel de Terry from Spain, who was living with us. Miguel was a young college student who enjoyed Tom as much as I did, and provided a leg up or a hand when Tom needed it.

When we got there mid-morning, we could see ducks dropping into our upper pond, but to get there we had to wade across the wash. My strong Spanish friend put his arm around Tom and helped him across, and his final shoot was a good one. He shot six green head mallards and one bull pintail—a limit.

That November, I had an invitation from Queen Beatrice of the Netherlands for the royal boar shoot at Apeldoorn in Holland. The shoot was hosted by Her Royal Highness Princess Margriet and her husband, Pieter van Vollenhoven. I was concerned about Tom's health, so I talked to Anne, and she talked to his doctor. They all felt I could make the trip safely before Tom died. Sadly, on the second day there, Ola called late in the evening to say that Tom had passed away. I immediately thought back to my departure from home when I had left for the airport and Tom, in typical fashion, had come over to see that I had everything I needed for the trip. I remembered the words he said to me many times, that "if in life you end with one great friend, that's all you can ask for." He was that great friend, and I shall always miss him.

In 1983, I had a telephone call from our board member and friend Jim Boswell saying that he and his wife, Ros, were going to be visiting clients in the textile world in Europe and would like very much to experience a driven partridge shoot in Spain. Could I arrange one, possibly with my friends the de Terrys in Andalusia? I contacted Fernando de Terry, and he seemed delighted with the prospect of entertaining one of the largest cotton growers in the world. Fernando received us royally when we arrived in Puerto de Santa Maria. He raised some of the finest white horses in Jerez, and had two of his Andalusians harnessed to a four-seater buggy. The four of us—Jim and Ros, Betty and myself—were seated and paraded through the streets of Puerto.

When we arrived at one of his bodegas on the riverbank, Fernando ushered us into his stables with their tile floors and five chairs set up for us with glasses of Fino Sherry on a silver tray. Fernando said, "My bodega here makes the very best Fino. Anyone can make most sherries but not everyone can make Fino. If you succeed with Fino you will have no problems." While Fernando toasted us and we sipped his wonderful Fino, we were treated to a marvelous dressage by his 15-year-old son, Miguel, one of the finest young horsemen in Spain, exhibiting his prowess on a high-stepping white horse.

Early the next morning, we were in for more excitement when Fernando picked up Jim and me from the hotel and drove us out to one of the ponds on his *finca*, a ranch, for a duck shoot. There were two boats, a gamekeeper, and his assistant who took us to separate ends of the pond where they shoved the boats into the reeds for a blind. We waited for the dawn flight of ducks coming for water out of the green fields. The wind was blowing, the ducks were coming high and fast, and we expended more shells than killed ducks, but the air was also full of our competitive yelling from one end of the pond to the other. Jim Boswell was shouting his excuse that the loaned gun from Fernando didn't fit him properly. I was shouting back, "Don't blame the gun, it's the man behind it that counts." By mid-morning we'd had an excellent shoot. Fernando arrived with another pickup with tables and chairs and quickly set them up under the olive trees. When you looked a second time, there was a white tablecloth and a complete setup for a mid-morning meal, of course starting off with Amontillado sherry and tapas with Spanish serrano ham. We were a little concerned by the smile on Fernando's face when his gamekeeper produced his notebook, detailing how many shots we had fired and how many ducks had been brought down.

We were all relaxing and enjoying the camaraderie when Fernando talked again about his horses for which he had a passion. He described the Arabian horse with the chest of a lion, the legs of a wolf, and the docile eyes of a gazelle. We were enjoying our sherry, looking out over the undulating hills, grasslands, and olive trees that were typical of this great *finca*, called San José Del Pedroso. Then Fernando said, "We're burning up time here, and I have another plan. Unless you men would like to return to the hotel and rest, my two gamekeepers are ready to take you on a rough partridge shoot over the hills." "Rough" is the word Europeans use for the type of hunting we do in America: walking with a dog. So we were off again.

At the end of the day, after much exercising and sport, we were ready for Fernando to pick us up. He congratulated us on a good bag and said, "There is no finer bird for the table than the red-legged partridge of Spain!" He also told us we'd have plenty of time for a hot bath or a shower since we wouldn't gather in the parlor until 10:30 p.m. for drinks and 11:00 for dinner. This was music to our ears. When Betty and I were preparing for dinner, she told me about the luncheon that Elisa, Fernando's wife, had arranged for Ros and herself to meet some of the ladies of Puerto. Betty was laughing about herself, saying how all the ladies and Ros were dressed in black with pearls and she arrived dressed in blue. She added, "At least I stood out!"

The dinner was in the beautiful villa of Fernando's mother, and it was exquisitely presented. The children were not present, and Fernando took the occasion to talk to Betty about his son Miguel, whom we'd enjoyed meeting at the stable where he rode so beautifully. Evidently he was having a struggle in school and was totally unhappy, so Betty suggested he come and live with us. She would help him finish high school and see that he was prepared for college. This became a reality, and he became a member of our family. He did graduate from high school, and with a little help from Jim Boswell, was admitted to the University of California at Davis where he graduated with a degree in viticulture.

The next morning, Fernando surprised us saying, "I have laid on a driven partridge shoot that I especially think you would enjoy. Several of my sons will join us." Jim had heard my descriptions of these driven partridge shoots when I had first been a guest of Fernando in 1972 and was living in Brussels at the time. Fernando also invited Betty and Ros. For Jim and me it certainly was a new picture to see a long line of beaters coming over the hills, flanked on both ends by white Andalusian horses. The riders had black Spanish hats and gaucho outfits, and for a moment you could see them but then they would disappear into a ravine. You could still hear the popping of their white flags as they tried to get the partridges to take flight. Suddenly, a covey of red-legged partridges burst over the knoll in front and headed for us. They veered just before reaching our post and went directly over Boswell and one of Fernando's sons. Four shots rang out, and three birds tumbled into the grass. Jim Boswell had scored his first Spanish partridge while Fernando had collected his double. Fortunately, there had been a good hatch and birds were plentiful, so everyone had their share of shooting. After three such drives we broke for lunch under the shade of the trees. We started with three different kinds of sherry, and Boswell and I both agreed that we saw many more birds after lunch!

The next morning, when we went by Fernando's mother's villa to say goodbye, she said to Betty, "I've heard of your offer to take Miguel into your home and family and help him finish his schooling. I can't tell you how appreciative I am and how much I back this idea." When we took our leave from Fernando, Elisa, and their children, Fernando said, "I hope to visit you one day." Shortly afterward we welcomed the whole family in Tucson.

My long and close friendship with Peter Voevodsky started in a most inauspicious way in 1975 when I pulled into the old wooden gas docks in the San Carlos Marina. A tall man with a white hat and tan shirt completely wet from perspiration but with a ready smile said, "I've just come over to have a look at your boat." My boat was a 28-foot Cary named the *Miss Jenny* that had recently been shipped to me from a close friend named Elton Cary. Elton wanted me to try this boat out for fishing in the Sea of Cortez. It was the prototype of a boat Don Arnaud and Elton were working on which eventually became the *Cigarette*®. Peter wasn't interested so much in that piece of news as he was in examining the engines in my boat—two Ford interceptor engines, 300 horsepower each, with turbochargers. Peter, as a race car driver, had watched the boat running out of the harbor that morning and was impressed as he went through the engines in detail. "Boy," he said, "This is some hunk of power. I'd love to have a ride." So we cast off the lines and went for a spin. After I got the boat up on plane, I turned it over to Peter. He came to life like a young boy with a new toy and took the boat through its paces at flank speed, and then brought it back into the dock. That was the beginning of our friendship, and we spent a lot of time that summer fishing together or separately, usually on our own boats. Peter had a beautifully appointed 25-foot Bertram. Betty and Peter's wife, Reyn, also enjoyed one another's company.

Peter was a most interesting man—tall, handsome, with a certain regal bearing that made him impressive wherever he went. I learned early on that Peter's father, George, had been the commander of the elite Chevalier guard of Tsar Nicholas II. He and his first wife, a Russian princess, fled during the Russian Revolution. Sadly, his wife died when they got to Constantinople, Turkey. Eventually, Peter's father made his way to the United States and ended up in Chicago where he knew no one. He was, however, an accomplished pianist, and on a special occasion when he was performing for a family who owned the Crane Plumbing Company, he met his future wife, Maroussa, their daughter. They raised their sons, Peter and Jack, in Lake Forest, Illinois. Both boys were endowed with their mother's social skills and their father's brilliance. Eventually the family moved to Tucson. Peter became a partner in a law firm, and Jack became a professor at Stanford University. I greatly enjoyed my friendship with both of them. Peter became a board member of Up with People and also the legal counsel of the company. Peter and his wife, Reyn, had two sons, Steve and Michael, and with our two daughters, Jenny and Katie, we did a lot together.

Peter and Jack joined me when I went to see Captain Gene Cernan's Apollo 10 launch at Cape Kennedy. On the way driving we stopped for breakfast. Being a Southern boy I suggested that my two friends try grits with their eggs, sausage, biscuits, and gravy. When the grits arrived, both Peter and Jack started to put sugar and cream on them. Our waitress observed this, and her eyes grew as wide as teacups. She said with astonishment, "Boys, this is not cream of wheat; this here is grits—you put butter and salt on them and you see how good they are." Unfortunately, the boys wouldn't give them a try!

Over the years, Peter became a man I totally trusted, and he shared my passion about the development of Up with People. Quite a few times his brilliance and expertise kept us out of legal difficulties. To his credit he also had the ability to win the trust and friendship of the other board members and quite often they would speak to him about matters that concerned them.

Both Peter and I loved big game fishing and since we both had boats, we often competed in tournaments and won a number of them. In those early years the largest sailfish on light tackle—a 28-pound test line—won first prize.

One year we invited the grand old man of the Sea of Cortez, the American actor Ray Cannon, to be our special guest at the next tournament. Ray had published the first authentic story of the wildlife in the Sea of Cortez. He was also the founder of the Vagabundos del Mar, a passionate group of fishermen who fished together in their small boats for safety. Some 12 or 15 of them arrived with Ray, trailering their boats from California. They were determined to go home with all the trophies. Since all is fair in war and fishing, Peter and I came up with quite a crooked plan known only to the two of us, and it worked like magic. Every hour on the hour during the tournament, each boat had to report on strikes, fish landed, and fish released, but in between there was much chatter. When there was a little bit of silence, Peter and I would strike up a conversation about the great schools of sailfish, dorado, and marlin we were encountering. Immediately, one of the Vagabundos would call back and ask for our position. Of course, as you can imagine, one of us—usually Peter, with his stronger radio—would give him a phony position. We'd say we were just off the mouth of the Yaqui River, and they would ask where the hell the Yaqui River was, and Peter would give completely fictitious directions. We of course were fishing miles from there, but that was way before fishing boats were equipped with a Global Positioning System. This worked well for the first two days of the tournament, but on the last day when they followed the false information, they got into more fish than any of us saw during the rest of the tournament. Fortunately, our team still won the tournament, but it was close. The good news is that our yacht club and friends fishing out of San Carlos remained close friends with all the Vagabundos—especially their founder, Ray Cannon.

One memorable occasion was in the Hawaiian Islands. Another good friend named Peter Fithian, the founder of Hawaiian International Billfish Tournament, invited me to put together a Mexican team and come fish in the tournament. So, Peter Voevodsky and I went to work and enlisted our friend from Guaymas, Ernesto Zaragoza, owner of a chain of supermarkets and a shrimp fleet. He, in turn, helped pick a team of leading local citizens, all of whom came eagerly with their wives. It was a festive time. The opening ceremony started with a parade; the six of us were seated in convertibles driving through town, along with 18 to 20 other national teams. When we reached Pearl Harbor, the teams were lined up in a big circle around the flagpole and the band. Each team was announced, followed by applause and the hoisting of the national flag on the yardarm of the flagpole while the band played that country's national anthem. It was quite a prestigious if somewhat solemn occasion. However, when the Mexican flag was hoisted and the band struck up the Mexican national anthem to the great surprise of Juan Belk and Pedro Voevodsky, our team sang the words at the top of their lungs. The picture the next day in the Guaymas newspaper showed the two *gringos* trying desperately to follow along. In the same picture there was the port captain of Guaymas singing away but his fly was down. The caption under the picture was, "The port of Guaymas is always open!"

Our Mexican group was the talk of the tournament, and since each day during the week we switched boats, all the captains were vying for them. We had one marlin strike during the tournament. The designated fisherman almost fell over backward when it struck but unfortunately the fish was not on the other end of the line. Still, it didn't matter to the Mexicans, who enjoyed every minute of the experience and were constantly thanking Peter and me for the arrangements. And at the final banquet, though they hadn't won anything, when the Mexican team was introduced they received the loudest ovation of the evening.

I would be remiss in talking about Peter and Reyn not to mention a wonderful barge trip we took in the south of France on the Canal du Midi. There was Bill and Sue Small; Bill was the owner and publisher of the afternoon paper in Tucson, *The Citizen*. They brought as their guests Jim and Betty Geehan; he was the lead editor of *The Citizen*. To be honest, I thought a slow trip by French barge would be boring and arranged an extra day in Bonn where I visited with Mrs. Hannelore Kohl, wife of the German chancellor. We were planning for one of our casts to participate with her favorite charity. However, when I arrived in France I was pleasantly surprised and excited to have a beautifully appointed barge totally at our disposal with a captain, superb cook, and steward. It was September and a full Moon when we celebrated Reyn's birthday. The barge floated in the canal among the farmland so each evening we sat on the upper deck for cocktails, enjoying the local wine and cheeses that were acquired each night when the barge was docked. Even at 8:00 in the evening it was still light, and we could see the workers in the vineyards on one side of the boat and on the other several small tractors cutting a large wheat field far from the hustle and bustle of the big cities!

Betty and I both believe that the older you get, the more you appreciate trusted friends. Peter and Reyn have been that for us, and we are forever grateful.

We're still planning for the future with a passion to pursue our unfinished dreams—never turn these loose—they keep you leaning into the wind and into the future!

Above: The Great House, home of J. Skottowe Wannamaker and his wife, Lillian. They were affectionately called Papoo and Mamoo by their grandchildren.

Below Left: The Reverend J. Blanton Belk and J. Blanton Belk Jr. after a duck shoot in 1933.

Below Right: Papoo Wannamaker and "Brother" Blanton Belk going fishing, 1929.

Above Left: The Reverend J. Blanton Belk with the prize turkey that he shot to celebrate the birth of his daughter, Jane, in 1926.

Above Center: Blanton and best buddy, Hence, embark on a hike up Mount Mitchell, 1935.

Above Right: Blanton at age 13 on his bike, delivering the *Richmond Times-Dispatch*, 1938.

Left: Cadet Blanton Belk, Naval V-12 Program, University of North Carolina, 1943.

Below: The Wilkes children all dressed up for Easter Sunday, 1943.

Left: Kay and Bill Wilkes, Betty Belk's mother and father, wintering in Florida, 1945.

Bottom: Blanton Belk marching with other international veterans at Mackinac Island, Michigan, 1946.

Below: Betty Wilkes, Summit High School sophomore, 1945.

Above Left: Jennie Belk and her son, Ensign Blanton Belk, in Richmond, Virginia, 1945.

Above Right: Bill and Kay Wilkes and their children, Peg, Ann, Tom, Bill, and Betty, in Summit, New Jersey, circa 1946.

Right: Carol Deane, Virginia Crary, and Betty Wilkes, train mates on the tour of India, 1952.

Below: Mr. and Mrs. J. Blanton Belk Jr. on the way to their wedding reception in Short Hills, New Jersey, on December 11, 1954.

Left: Charles P. Howard greets newlyweds Mr. and Mrs. J. Blanton Belk Jr. while Betty's sister Ann looks on, December 11, 1954.

Center Left: Prince Richard of Hesse-Kassel, Blanton Belk, Erich Peyer, and Ernst Reinecke attend Chancellor Konrad Adenauer's funeral in Bonn, West Germany, April 1967.

Below: Guest book page signed by Dr. Martin Luther King Jr, his father Rev. Martin Luther King Sr., and Rev. Ralph Abernathy at a dinner hosted by J. Blanton Belk in Washington, DC, May 17, 1957, after Dr. King's first speech given at the Lincoln Memorial during the Prayer Pilgrimage for Freedom.

Right: Cast member Emiko Chiba of Japan being greeted by Chancellor Adenauer in Bonn, May 1966.

Above: President Dwight Eisenhower and Blanton Belk watching a performance of Sing-Out/Up with People in Indio, California, on February 13, 1967.

Below Left: Her Majesty Queen Fabiola of Belgium escorted by Jean Wittouck greets the cast of Up with People, June 1969.

Below Right: Betty and Blanton Belk at the White House where an Up with People cast performed for the National Governor's Conference, February 1971.

Above Left: Former Mexican President Miguel Alemán Valdés and Blanton Belk in México City, spring 1975.

Above Top Right: Blanton Belk talking to Chinese students in Peking, China, May 1978.

Above Bottom Right: Blanton and Betty Belk with astronaut Captain Eugene Cernan in St. Peter's Square, April 1984.

Below Left: The four Belks—Betty, Blanton, Jenny, and Katie at home in Tucson, Arizona, 1977.

Below Right: Lunching with Lila and DeWitt Wallace, founders of *Reader's Digest* at their home, High Winds, April 1978.

Top: Up with People performance at the Super Bowl XIV halftime show at the Rose Bowl, Pasadena, California on January 20, 1980.

Above Left: Jesse Owens signing autographs for cast members at the ARCO Jesse Owens Games, August 1978.

Above Right: Manuel and Marie-Therese Arango following the Papal Audience with John Paul II in Rome, April 1984.

Below: Ros and Jim Boswell with Blanton and Betty Belk on the West Lake in Hangzhou during the first tour of China in May 1978.

Top, Above Left, and Above Right: Up with People archives (MS 491). Special Collections, University of Arizona Libraries. ©Up with People. Below: Courtesy of Anna Carlberg-Belfrage.

Above: Board Members Pieter van Vollenhoven, Wes Dixon, and Jim Boswell at the home of Jean Wittouck in Brussels, November 1983.

Left: Up with People's performance at Alken, Belgium, in November 1983 was attended by Their Majesties King Baudouin and Queen Fabiola of Belgium together with Her Royal Highness Princess Margriet of The Netherlands and her husband, Pieter van Vollenhoven.

Below Left: At the invitation of Their Majesties King Hussein and Queen Noor of Jordan an Up with People cast participated in the Jerash Festival, August 1984.

Top Left: Blanton and Betty Belk with Peter and Reyn Voevodsky on a trip to Europe in 1984.

Top Right: Betty Belk with Jim and Betty McDonald at Turtle Lake, Michigan, in fall 1985.

Above: Betty and Blanton Belk meet again with Mr. Wang Chinchen, Beijing, China, in December 1985.

Right: Betty Belk enjoying the sunshine in the moors of Scotland.

Above: Blanton Belk welcoming Her Royal Highness Princess Margriet of the Netherlands and her husband, Pieter van Vollenhoven, to the 25th Silver Anniversary Celebration in Denver, Colorado, July 1990.

Below Left: Mr. and Mrs. Preston Keevama of the Hopi Nation with Don and Maya Saul and Betty Belk in Santa Fe, New Mexico.

Below Right: Betty and Blanton Belk being received by Pope John Paul II at the Vatican in June 1990.

Above Right: Dinner for Tom Via on his retirement, with his wife Anne, and the Belks, January 8, 1984, Tucson, Arizona.

Right: Chancellor and Mrs. Helmut Kohl receiving the Founder's Award for Konrad Adenauer's contribution to the founding of Up with People in Bonn, May 1992.

Below: Blanton Belk with Eduard Malayan, Soviet diplomat and friend at the 25th Silver Anniversary Celebration in July 1990. Also present, Peter Coors, Chairman of the Board, Coors Brewing Company.

Above: Members of the Up with People Board of Directors after having lunch with Chancellor and Mrs. Helmut Kohl at their residence in Bonn, May 1992.

Left: Betty and Blanton Belk dancing into the future at their Golden Wedding Anniversary in Tucson, Arizona, December 11, 2004.

Below Left: Wes and Sue Dixon receiving the Founder's Award from Blanton Belk as daughter Lynn and Board Member Tom Cruickshank look on, summer 1993.

Below Right: Dr. and Mrs. Shoichiro Toyoda and Blanton Belk at Expo 2005 Aichi.

Above: Blanton Belk with his sisters, Lillian Youell, Jane Moncure, and Barbara Tinsley, and their mother, Jennie Belk, circa 1993.

Above Right: Jenny Belk's wedding to Ajay Gupta with Maid of Honor Katie Belk, Blanton and Betty Belk, at the Belk home in Tucson, Arizona, March 26, 1994.

Right: Katie Belk's wedding to Miguel Arenas with Matron of Honor Jenny Belk, Best Man Ajay Gupta, Betty and Blanton Belk, Tucson, Arizona, January 8, 2000.

Below: John M. Belk, Chairman of the Belk's Department Stores, and wife Claudia with Betty Belk during a tour of Italy, May 1998.

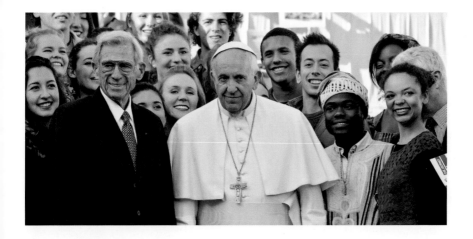

Above: Blanton Belk with Pope Francis I and a cast of Up with People, December 2015.

Below Top Left: Larry and Beatrice Lunt on vacation with Blanton and Betty Belk in México, 2005.

Below Bottom Left: Blanton Belk on *La Palomita*, San Carlos, Sonora, México.

Below Bottom Right: Blanton and Betty Belk at Sandhill Farm, 2010.

Below Top Right: The Colwell Brothers and Herb Allen at Big Mama's Karaoke Café in Seymour, Tennessee, in July 2003.

Above: Blanton's 95th birthday, February 2020.

Right: Annual Belk-Arenas Holiday Party, December 2019

Below: New Year's Eve 2017, Tucson, Arizona.

32

Our Daughters' Weddings

"Where the Roads Come Together"
Ev'ry heart beats a little differently.
Each soul is free to find its way
Like a river that winds its way to the sea.

Jenny, our first daughter, is a wonderful mixture of Betty's Yankee heritage and my Southern roots—she has the best of both. She is beautiful, forceful, intelligent, a keen observer of people, a voracious reader, and outspoken. When she was younger she became known as "The Band," meaning that she always had a plan and inspired all to go along with her. She loved fashion and was sartorially perfect in her dress. During her first year at the University of Arizona, she got to know two cousins from Iran. They were fellow students and the owners of a newly opened Benetton store in the Tucson Mall. Benetton was the fashion-forward Italian knitwear company that was all the rage in Europe. They recognized her sense of style and hired her. That became her first taste of the retail business. Jenny loved her job and soon became the store manager. She worked almost full time there while going to school.

During her sophomore year, Jenny interviewed in the spring 1985, was accepted and traveled with Up with People in Cast 85C. Jenny's cast traveled extensively in the Western US and Canada. They joined four other casts to perform the halftime show at the 1986 Super Bowl in New Orleans. Her cast spent the spring in Sweden, Norway, and Finland, and ended the year in the Eastern US and Canada. Jenny credits her year with Up with People as a turning point for her, and she came back with a new maturity and excitement for her future. She loved her time with Up with People and remains in close touch with many castmates to this day.

After she graduated from the University of Arizona with a BA degree in 1989, she pondered what to do next. So we got out a big map of the United States and she studied all the major cities. Finally, she picked Chicago. She had a great friend from her Up with People cast there, but otherwise, she was on her own. She decided to try her luck anyway, as she felt it was time to get to a big city. Betty and I knew it took all of her courage to step out on her own into the unknown. However, she did it and ended up being hired as a manager at the Gap store on Michigan Avenue for two years and later, manager at the Crabtree and Evelyn shop in the Water Tower Place.

One day, a childhood friend living in Chicago connected with her. He was Mike Voevodsky, who had just finished his business degree at Harvard University and had been hired by Quaker Oats to develop their Gatorade division. Mike's wife, Therese, invited Jenny to a surprise party for him. The day after the party Jenny telephoned Betty to say she had met a nice guy the previous evening. We took interest, but nothing developed immediately. A month passed and Jenny called Betty again, this time saying that the nice guy she had met was Ajay Gupta. He was originally from India, a recent MBA graduate with a degree in mechanical engineering from Illinois Institute of Technology. She then went on to say that Mike and Therese had invited her to a party being thrown by Ajay that night. She added that she was very tired but she thought she'd go anyway. Later, she found out that Ajay had the party just to have a chance to see Jenny again. That was the beginning.

Ajay had grown up in Lucknow and New Delhi, India, and went to school at Birla Vidya Mandir Nainital in Nainital, a beautiful town in the Himalayas. His father, Mohanlal Gupta, worked with the World Health Organization, specializing in developing clean water systems in many countries around the world.

Jenny was keen that we come to Chicago and meet Ajay, which we did. We quickly saw why Jenny had fallen in love. He was six foot two, trim and handsome with perfect manners. A few months later we returned to

Chicago, this time to meet Ajay's parents who were visiting from New Delhi. Betty charmed Ajay's mother, Sushila, and soon we were all great friends. When Ajay came to me to ask for Jenny's hand in marriage a few months later, I was delighted to give him our blessing. It was with the understanding that the wedding had better be in the spring, because fishing season and a busy summer were on the horizon. The Gupta's too, had a busy schedule so Betty and Jenny put together a wedding within several months. Jenny and Ajay were married on March 26, 1994, at our home in Tucson. Ajay's parents flew in from New Delhi. It was in the middle of the NCAA men's basketball tournament, and the University of Arizona was hoping to play in the Final Four. The day before, Jenny made me promise that there would be no TV blaring during the festivities and that the unseasonable rain would stop on the day itself. I said "yes" to both, and miraculously the rain stopped just before the wedding. Dr. Morris Martin, a dear English friend, conducted the service. The first thing he did at the start of the ceremony was announce that Arizona was in the Final Four. At that point the sun broke through the clouds and everyone cheered. The wedding was held outside. It was packed with friends and relatives, some sitting on chairs in the patio and others sitting in the living room with the French doors wide open.

Jenny did a masterful job in melding it all together and she looked beautiful in Betty's heirloom wedding dress. She had asked Dr. Martin, who she adored and greatly admired to participate in the ceremony. He had given the address at Betty's and my wedding in 1954, too. Also, he was completely at home with the Guptas. He had experienced living in India and had friendships with many of the leaders of India. Former President Rajendra Prasad had been a classmate of Morris's at Oxford—which helped him make a strong connection with Ajay's family.

Ajay was dressed in a traditional *shervani* suit that the family had brought from India for the wedding. When he tried it on in Tucson the day before the wedding it was much too small. His measurements at the tailor in New Delhi were from years earlier when he was just a 17-year-old boy and now he was a 30-year-old man! When he came out looking like he had squeezed into a child's suit, Jenny had a fit. Luckily for all of us we had a friend who was a seamstress and she spent much of the night reconstructing it—Ajay looked dashing, as did his brother Sanjay, as Best Man. His good friend Siddhartha Chadda, who had also married a wonderful American girl named Anne, started the ceremony. He read the most important rite of a Hindu marriage ceremony called the Seven Steps. In Hindi and Sanskrit the word *Saptapadi* means "seven steps." Following this, Jenny's close friend Kish Pisani read 1 Corinthians 13 from the New Testament. Bonnie Gradillas followed by a reading from the famous poet Kahlil Gibran. Then, Morris spoke directly to the young couple about marriage. Ajay's parents paid tribute to the coming together of two people representing different cultures and customs. Now they were united in their shared mission of life. Judge Joseph Livermore, a friend of Morris's led them through their marriage vows and then pronounced them husband and wife. Great applause followed when Ajay in the Western tradition kissed the bride. The whole event had come together beautifully. Afterward there were many toasts and dancing on the patio.

Some skeptics said that a marriage of two people from different cultures would never last, but we're happy to say that Ajay and Jenny have celebrated their 25th wedding anniversary. Part of their legacy is two wonderful daughters named Chameli and Surina, who will make their own marks on the world. Jenny's Maid of Honor was her sister Katie, our younger daughter. She was a shining star and the greatest support to her sister Jenny.

There is a legend about Katie Belk that we found her under a mushroom. She very quickly developed a cloud of blond hair, which suited her blue eyes nicely. Also, she was our athlete, loving to jump on the trampoline, ride horseback, and go scuba diving. Katie is definitely our best spincaster—an important skill in our fishing-loving family. When she was five, we moved to Brussels, Belgium, and enrolled her in a local nursery school. When the sun went down each week night, Katie would start to cry, knowing the next day she would be immersed in French, and not able to understand the nuns or the other students at all. It broke our hearts, but we knew it was her first big challenge in life and she would survive. When we returned to Tucson, she always did well in school and graduated from Salpointe Catholic High School. Katie applied and was accepted to travel with Up with People in 1988. Like her sister Jenny, Katie had a life-changing year on the road, and forged lasting friendships with many of her castmates. They traveled and performed in Belgium, West and East Germany, the Netherlands, Luxembourg, Quebec, Canada, and the Eastern United States. After returning from Up with People, she soon graduated from the University of Arizona with a BS degree in Business Administration in 1990. Katie then was hired by the Toyota Motor Company headquartered in Torrance, California and began working there in 1991. Katie had a cute apartment in nearby Long Beach and, of course, a sporty Toyota car. She loved living in Southern California, even after living through the tragic race riots with the whole city shut down for two days and despite the 6.7 magnitude Northridge earthquake in 1994.

Katie learned a lot at Toyota, working as a fledgling in their customer service call center. She was on a managerial track and could have moved up the corporate ladder there, but she felt she was meant to do something else with her life. Like me in my early years, she was searching for a purpose.

It was at that point that Katie ran into a friend from Tucson, Tom and Ann Via's daughter, Kelly. She was inspired by the work Kelly was doing as a therapist. Something in their conversation deeply touched Katie, and after doing some research she felt excited that she had found her calling. It would combine her love for fitness with her desire to heal and help people. Returning to Tucson, she enrolled again at the University of Arizona and spent the next two years completing required science courses. She was accepted to Regis University in Denver where she spent two intensive years earning a master's degree in physical therapy.

Toward the end of her time at Regis, Katie called her mother to say that she had finally met a wonderful guy named Miguel Arenas. He had graduated with honors from medical school in Peru and had been given a Permanent Resident Card to come to the United States. The next night she called saying, "We have a date for dinner tomorrow night!" So it started. Several days went by, and Katie and Miguel were spending more and more time together getting to know each other. Betty was in Tucson but I was in Denver at the Up with People office, so Katie invited me for coffee and bagels, saying, "This is nothing very serious, Dad. I just want you to meet this guy." Right away, I was impressed with this young doctor from Peru. I could tell immediately that the two of them were falling in love! Even with his medical degree from Peru, he was required to do another internship in the United States to be able to practice medicine here.

Miguel had not been in Peru since his father had died, and he needed to return home to see his family in Arequipa. He left her in Denver with the words, "Wait for me, I think we're meant to be together." After a whirl-wind courtship, he asked Katie to join him on a trip to meet his friends and family. Miguel showed Katie around Peru, including a visit to Machu Picchu and Lima. Miguel was a fine musician and played the mandolin with a *tuna* group from his college. Near the end of the trip, on his mother's birthday, he surprised both his mother and Katie by appearing outside the house in his ribboned *tuna* cape with his *tuna* group. They played a few songs and serenaded his mother and Katie. Then, Miguel went down on his knee in front of a crowd of family and friends and proposed marriage to Katie as she stood in the doorway. Needless to say, she was floored and thrilled. Katie didn't hesitate, and they were engaged.

Once they were back in the US, Katie landed her first job as a physical therapist in Crescent City, California. While Katie was at work, appar-ently, in between studying, Miguel put their mattress against the wall and practiced his golf swing—a new hobby. Miguel was studying for his board exams during this period. Crescent City was beautiful and very remote but soon but she was offered a job in Fremont, California, so they moved there. After all this moving around, Miguel was accepted as an intern at Tucson Medical Center and Katie landed a job as a full-time physical therapist. They were at last established and began to make plans for a wedding in Tucson on January 8, 2000. Isabel, Miguel's mother, and his Aunt Yolanda, came from Arequipa. Miguel wanted a Catholic ceremony so they decided on a wedding at the St. Thomas More Catholic Newman Center at the University of Arizona. Jenny was Katie's Matron of Honor, and Ajay was

Miguel's Best Man. Our eldest granddaughter, Chameli, age two, was the flower girl. Morris Martin suggested that Father Robert Burns would be a great help in planing and performing the wedding service. He made Katie, who is not Catholic, feel comfortable and welcome. It was a lovely ceremony with a reception at the Mountain Oyster Club. Every table in every room was full. A panicked event coordinator was trying to arrange a few extra seats for the overflowing crowd. In the end many of our family gave up our seats and just mingled including the bride and groom. Katie was such a beautiful bride and, like Jenny, wore Betty's heirloom wedding dress. As with our wedding 46 years before, they had Dr. Morris Martin speak and bless them on their way.

Miguel was finishing his residency in internal medicine but he really wanted to specialize in gastroenterology. His dream came true when he was accepted into the fellowship program for gastroenterology at the University of Arizona. This made it possible for him to settle permanently in Tucson. Meanwhile, Katie worked as a physical therapist and during this time their two sons, Thomas and Mateo, were born. So we were doubly glad that we lived nearby and not only to be part of their daily lives, but help with our two active grandsons! Miguel worked for some years with another doctor before he and Katie decided to open their own clinic and surgery center. What a leap of faith! Miguel is a superb gastroenterologist, and Katie has used her financial skills and great business acumen to build and manage the business from the ground up. With the dedication of these two, it has been a huge success.

With our multicultural family our horizons have been greatly expanded. We've enjoyed getting to know the countries of our sons-in-law. We have been privileged to enjoy wonderful trips to India and Peru together.

33

The Next Frontier

"Unfinished World"
There's still so much to do,
So far to go.

There's a statement that lingers with me and it was said on the night before it became the 21st century. I was inspired by something that the Librarian of Congress said when he was being interviewed on national TV and it goes something like this: When he was asked, what do you think will be the vital issue of the 21st century? He answered, I think the biggest issue facing us is whether the youth of the Western world can reach out and build trust and friendship with the youth of the Muslim world. We had felt that same urgency to reach out to the Muslim youth. In March 1975, we were invited to Morocco. The cast started in Tangier, went on to the capital city of Rabat, and then to the port city of Casablanca. The last two cities were El Jadida and Fez. They received a great welcome on their tour and cultural differences seemed to melt away.[1]

In March 1984, Her Majesty Queen Noor of Jordan was on a speaking tour of the United States sponsored by the Council on World Affairs. Dr. Landrum Bolling, representing the Jordan Society, accompanied her. On the Dallas, Texas portion of the tour, Dr. Bolling spoke to the group about the Jerash Festival, which was an important project to the queen. She wanted to have American groups participate in the Festival that year. Queen Noor hoped that Up with People might be available for such a performance in the summer and that they could find the needed funding. Thomas H. Cruikshank, President and CEO of Halliburton was in the audience and came forward to say that his company would be interested in sponsoring Up with People to perform at the Festival. I was excited when I heard this news and I felt compelled to fly to Dallas and thank Mr. Cruikshank personally. Tom later declared "Belk didn't even let the ink dry on my check before he was at my office." That was totally incorrect, it was that afternoon! It was the beginning of a great friendship. Tom Cruikshank became a board member of Up with People and a tremendous supporter.

In August 1984, 45 members of a cast who were touring Europe were privileged to perform in one of the oldest Roman cities in the world—Jerash, Jordan. They were invited to participate in the Jerash Festival of Culture and Arts. The site was the South Theater, which was built between 90-92 AD and seated 3,000 people. At the opening parade, 12 members of the cast were able to present to King Hussein and Queen Noor, patrons of the Festival, an album of their show. It was a close-to-capacity audience for the first show Up with People had performed in Jordan. Their three children attended the show on the second night. *Jordan Times* reported the great success of Up with People saying, "…the show was divided into sections which featured international folk dancing and songs, hit tunes and original music all of which carried the message of brotherhood of man and attempt-ed to instill a sense of hope among members of the audience."[2] At each of the two shows, students and members of the audience rushed to the front of the stage to meet the cast members and inquire about the possibility of participating in the program. Rajean Shepherd, cast co-manager said, "The people went wild when we sang in Arabic 'Safir Ya Habibi Wir-Dja,' the popular Jordanian song. We even had to do an immediate reprise of that song because of the wild cheers."[3]

Five years later, we received another invitation from Her Majesty Queen Noor to participate in the Festival, which we were delighted to do.

There was a beautiful song titled "The Last Embrace" in the Festival show in 1995. I inquired of Paul Colwell, what the storyline was behind it. He recounted, *When the Cold War ended new nations emerged and ethnic and sectarian conflicts erupted. I was particularly moved by a photo shown on the news around the world in 1993 from the Siege of Sarajaveo. A year later I learned the details of the story from a TV documentary. A young couple lay together, mortally wounded, on a bridge in "no man's land." The girl, a Muslim, and the boy, a Christian, were engaged to be married and were trying to escape the war in their "beloved" city. To me they symbolized the hopes of the young generation for a world that embraces diversity and human dignity. "The Last Embrace" was recorded in London and very fittingly sung by two sisters from Serbia.*

In 1996, a cast of 40 toured Turkey and performed shows in Ankara and the Cappadocia Region. They were based at the University of Ankara and the students of Up with People were paired up with Turkish students who acted as hosts for the visit. Assistant Cast Manager Kent MacLennan said, "It was a great opportunity to really get a sense of what young people were thinking about growing up there…."[4]

I had always known that Israel was an important country and I had long promised the students of Up with People that we would go there. We needed to find an opening, which we did through Board Member Bob Marbut. A delegation of 101 strong representing 18 countries, including many alumni who wanted to participate in this historic moment, arrived in Israel in June 2014. The two-week tour was to include two performances and community service with five organizations.[5]

The invitation had come from Roni Chaimovski, a former cabinet minister and naval commander of a PT boat combat flotilla. Bob and Roni were partners in building a new corporation that would provide security for very large companies. Betty and I were flying from Tucson to Tel Aviv via New York but were held up there. We finally landed some three to four hours late. Our tour coordinator Paul Whitaker was there with a car to meet us. He did his best driving us to Tiberius, which was 50 or 60 miles up the road, where the cast was performing. However, we arrived in the midst of the intermission. As we walked in the lobby of the theater a man broke from his conversation and came towards us with a loud voice, "Here come two friends, Blanton and Betty Belk, welcome." It was our host Roni Chaimovski. Then we were welcomed by Bob Marbut and his wife, Jan. At the end of the performance, there was a solid ovation.

The next morning we looked out our hotel windows across the gleaming Sea of Galilee. I was carried back to the many times I'd heard my father preach about the sea where Jesus walked on the water. Shortly thereafter, we were invited to join the cast and guests for a boat ride and lunch on the Sea of Galilee.

Bob had introduced us some years previously when Mr. Chaimovski was visiting New York, and I liked him right away—another navy man full of life and energy with many stories. The second night we were in Israel, Roni invited Betty and me along with Bob and Jan Marbut for dinner at a wonderful restaurant in downtown Tel Aviv. I was seated next to Tami, Roni's charming wife, who kept telling me how excited she was having experienced the first performance of Up with People in Tiberius.

During the second course Roni turned to me and said, "How's it going for you, Blanton?" I told him how impressed I was with the hospitality of everyone we met but added, almost in jest, "I haven't met any navy men yet." Roni got right up from the table and walked to a quiet corner, speaking into his cell phone. When he came back to the table he said, "You have a date with Vice Admiral David Ben Ba'ashat who had been our commander of the Israeli Navy from 2004 to 2007." I was taken aback because as a naval lieutenant I didn't often hobnob with vice admirals. Still, the next morning I had a delightful hour with Vice Admiral Ben Ba'ashat. He was a super human being who had a love affair with the United States. He was a graduate of the US Naval War College. Also, Ben-Ba'ashat had been awarded the United States' highest decoration for a foreign military officer, the Legion of Merit. He was keen to know what he described as "this thing called Up with People that Roni has gotten himself involved with." He and Roni were close friends. The admiral wanted a full briefing from me, and I was happy to oblige weaving in General Dwight Eisenhower and General Curtis LeMay. Vice Admiral Ben Ba'ashat was impressed with our mission to prepare our students for global leadership. They would gain special skills to meet the needs of their cities and communities.

The next day all 101 of us were transported by bus from Tel Aviv to Jerusalem. We had lunch in the Old City with a briefing on the situation in Jerusalem, over which both Palestinians and Jews claim ownership as their capital. Of course, there were many photographs taken along the Wailing Wall. When we returned to our hotel in Tel Aviv my phone was blinking away with messages, all from the admiral wanting me to telephone. When I did, he said, "I've been continually thinking of our conversation yesterday and I have some thoughts. Please bring your wife and join me and my brother, Samuel, at the Hilton Tel Aviv lounge tomorrow afternoon at 5:00 p.m. sharp."

Betty and I were there waiting for them when they arrived. I've always held the conviction that those who get there earliest win! We were introduced to David's brother, Samuel Ben Ba'ashat. He and Roni had served together in the Israeli Navy and were close friends. A quite charming young woman from the US Embassy who represented the Fulbright Scholarship Program also joined us. She immediately said, "When I heard you were here with Up with People I telephoned my friend, Shahnee Barak Chen-Zion in Los Angeles who is an alumna of your program so I'm all up to date." Our new friend Samuel dove right in saying, "My brother shared with me your vision to have young Israelis and young Palestinians travel together in your program. I have thoroughly checked you out, and Israeli security confirms that you are totally apolitical and nonsectarian. A year in your program would give training to our young people. They would return prepared to take leadership in their communities. Furthermore, if we could succeed in getting our government to recognize officially that you provide this type of leadership training then, we could have our young Israelis travel with you. Perhaps receive one year's credit for their military obligation." He then added, "There are official links with the Palestinians and although it would be difficult, I think we could secure an equal number of their young people to travel. Perhaps, just perhaps, they and the young Israelis might become friends and bond together with new ideas for the future of our countries." The young woman from the embassy spoke up saying, "Mr. Ben Ba'ashat, you are so well-recognized and positioned in Israel that I think you could urge the Israeli government to give official recognition to this program."

On June 19, Roni and our military friends were given permission for us to set up our equipment in a popular square in Ramat Gan, a city in the Tel Aviv District, and put on our performance. The word that came down from the government officials that Up with People and the spirit and hope represented was needed more than ever before—go on with the show!

Up with People had been fortunate to be able to perform in Israel. Before we left, Roni and his committee deemed it a success and said they were happy with the response of young and old alike. They considered this trip the beginning of a long-term relationship. Vice Admiral Ben Ba'ashat also assured me that when the time was ripe he would raise the possibility of an official recognition of our leadership program.

Betty and I sent special thanks to Charles Jarrett, Chairman of Up with People's Board of Directors and a distinguished alumnus who joined us with his daughter on this trip. He had invited us personally and contributed generously to the funding for the project. We also thanked Bob Marbut for his leadership role with his close friend Roni in securing an invitation. Bob's commitment over the years finally culminated with this trip to Israel. Our staff and management remain alert and committed to finding a way to continue this opening with Israel.

Fulfilling my long-standing commitment to get Up with People to Israel was one important milestone of the second decade of the 21st century. Another was to get a cast to Cuba. As with visits to China and the Soviet Union, I had been pledging to casts of Up with People from the beginning that they would have the chance to link up with the young people of Cuba. Once I made that promise, I carried it with me, always looking for openings that could bring it to fruition. With regard to Cuba, I found just that through the provost. In 2012, Arizona was celebrating its 100th anniversary, and I felt we should use the occasion to strengthen our ties with our neighbor México. My colleague, Arch Brown, and I visited with the provost of the University of Arizona, Dr. Jacqueline Mok, who had taken a great interest in our program since the university library had accepted Up with People's Archive for their Special Collections. I informed her that I was going down to México City to invite the First Lady of México, Señora Margarita Zavala de Calderón, to be our special guest in

Tucson. Dr. Mok immediately suggested we meet with the assistant vice president for US-México affairs, Dr. José Lever, who was based in México City. She arranged an email introduction and I flew to México City with Korey Riggs, a Spanish-speaking alumnus.

It was a fortuitous connection, and Dr. Lever was captured with the concept of celebrating the relationship between our two countries. He literally took the next three days off to take us around the city and introduce us to academics, government people, and his personal friends in the US Embassy. At one point he said, "You've told me all about your visits to China, the Soviet Union, and other countries but you have not mentioned Cuba—do you have any interest in going to Cuba?" Of course that opened the door for me to tell him that we would be tremendously interested in his help. He immediately responded that he had a long friendship with Fernando Rojas, the Vice Minister of Culture, and he would be happy to serve as the go-between. México had kept their diplomatic and economic relationships with Cuba, and José would be a perfect representative—at long last we had found our man and our opening to Cuba!

Korey Riggs and I had a most interesting and delightful visit with Senora Zavala de Calderón at Los Pinos, the White House of México. When we walked into her drawing room she stood up and started singing, "Up, up with people, you meet them wherever you go!" She told us when we were seated that when she had first seen Viva la Gente—our brand in Latin America—as a young girl she had wanted to participate. We thanked her for receiving the cast at Los Pinos when they were in México. When we invited her to be the guest of honor at our gala in Tucson celebrating our two countries, she became quite thoughtful and serious. She immediately wanted to know whether the governor of Arizona would be present. She was not a fan of our governor but she seemed to be interested in coming, and she assured us she would talk it over with her husband and let us know. Sadly, she was advised that it would be unwise for her to go in person—however, she sent a very thoughtful video to be shown at our gala.

Along with celebrating the 100th anniversary of Arizona, we planned to pay tribute to the University of Arizona and their decision to house Up with People's Archive in their Special Collection. Arch Brown and I were both on the board of the Friends of the Library at the university and went to work to raise funds for processing our archival collection. We had an amazing response to our efforts to sell advance tables of eight for $5,000 each. Everyone we approached bought a table—it was 100 percent, not one single no! When we visited with a friend, one of the leading philanthropists and real estate leaders in the community, he asked how much? When I said $5,000, he said immediately, "I agree—I know if I don't agree quickly you'll be asking for bigger money!" Another good friend said, "Is that all you want?" While we were thinking how to respond, he said, "I'll buy three tables for my family and friends." We were constantly reminded of the value Tucson placed on Up with People.

The celebration was filled to capacity. People wanted to show their backing for the relationship between Arizona and our neighbor to the south, México. It was a spectacular opening with the cast of Up with People parading in with the flags of the nations, ending on the stage with the Stars and Stripes next to the Mexican national flag. Everyone stood as the cast sang together our national anthem and then the national anthem of México. This was followed by the video from Senora Margarita Zavala. It was done in both Spanish and English, and she spoke from the heart.

Continuing with our plans for Cuba, during the next months, José Lever made several trips there to see his friend Fernando Rojas. He was interested but cautious. Dr. Lever answered all of the vice minister's questions as best he could. He underlined that Up with People did not belong to the US State Department or any other branch of the US government, that it was completely apolitical and nonsectarian. Finally, Vice Minister Rojas wanted to test the waters himself and invited me as the founder and Dale Penny as CEO of the organization to come to Cuba. So we went. We were both struck immediately with the widespread poverty in the country, but at the same time the most open and hospitable people. The first morning we were taken in to meet Vice Minister Fernando Rojas in his government office building. We had worked on our presentation and were prepared to answer his questions, but lo and behold there were no questions. He welcomed us with a handshake. As soon as we were seated, he started complaining bitterly about our tour coordinator, Paul Whitaker. It was a tirade, accusing Paul of not giving him accurate figures as to how many were coming and what their category would be when they arrived. He wanted to know if they would be students, musicians, educators, or what? Furthermore, were they coming from the United States or elsewhere? The more the vice minister paced the floor and attacked Paul, the more obvious it became he was demonstrating his power. When it ended, Dale and I sat there until he stood up and said, "Thank you for coming." We were dismissed. We grabbed a cab and went back to our hotel, both feeling we had wasted a trip coming to Cuba.

Later that evening, Paul telephoned, saying he had just had a call from Fernando Rojas who told him, "I like your two top men and I would like to host a dinner party in their honor at my club at 9:00 this evening." We were completely astonished but relieved. Somehow, we had lived through a test by not jumping in to protect our man and leaving him on his own.

The dinner party was a success and Vice Minister Rojas was a completely different personality, full of charm and civility. He was introduced to our staff and impressed us during the meal by remembering each person's name. He said at one point, "I have been talking to José and understand you're incorporated in México. I would suggest you come to Cuba as Viva la Gente." Towards the end of the meal he turned to me and said, "Since you are from Arizona do you know Senator Jeff Flake?" When I responded that I did, he asked that I invite the senator to come with the cast to Cuba. I replied that it would be helpful if he could put the invitation in writing, at which point he clapped his hands and asked for paper and pen. While we all watched, he penned a letter to Senator Flake, folding it up tightly and handing it to me, saying, "Please give this to the senator." The point registered that he did not want the letter to go through the mail since it was a no-no for a Cuban cabinet minister to have a personal link with a US government official.

After many toasts with Cuban mojitos and hugs we departed. The first thing I did when we returned to the United States was to telephone

Senator Flake's chief of staff in Washington and brief him on what had transpired. He understood Vice Minister Rojas's desire not to go through the mail and said he would talk to the senator and get back in touch. Several days later he telephoned asking if Betty and I could meet the senator in Nogales, Arizona, the following Wednesday when the senator was flying in for meetings. When Senator Flake arrived he was met by an official delegation, and then he spotted us and came straight over saying, "I hear you have a message from my friend Vice Minister Fernando Rojas." He promptly read the letter and asked, "When are you going back?" I said, "Next Tuesday." He said, "I can't go until after the elections, but I will go in November. How many are going?" I told him 112 from 14 to 16 different countries. He said, "That's terrific! We need more and more of this international cultural exchange." He thought it was a good idea to have one of his staff take a picture of us delivering the letter, which we could take back to Vice Minister Rojas in Cuba. His staff took the picture, which I passed along to him.

The senator and his staff were great help on our trip to Cuba in briefing the US State Department and sending direct word to Jeffrey DeLaurentis, the section chief of the US Interests Section Havana. When one of our distinguished board members, Tom Cruikshank, heard of this exchange between Fernando Rojas and Senator Flake, he said to me, "I'm so glad to hear at your age you've found a new job as a courier!"

Paul Colwell remembered: *While we had long since passed the torch of show productions to our younger colleagues, we were still consulted on some of the writing. In 2014, Ralph and I were asked to help write a song for Cuba. Our friend and Up with People Board Member, Larry F. Lunt, who had lived in Cuba for a time as a boy, set up a writing/recording session in New York City. Among others, we collaborated with Grammy-winning record producer Andres Levin from Venezuela, Ken Ashby, and our two sons, Jeb and Clayton, to produce "Cuba en mi Corazon." We traveled to Cuba with the cast, and with our sons, performed the song in the shows. A truly unforgettable experience.*

When I telephoned another of our board members, Manuel Arango, in México City and briefed him on the situation, he said, "I want to go with you. My mother was born in Cuba, and I've never been there. Why don't you and Betty join me in México City and fly in my private plane?" He then added, "I'll invite 4 or 5 of my closest friends to come. It'll be a great adventure."

We took Fernando Rojas's advice and flew 112 people from México City to Havana.[6] Sixty-nine of these were with the Up with People cast representing 14-16 nationalities. The guests all lived in five-star hotels, but our students lived with university students in a school where there were 25 or more students for every bathroom. The trip turned out to be a great learning experience for our students and the Cubans they met. The last evening, the music and dance school where the cast had been living gave an outstanding performance for our cast. Following that, Up with People performed for them. There was electricity in the air as the young Cubans and our students came together.

Our first show was by invitation only, issued by the government, and it was definitely planned that way so the leadership of the country could check us out. At intermission, Jeffrey DeLaurentis came over and said to me, "I hope someone will tell your students what they have accomplished tonight. What you have demonstrated is something very new for the youth of Cuba, who have never seen anything like this before. They have been schooled that North America is the big devil and that they have no friends in the world. Here you are with your young Americans performing with their friends from other countries. Thank you for coming."

Our main public performance was at the soccer field in Havana, and it poured rain for the previous 24 hours. It was a tropical storm out of the Caribbean, and we all went to bed that night thinking it would be impossible to have an outdoor performance. During the day it continued to rain, and Paul Whitaker kept stretching it as far as he could by changing the opening from 8:00 to 9:00 p.m. We held our breath. Betty and I were seated with Manuel and his guests on the second floor that overlooked the soccer field. Promptly at 8:15 p.m. the storm stopped and the skies cleared. Suddenly, from a completely empty soccer field people poured out from under the trees and umbrellas and the show started. Within five minutes several drummers had appeared in the audience drumming with the beat coming off the stage. At that point one of Manuel's friends grabbed him and said, "Come here and look down at the audience! There is another show going on there. They are all singing and dancing in the aisles."[7]

The next day, according to Manuel, he lived through quite an emotional moment when he went alone to stand in front of the house where his mother had been born in Havana. That afternoon we flew with him back to México. Everyone was animated, discussing what we had seen and done. Manuel was particularly concerned that México be a good neighbor to Cuba and help them where possible when the country truly opens up and materialism and money come pouring in. He said, "I'm already considering bringing some of our top CEOs from México. That might help them through such a transition."

When Betty and I arrived back in Tucson we received an email from Manuel saying, "I have known you and been involved with Up with People for some 40 years but what I experienced in Cuba convinced me that in many ways Up with People has come of age. I believe with the right backing it can play a part in bringing countries together."

34

Sandhill Farm

"Walk Lightly"
Walk lightly [on the Earth]
Such a beautiful sight
It wouldn't be right to let it go.

To begin with the name, Sandhill Farm is a misnomer because it is not a farm. It is a piece of property we purchased incrementally in Cochise County in Southern Arizona beginning in 1987 with the purpose of creating a conservation easement. The name "Sandhill" is a tribute to the 30,000 to 40,000 Sandhill cranes that winter in our valley, the Whitewater. On some days, particularly when it's very windy, 4,000 or 5,000 of these magnificent birds use our property. Their wonderful call gives one a feeling of antiquity. At this writing, we own 1,000 acres of deeded land that has been acquired parcel by parcel over the years. Very important to us and included in this parcel is 112 acres of seasonal wetland and 12 acres of irrigated farmland. We have two miles of the Whitewater Draw, headwaters of the Mexican Rio Yaqui, which runs through México into the Sea of Cortez. The Whitewater Draw attracts many migrating bird species, a wide variety of waterfowl, and upland game. It is also a habitat for threatened and endangered species. We have received a grant from the US Department of Agriculture to save the endangered southwestern willow flycatcher. This entailed planting (so far) 640 Goodding's black willow trees to attract the willow flycatcher for nesting.

So how did I get involved in such projects? The answer is quite simple. Growing up in Virginia I developed a passion for duck hunting. When I came west to Tucson and saw the endless miles of dry desert land, I thought my duck hunting days were over. I didn't give up, however, but started snooping around. I learned that even though Arizona is not on a main flyway of the duck migration, it is on the edge of the Pacific Flyway. If there is water, it's like a magnet to waterfowl flying over Arizona on their way to the rice fields in México. I was most fortunate to have Tom Via as a best friend. Even though at that point he was not experienced in duck hunting, he soon caught my enthusiasm. Our search took us to interesting people and interesting wetlands and ponds. We made friends with Jim Glover, a cotton farmer and crop duster pilot in the Avra Valley, which is known for its longleaf Pima cotton. Since he was flying around the valley with his crop dusting, we asked him if he was spotting any wetlands or stock tanks. He answered, "I've seen quite a few but I also have two ponds at the back of my property that sometimes hold quite a few ducks." That was the beginning. There were great shady trees around the ponds, and it became a destination point for our family picnics. Of course, we built duck blinds in both ponds. It was an ideal spot only 35 minutes from my house and Tom's. We could drive there and have a morning shoot and be home by 9:30 a.m. Sadly, civilization and new homes being built eventually brought an end to that.

Sometime later, Tom and I started our Buenos Aires (BA) Duck Club and developed our friendship with George Vensel and his wife, Linda. When I informed Jim Boswell that I had secured a hunting lease on the BA Ranch, he played it very cool. He said he would like to fly over and hunt quail with me, which he did the following weekend. I picked him up at the airport where he landed in his Cessna Citation jet. He came out with his hunting clothes and boots on, carrying one of his 20-gauge side by side guns. It was one of the matched pair he had acquired when we had shot red-legged partridges in Spain. He was anxious to get in a full day of hunting since he planned to fly back late that afternoon, so I stepped on the gas. I had hunted with George the preceding weekend so I got Jim to the birds quickly. We both shot well but I think I was one bird over him. When we went back to the pickup for a cold drink, he said oh so casually,

"I'm glad to see the old BA Ranch again. I used to own it along with the Gill brothers." I answered equally casually, "Oh, really." He was caught off guard and thought I hadn't heard him so he repeated saying, "I said I used to own this ranch with the Gill brothers." I answered, "Yes, I know, you just told me that." This was the game we played together called "one-up-manship," but that was one of the few times I held my own.

My shorthair pointer dog, Duke, greatly impressed Jim. When he made a nice crossing shot on a Gambel's quail, the dog went out to retrieve the bird. Suddenly Duke rose on point while holding the first bird in his mouth. He stayed that way until Jim walked in front of him and shot the second bird. All in all it was a perfect day for both of us. We had enjoyed poking fun at each other especially when one of us missed a shot. The other would say, "I don't see how you could miss such an easy shot as that!" We soon hit our limit of 15 quail each, and we went back to the car and had a nice cold Bohemia Mexican beer. Before we could relax he said, "Come along with your beer. We're going to collect some mesquite wood. There's no wood like it for the barbecue, and I promised Ros I'd bring a load back." Once we loaded the wood into the nose compartment of the Citation, we cleaned the birds putting them in Ziploc bags on ice. He quickly agreed when I said, "Take my 15 as my gift to Ros." His faithful pilot, Al Stern, had the plane all ready to go. When Jim thanked me for the day he said, "Let's do it again soon, and I hope you'll shoot better next time!"

I always enjoyed having a place like the BA Ranch that I could share with friends, board members, and staff. Wes and Sue Dixon came from Lake Forest, Illinois, quite a few times and shot what we call a grand slam—Gambel's quail, Scaled quail, and a Mearns quail—and later had the three of them beautifully mounted.

After eight or nine wonderful years I had a telephone call from the ranch's manager, Jim Patton, saying, "Sad news—Arizona Game and Fish Department bought the BA Ranch in an attempt to save the Mexican masked bobwhite quail." Of course, it was a sad day for Tom, myself, and other good friends when we picked up our duck boats, closed down our campsite, and said goodbye to Jim and the ranch. When Tom and I went by to thank George for our unforgettable times at the BA, he said, "Call in about a month, I might have a thought for you for the future."

A month later, almost to the day, I telephoned George who said, "If you're free this weekend I'll take you down and show you my in-laws' ranch in Cochise County. The wildlife there might be of interest to you." George's father-in-law, Bill Cowan, met us with saddled horses and we had a terrific morning riding up the Whitewater Draw flushing ducks and quail as we went. I became more and more convinced that we had found our next area to develop. It was definitely a tipping point that led to over 30 years of building long-lasting friendships with ranchers, farmers, Ducks Unlimited, the Arizona Game and Fish Department, and the US Fish and Wildlife Service. Tom Via and I had lots of adventures getting to know the heads of all these organizations, ranches, and farms. The parcel that we had eyes on was owned by Bob Cowan, Bill's brother, and we acquired a foothold on this seasonal wetland when he agreed to our purchasing 20 acres of deeded land—the start of our Sandhill Farm—with Tom and I splitting ownership equally. At the same time, Carl Miller, a neighbor who earlier had acquired a section of land contiguous to our 20 acres, agreed to a long-range hunting lease on his 640 acres. Tom located an old trailer for our headquarters.

We thought we were well on our way when George Vensel came for a visit and reminded us that we needed water if we expected to attract waterfowl. He gave us the sad news that we had only inherited the rights for 10 acre-feet, which means 1 foot of water on 10 acres. He did have some good news: he'd found an old dike that was originally installed in 1950 and it could be grandfathered in, meaning we could legally fix it up. We got busy and found a new friend in the valley who had a large Caterpillar tractor and he fixed our dike. Water is like gold everywhere but especially in the desert.

We purchased the first 20 acres from the Ralph C. Cowan Ranch Ltd. The second transaction occurred in September 1999 for 60 deeded acres with two irrigation wells and irrigation authority for 13.6 acre-feet. In early 2000, Betty and I were both moved when Anne Via, the widow of our friend Tom, said that she had directed her lawyer to arrange for a quitclaim deed to transfer their half of the original 20 acres of Sandhill Farm over to us. We gave her a big hug and told her how much we missed Tom. The next transaction occurred in October 2001. This purchase included 760 acres and a 15-foot easement. In November 2004, we bought two more 80-acre parcels, which completed 1,000 acres of deeded land known as Sandhill Farm LLC. Joining me in the LLC were Betty Belk, Jenny Belk and Ajay Gupta, Katie Belk-Arenas and Miguel Arenas, David Gardner and Herbert Kai. When Carl Miller and his family ran into financial difficulties and put their 760 acres up for sale, the man who said "Buy it!" was Tommy Thomas, one of our Up with People Board Members from Albuquerque, New Mexico.

Tommy also urged me as the manager of Sandhill to encourage the members of the limited liability corporation to place a conservation easement on the property. I signed the deed of conservation easement for Sandhill Farm LLC to the Arizona Land and Water Trust, Inc. in May 2011. The purpose was to forever conserve the open space character, agricultural productivity, wildlife habitat, and scenic qualities of the subject property. Sandhill Farm LLC is primarily open rangeland, wetlands, and some seasonal sacaton prairie and agricultural land, and is an important part of the productive agricultural land still remaining in Cochise County. It is also used by landowners and a limited number of guests for observing wildlife and hunting during the legal seasons. Our property includes natural habitat with a variety of wildlife species, including Sandhill cranes, migrating waterfowl, ducks, geese, raptors, quail, dove, and several species of owls including the great horned and barn, as well as mule deer. The historic wetlands have been enhanced with a series of constructed dikes and earthen berms.

I spent four years working with the Arizona Water Resources Department in Phoenix to acquire more water for wildlife. Once we signed the deed for a conservation easement they took a new look. At the end of this time we had acquired 84 acre-feet of water, up from the original 10 acre-feet. In turn, the Natural Resources Conservation District wanted to work with us after we obtained the conservation easement and new water rights. We were given a grant to install sprinklers in our 13.5-acre agricultural area and provide fencing for the periphery of the 1,000 acres. Since the management of this grant fell on my shoulders, I immediately hired Neil Grantham, the top fence man in Cochise County, and others to put in the underground piping and sprinklers. Then 60 acres was ripped up and planted with native seeds.

Following the granting of the easement, Betty and I were hosting the state conservationist for Arizona from the Natural Resources Conservation Service. As we were driving her around the property she noticed our Goodding's willows. She said, "This is just what we're looking for as habitat for the endangered southwestern willow flycatcher. Perhaps we can collaborate on this project." Shortly after that the Department of Agriculture called and proposed a three- to five-year contract to plant 750 willow trees. In return, they would give us a solar water pump. The Sandhill LLC Board of Directors unanimously approved the request.

I must pay particular tribute to a true friend, water expert, and lover of all trees, shrubs, and bushes who came along and guided all of us volunteers in how to make this effort a success. Jim Davenport was in his element in February 2018 when 60 or 70 volunteers appeared at Sandhill Farm shortly after daylight to assist in planting the willow trees. Jim handled the troops beautifully, particularly the teenagers who came from two different high schools. It was a sight to see—some planting the willow branches, others putting in rich topsoil and tapping it down, and finally a group pouring water into the roots. Against all odds the job was finished by noon the following day. Jim organized and led this effort. Since then he has digitally tabulated all the trees that were planted and constantly checks on their growth.

One Friday after school and soccer practice, I picked up our two grandsons, Tommy and Teo, then ages 16 and 14, and drove us to Sandhill Farm. After a short but good night they were up for coffee, sweet rolls, and a trip in the Jeep to the duck blind. It was already cold but early in the season, before a migration of waterfowl had hit our area. As dawn snuck in they were sitting together in the blind and I was in the chair in the bushes some yards away. I thought of all I had learned from my father so many years ago sitting in a duck blind together, saying nothing but communicating on a deeper level. Silently, I watched our two grandsons through the underbrush and listened as they quietly sang together some of the most popular songs of the day. It was quite a magical moment for me as a grandfather. Suddenly my reverie was abruptly ended by the cacophony of the cries of 1,000 Sandhill cranes coming off their night's roost in flight to the cornfields. The boys were on their feet staring into the dawn sky at this happening. I was moved and thought that all the years of work developing Sandhill was worth this moment—a moment far greater than anything high-tech has created! The cranes, like sharks in the sea, are our touch with infinity. They have survived all, and we must claim a faith for our children and grandchildren that they too will survive and find their future.

EPILOGUE

When I, like you, watch the evening news, I'm carried back 55 years when America and the world were being torn apart by race riots. We are back at that point again, with the news of the horrendous murder of George Floyd in Minneapolis, Minnesota, seen by the world on television and on social media. Those scenes have gone viral. The whole world is watching.

My grandfather's words are still ringing in my ears: "Do something about the evil in our land." I believe he was talking about the enslavement and suppression of a whole race of people. I also remember Dr. Martin Luther King's assertion that character is more important than color. This set me on my life's work with Up with People.

We can't go back and change history, but we can commit ourselves to creating a society that is inclusive of all. We cannot put this on our government or even our neighbor. This is on all of us. We need a renewal to a commitment of what really matters. An understanding of those not like us, and a heartfelt understanding of those who are like us. It's not an easy task, but it's essential during this divisive time to do our best to build bridges of understanding. Always keeping in mind that peace is not just an idea. It is people becoming friends. It's an unfinished world and it's still in the making and all of us can play a part.

We are living in a most insecure time for the young as well as the old. Our four grandchildren are all with us now and we have learned a lot by listening to them---take interest in what the youth have to say!

Some years ago Jenny took her daughters, Surina, six months old and in a stroller, and three-year-old Chameli, to a book signing. They stood in a long line, waiting to meet renowned Mexican-American author Victor

Villaseñor. When they finally made it to the front of the line, he reached down, lifted Surina out of the stroller, and took her in his arms, and said to Jenny, "Listen to the little ones. They remember Heaven and will tell you about the angels."

May the Great Spirit be your guide and protector. We face an unknown future but we face it together with compassion and care for one another and the firm belief that we will have a future! It is proper to give the last words in this memoir to those whom it is dedicated, our grandchildren, who are the future.

As young people, we are frequently celebrated as "the future," but we think the world would be a better place if we were treated as the present. As we enter into adulthood, we are filled with anger and frustration at the division and destruction we have inherited from those before us. Our exceptional grandparents have taught us, not to ignore that anger, but to channel it into action. We are part of a fired-up generation, but also a hopeful, motivated, and united one. We refuse for our voices to be ignored until the future; we are ready to be heard now.

Chameli Belk-Gupta, age 22, and Surina Belk-Gupta, age 19

The glue that holds our turbulent world together is a dream: ideas of what the world could be. For us, our dream for the future is that one day all voices of every person no matter race, religion, sexuality, or gender will ring loud and clear in the halls of Congress. We will fight for our dreams but, in the meantime, dream on.

Tommy Belk-Arenas, age 18, and Teo Belk-Arenas, age 16

ACKNOWLEDGMENTS

Our eldest grandson said to me, "JB, when are you going to finish this memoir? I don't want to be your age when I read it!" So Tommy, if all goes according to plan you will have a copy of this book by the fall of 2020.

So many people—family, friends, board members, and alumni of Up with People have contributed to this story. There would never have been this memoir if it had not been for Betty Belk, my wife, partner, inspiration, and soulmate for over 65 years. On being informed that I was dedicating this book to her she said, in typical Betty Belk fashion, "Nonsense! your life and passion are a call to action for the young world and our grandchildren represent that future—it belongs to them!" Even as I write this, Betty with our good friend and Up with People archivist and alumna Elaine Crepeau are working tirelessly on the manuscript. They are verifying names, dates, and places. Elaine reached out to archivists and librarians in presidential, national, and state archives for information.

A heartfelt thanks and gratitude to our two daughters, Jenny Belk and Katie Belk–Arenas. No parents could ask for any more support and encouragement. They have been totally committed to making sure the book is published. We have also had the perspective of Jenny's husband, Ajay Gupta and Katie's husband, Dr. Miguel Arenas. Three years ago, the Arenas family invited us to live with them. What a perfect place it has been to finish this manuscript. Jenny visited us frequently from Houston and helped add humor and perspective to the book.

Our families supported us in every way. My cousin, the late John M. Belk, Chairman of the Board of Belk's Department Stores, was interested that I was writing this book. He gave a generous donation from the Belk

Foundation for which we are deeply grateful. We were glad that he and his wife Claudia traveled with us to Rome when Up with People performed for Pope John Paul II. Betty's extended family has been equally supportive. Her older sister, Ann, and husband Bob Hogan made a generous contribution at the beginning of this project. Their daughter, Margaret Hogan, a freelance editor, kindly offered her professional knowledge. We owe her a debt of gratitude for her help. Thank you, Margaret!

I must thank the late Ola Cook Henry, my executive assistant for many years. She kept me organized and maintained all my records. Those records have been invaluable as I write this story.

We thank the late Penelope Niven for all of her inspiration and help as we began this memoir. When Penny died in 2014, we lost heart and put it aside. My friend and alumnus of Up with People John Gonzalez strongly encouraged me to start writing again feeling that this story needed to be told. That was a defining moment! Betty joins me in gratitude and thanks to him.

Board member John Fuller and his wife Jeannie were among the first to commit funding for this book. Thank you, John and Jeannie! A special thanks to the James G. Boswell Foundation and to the late Jim and Ros Boswell for their very generous support and encouragement. Wholehearted thanks to long-serving board member, the late Jerry Jarrett and his late wife Martha for their generous contribution. Kelly Via Mollison and her husband Mark, and Tracy Via Tolmie and her husband David made a generous gift in memory of their parents, our dear friends Tom and Anne Via. Thank you! Thank you, General Steve and Danielle DeConcini Thu for your wholehearted backing and support. We thank our dear friend, the late A. E. "Tommy" Thomas for his generosity.

My very dear friend and one of our musical founders, the late Ralph Colwell, listened to the many readings of the chapters. After one occasion he said, "I've never heard these stories before. I'm sure it will be a revelation to all the present and former Up with People staff and alumni to learn what you and Betty were actually doing over the years." Ralph's personal archival papers have been shared by his wife Debbie, who has also been a great support. Thank you, Ralph and Debbie!

Our thanks go out to Paul Colwell, another friend and musical founder for weaving Up with People song lyrics into our chapter headings and for generously providing his recollections of the development of the whole musical component of Up with People. It was a labor of love and we thank him.

Thank you to all, from the earliest to the current writers who have created the music and the lyrics of over 375 songs. They have inspired millions with their musical genius and inspirational wisdom. My gratitude to the late and great Herb and Jane Allen, Frank Fields, Ken Ashby, Pat Murphy, Cabot Wade, John Tracy, Dick Smith, Tim Clark, David Mackay, Eric Lentz, and Michael Bowerman.

We also want to thank the University of Arizona Libraries Special Collections for their research cooperation and their stewardship of both the Up with People Archive and the J. Blanton and Elizabeth (Betty) Belk Jr. Papers. It's been invaluable.

Thank you to our friend John Humenik for finding us such a great publisher. Our thanks to Pediment Publishing for leading us through the process to a great finish.

Thank you to Up with People for giving us permission to use their images and music lyrics in this work.

A SPECIAL THANK YOU

From my first thought of writing a memoir, I was sure I would need help. Luckily, I have gotten lots of it. However, one source stands out. She is Elaine Crepeau. Experienced librarian and archivist with prior experience in book production. She is also an enthusiastic and active alumna of Up with People.

Elaine has been a godsend as I worked to complete this memoir. No fact has gone unchecked, twice! No spelling or grammar mistakes have been overlooked. She has been selfless in her help and made time when some-times there was none. She has left no stone unturned yet has not sought remuneration for her colossal contribution to this project. (We intend to rectify this once the dust settles.)

Elaine is a global personality. She lived many years in Japan, and married Nubuo Kodama in 1987. There, they raised their son, Kenta, who was educated both in Japan and the US. He graduated from Boston College and is a software engineer. However, Elaine is as comfortable in Europe as she is in Japan or the United States. She appreciates the many diverse cultures in which she has been immersed over the years and is knowledge-able about them all.

Elaine M. Crepeau has enjoyed a lengthy and diverse career as a profes-sional librarian, archivist, and information consultant both in the US and Japan. During a college gap year, Elaine traveled with Cast 68C as an Up with People High School teacher where she found a passion for helping students with research and discovered her profession. Elaine went on to earn a BA in English Literature in 1972 and MS in Library and Information Studies, both from Florida State University, in 1973.

Since 2013, Elaine has been the corporate librarian/archivist for Up with People and performs in-depth historical research for the organization, its alumni, and the general public. She's the liaison between Up with People and Special Collections at the University of Arizona, where the Up with People Archive is housed. Prior to Up with People as archivist, Elaine was Head of Technical Services at the Belvedere-Tiburon (California) Library from 1997-2013. In Japan, she was the Senior Foreign Language Cataloging Librarian at Sophia University Library (Tokyo) from 1978-1992. Prior to accepting the position in Japan, Elaine was the Head of the Cataloging Department at Duke University Law Library (Durham, North Carolina).

Elaine has become part of our family. She is a trusted advisor and friend, and Betty, Jenny, and Katie all join me in expressing our gratitude for all she has done to get this memoir published. She has traveled back and forth in time with us, guided us with infinite patience and good humor all along the way.

Artwork by Surina Belk-Gupta.

MUSIC PERMISSIONS

"The Old Man and the Boy." (page 9) Music and lyrics by Paul Colwell and Bill Cates. ©1974 by Up with People. Used by permission.

"It Takes a Whole Village." (page 20) Music by Paul Colwell and Herbert Allen, lyrics by Pat Murphy, Paul Colwell, and John Kagaruki. ©1993 by Up with People. Used by permission.

"Home Foundation." (page 29) Music by Pat Murphy, Paul Carman, and Peter King, lyrics by Pat Murphy and John Kagaruki, ©1993 by Up with People. Used by permission.

"Mabuhay Pilipinas!" (page 34) Traditional Filipino melody, lyrics by Steve, Paul, and Ralph Colwell. ©1956 by Steve, Paul, and Ralph Colwell. Used by permission.

"We'll Be There." (page 46) Music by Stuart Leathwood and Gary Sulsh, lyrics by Paul and Ralph Colwell. ©1985 by Up with People. Used by permission.

"There's Gonna Be Another Day." (page 49) Music by Paul and Ralph Colwell, and Herbert Allen, lyrics by Paul and Ralph Colwell. ©1978 by Up with People. Used by permission.

"Room for Everyone." (page 58) Music and lyrics by Paul and Ralph Colwell, Herbert Allen, Pat Murphy, Ken Ashby, and Tom Sullivan. ©1984 by Up with People. Used by permission.

"Tomorrow's a Picture." (page 68) Music by Ken Ashby and Doug Holzwarth, lyrics by Ken Ashby. ©1977 by Up with People. Used by permission.

"We Shall Overcome."(page 73) Highlander Folk School songbook, 1948.

"Common Beat II." (page 79) Music and lyrics by Ken Ashby, Pat Murphy, and Guy Moon. ©2000 by Up with People. Used by permission.

"Does It Really Matter." (page 91) Music by Tim Clark, Pat Murphy, and Gregory Wachter, lyrics by Tim Clark and Pat Murphy. ©1989 by Up with People. Used by permission.

"Freedom Isn't Free." (page 99) Music and lyrics by Paul and Ralph Colwell, lyrics by Paul Colwell. ©1965 by Up with People. Used by permission.

"We Will Stand." (page 105) Music and lyrics by Cy Frost and Doug Olson. ©1997 by Up with People. Used by permission.

"Let the Rafters Ring." (page 113) Music and lyrics by Dick Smith. ©1966 by Up with People. Used by permission.

"Up with People." (page 122) Music and lyrics by Paul and Ralph Colwell. ©1965 by Up with People. Used by permission.

"Keep Young at Heart." (page 131) Music and lyrics by Glenn Close, Paul Colwell, and Herbert Allen. ©1966 by Up with People. Used by permission.

"The Beat of the Future." (page 136) Music by Herbert Allen, Ken Ashby, and Pat Murphy, lyrics by Ken Ashby, Paul and Ralph Colwell, and Pat Murphy. ©1985 by Up with People. Used by permission.

"The Further We Reach Out." (page 148) Music and lyrics by Paul Colwell, Frank Fields, and Ken Ashby. ©1971 by Up with People. Used by permission.

"With Everything Changing." (page 164) Music and lyrics by Paul Colwell and Bill Cates. ©1970 by Up with People. Used by permission.

"Can We Sing a Song of Peace?" (page 168) Music by Ken Ashby, lyrics by Paul Colwell and Ken Ashby. ©1981 by Up with People. Used by permission.

"Pays de Coeur/Hartelijk Land," (page 174) Music by Herbert Allen, Paul and Ralph Colwell, lyrics by Ralph and Paul Colwell and Chantal de Limelette. ©1980 by Up with People. Used by permission.

"In a Sacred Manner I Live."(page 186) Music and lyrics by Frank Fields. ©1972 by Up with People. Used by permission.

"Moon Rider." (page 191) Music by Paul and Ralph Colwell, and Herbert Allen, lyrics by Paul and Ralph Colwell. ©1977 by Up with People. Used by permission.

"Two Hundred Years and Just a Baby." (page 202) Music by Paul and Ralph Colwell, Herbert Allen, and David Mackay, lyrics by Paul and Ralph Colwell. ©1975 by Up with People. Used by permission.

"We Are Many, We Are One." (page 207) Music by Paul and Ralph Colwell, Herbert Allen, and Doug Holzwarth, lyrics by Paul and Ralph Colwell. ©1979 by Up with People. Used by permission.

"El Puente." (page 217) Music by Paul Colwell and Ken Ashby, lyrics by Paul Colwell and Marshall Cartledge. ©1977 by Up with People. Used by permission.

"Wó Men De You Yi Shēn Yòu Cháng." (page 223) Music by Paul Colwell and Herbert Allen, lyrics by Yao Tao Tsung and Paul Colwell. ©1978 by Up with People. Used by permission.

"Hearts Still Beating." (page 235) Music by Paul Colwell and Herbert Allen, lyrics by Paul Colwell. ©1989 by Up with People. Used by permission.

"The Day the People Came Together." (page 244) Music by Pat Murphy, Ralph Colwell, and Herbert Allen, lyrics by Paul and Ralph Colwell. ©1995 by Up with People. Used by permission.

"Cielito Lindo." (page 255) Music and lyrics by Quirino Mendoza y Cortés. 1882.

"These Are My People." (page 266) Music by Pat Murphy, lyrics by Paul Colwell. ©2000 by Up with People. Used by permission.

"Where the Roads Come Together." (page 279) Music by Paul Colwell and Herbert Allen, lyrics by Paul Colwell. ©1971 by Up with People. Used by permission.

"Unfinished World." (page 286) Music by Herbert Allen and Pat Murphy, lyrics by Paul Colwell and Pat Murphy. ©1987 by Up with People. Used by permission.

"Walk Lightly." (page 298) Music by Paul Colwell and Herbert Allen, lyrics by Paul Colwell, Ralph Colwell, and Ken Ashby. ©1983 by Up with People. Used by permission.

ENDNOTES

Some citations are to materials restricted at the time citations were made. The terms under which those restricted materials will be released is per agreements with University of Arizona.

PROLOGUE My Grandfather's Funeral

1.   James Newton. "Amazing Grace." In The Presbyterian Hymn: Complete Concordance and Indexes, edited by David Eicher. (Louisville, KY: Westminster John Knox Press, 2013), 649.

CHAPTER 1 The Preacher's Son

1.   James A. Moncure, ed., The Poems of George Washington Belk (Seven Lakes, NC: Privately Printed, 1988), [13].

2.   George McMillan, "Promised Land in North Carolina," *New York Times*, May 31, 1987, 650.

3.   Daniel de Marbelle. "When They Ring the Golden Bells." https://hymnary.org/media/fetch/127007

CHAPTER 3 Growing Up in the South

1.   J. B. Belk, *A Faith to Move Nations* ([n.p.]: Moral Re-Armament, Inc., 1969), 96.

2.   Ibid., 21.

3.   Ibid., 97.

4.   Louis A. Skidmore, and Chloris B. Lohl. *A History of St. Giles' Presbyterian Church* ([Richmond, VA?], n.p. 1987), 11.

5.   Belk, *Faith*, 21.

CHAPTER 4 Navy Days

1.   William L. Pendergraph, *Training Programs of the University of North Carolina for the U.S. Navy During World War II* ([Chapel Hill, NC?]: n.p., 1993). 5.

2.   Richard M. Connaughton, John Pimlott, and Duncan Anderson. *The Battle for Manila* (London: Bloomsbury, 1995). 15.

3.   Charles A. Bartholomew and William I. Milwee Jr., *Mud, Muscle, and Miracles: Marine Salvage in the United States Navy*. 2nd ed. (Washington, DC: Naval History & Heritage Command, Naval Sea Systems Command, Dept. of the Navy, 2009). 174-175.

CHAPTER 6 Peacetime

1.   Charles Moore, *Daniel H. Burnham, Architect, Planner of Cities* (Boston: Houghton Mifflin, 1921). 72-73.

CHAPTER 9 Charles Preston Howard

1.   "We Shall Overcome." https://en.wikipedia.org/wiki/We_Shall_Overcome

2.   Gentleman About Town, *Immortalia: an Anthology of American Ballads, Sailors' Songs, Cowboy Songs, College Songs, Parodies, Limericks, and Other Humorous Verses and Doggerel Now for the First Time Brought Together in Book Form* (Privately printed, 1927). 98.

3.   Ellen Daugherty, "Negotiating the Veil: Tuskegee's Booker T. Washington Monument." *American Art* 24, no. 3 (fall 2010): 67.

4.   "The Crowning Experience," *Arizona Sun*, Januanry 9, 1958, https://azmemory.azlibrary.gov/digital/collection/arizonasun/id/5520/

CHAPTER 10 The Statesman's Mission

1. Basil Entwistle, *Japan's Decisive Decade: How a Determined Minority Changed the Nation's Course in the 1950s.* (London: Grosvenor, 1985), 128.

CHAPTER 11 Meeting Dr. Martin Luther King Jr.

1. David L. Lewis and Clayborne Carson, "Martin Luther King Jr.," *Encyclopaedia Britannica*, January 11, 2020, https://www.britannica.com/biography/Martin-Luther-King-Jr

2. James L. Hicks, "King Emerges as Top Negro Leader," *New York Amsterdam New*s, June 1, 1957, 1.

3. Ely guest book. Albert Heman Ely Jr. Family Papers (MS 1843). Manuscripts and Archives, Yale University Library, Box 24.

CHAPTER 12 Washington, DC, and Eisenhower

1. *History, Art & Archives, U.S. House of Representatives*, "Timeline of 1954 Shooting Events," https://history.house.gov/Exhibitions-and-Publications/1954-Shooting/Essays/Timeline/ (May 14, 2018)

2. Asia Center Odawara, *Post War Japan and the Work of Moral Re-Armament: 40th Anniversary Publication.* (Tokyo: MRA House, 2008), 36.

3. Ibid., 39.

4. "Japanese Apologize to Eisenhower for Rioting," *Los Angeles Times*, March 30, 1961, 2.

CHAPTER 13 *The Tiger*

1. "Two Brazilian Political Foes Unite: Give Nation MRA," *Public Opinion* (Chambersburg, PA), January 15, 1962, 8.

2. "Frank Buchman of MRA is Dead," *The New York Times*, August 9, 1961, 1, 33.

3. "Meeting with Pres. Eisenhower, New York City, December 6, 1962," Belk, *Papers*, Box 32.

CHAPTER 14 "Tomorrow's America" Conference

1. "Mackinac Island Program, 1964," J. Blanton and Elizabeth (Betty) Belk Jr. Papers at the University of Arizona Libraries, Special Collections, Box 9.

2. "How to Build," *San Francisco Examiner*, June 30, 1964, 30.

3. "Mackinac Island Speakers, 1964," Belk *Papers*, Box 10.

4. "Eager Beaver All Dolled Up to Barge Into Harbor Springs," *Tomorrow's American News*, July 18, 1964, 3.

5. Moral Re-Armament, Inc. *Annual Report 1965.* (New York: Moral Re-Armament, 1966). 10.

6. Ibid., 16.

7. "Mackinac College Opens," *Tomorrow's American News*, October 10, 1966, 1-2.

8. *Annual Report 1965.* 20.

9. "Peter D. Howard Dies in Peru, Leader of Moral Re-Armament," *The New York Times*, February 26, 1965, 29.

CHAPTER 15 Sing-Out Explosion

1. "Student Heads Plan Mackinac," *Tomorrow's American News*, April 19, 1965, 1.

2. "Indians Open Mackinac Demonstration," *Tomorrow's American News*, June 14, 1965, 1.

3. "Showboat Sets Sail July Fourth," *Tomorrow's American News*, July 3, 1965, 1.

4. *Activities Report, Ezio Pinza Theatre July 1, 1965 to June 30, 1966*, (Stamford, CT: Stamford Museum and Nature Center, 1965). 3.

5. "Sing-Out '65 in Washington Hailed by Diplomats, Senators," *Tomorrow's American News*, August 27, 1965, 1.

6. Ibid., 2.

7. "L.A. Plea for MRA Musical," *San Francisco Examiner*, September 7, 1965, 3.

8. "Sing-Out '65 Scheduled at Bowl Tonight," *The Valley News* (Van Nuys, CA), September 19, 1965, 1, 4.

9. "Watts Hails Sing-Out," *Tomorrow's American News*, September 20, 1965, 1-2.

10. "130 Fly to Japan," *Tomorrow's American News*, September 27, 1965, 1, 3.

11. Asia Center Odawara, 49.

12. Ibid., 50.

CHAPTER 16 Chancellor Konrad Adenauer

1. "100 German Youth Join Sing-Out Cast," *Tomorrow's American News,* June 6, 1966, 3.

2. "Giving the Right Idea to Germany," *Tomorrow's American News,* November 28, 1966, 6.

3. "Leadership, Press and Youth in the Thousands Spark to Sing-Out," *Tomorrow's American News*, May 16, 1966, 3.

4. Charles Williams, *Adenauer: the Father of the New Germany* (London: Little, Brown, 2000). 538.

CHAPTER 17 Growth and Incorporation of Up with People

1. David B. Allen and Robin Hoar, *How to Create Your Own Sing-Out* (Los Angeles: Pace Publications, 1965), 6.

2. Local Sing-Out statistics are from a card file retained by Up with People beginning in 1967.

3. Tom Watson, "Up with People Smash Hit," *Desert Sun*, February 13, 1967, 1.

4. Dwight and Mamie Eisenhower, 1962-1990. Correspondence and reports. Belk, *Papers*, Box 32. Note: The official text of President Eisenhower's speech and the text that appeared in *Tomorrow's American News*, February 20, 1967, are slightly different as to arrangement and word usage. The official text was quoted.

5. Dwight D. Eisenhower to Blanton Belk Monday, April 17, 1967. Post-Presidential Paper's, Appointment Book files 1967, Box 2, Eisenhower Presidential Library. Eisenhower called Belk to talk about the Sing-Out group at 11:05 a.m. Monday, April 17, 1967.

6. Moral Re-Armament, Inc. *Annual Report 1967* (New York: Moral Re-Armament, 1968). 9.

7. "Black-Tie Audience Packs LA Music Center," *Tomorrow's American News*, December 16, 1968, 1, 3.

CHAPTER 18 The Further We Reach Out

1. Clarence W. Hall, "Sing Out, America!" *Reader's Digest,* May 1967, 49-54.

2. "Reader's Digest Show," *Tomorrow's American News*, August 28, 1967, 3.

3. "Up with People!" *TV Guide*, August 17-23, 1968, A66-A67.

4. "Reader's Digest Donates $1,000,000 to Scholarship Fund," *Silver Celebration Report: Denver 1990* (Tucson, AZ: Up with People, 1990). 17.

CHAPTER 19 A Show at the White House

1. "Up with People at the White House." *Up with People Perspective*, March 2, 1971, [1].

CHAPTER 20 Jesse Owens and the Munich Olympics

1. Simon Reeve, *One Day in September* (New York: Arcade Publishing, 2011). 79.

2. Jean Weathersby Wysocki Journal, 1972. "*September 6, Memorial Service.*"

3.   Ibid., "*September 6, Marcie's Memories.*"

4.   Ibid., "*September 8, Olympic Village.*"

5.   "Jesse Owens," *Wikipedia*, last modified July 27, 2019. https://de.wikipedia.org/wiki/Jesse_Owens

CHAPTER 22 First Americans/First Nation

1.   Jan Sturges, comp, *Special Report to Staff and Cast Members, Up with People 1975-76.* ([Tucson, AZ]: Up with People, [1976]). [86].

2.   Jan Sturges, "Laguna and San Juan Homeland of the Pueblo Indians," *Up with People News*, October 1975, [4].

CHAPTER 24 Bicentennial Year and Super Bowls

1.   "Superbowl 10: Anthem with Tom Sullivan." Filmed January 18, 1976. YouTube video, 2:52. Posted January 25, 2015. https://www.youtube.com/watch?v=zd8OPb-s-Q4

2.   "Tom Sullivan: Blind Entertainer, Author, Athlete, Actor & Producer, YouTube video, 5:07. Posted July 31, 2012. https://www.youtube.com/watch?v=DQ8JRWcbhQc

3.   Sturges, *Special Report*, [11-13].

CHAPTER 25 Board of Directors

1.   Peter Voevodsky, "Finance Committee Meeting Notes, 1976," Belk, *Papers*, Box 57.

2.   Alexander von Plato, *The End of the Cold War?: Bush, Kohl, Gorbachev, and the Reunification of Germany*, trans. by Edith Burley (New York: Palgrave Macmillian, 2015). 26.

3.   Ken Connors, "Special Report: Cast E was a Witness to History," *Cast E '89 Up with People World Tour* (Indianapolis, IN: Herff Jones, 1990). 93.

CHAPTER 26 México and Up with People

1.   "México," *Up with People Perspective*, November 11, 1969, 1.

2.   Ibid., 2.

CHAPTER 27 People's Republic of China

1.   "China," *Up with People News*, spring 1978, 7.

2.   *Up with People in the People's Republic of China 1978* ([Tucson, AZ: Up with People], 1978) 4.

3.   Vere James, *Up with People in China: December 1985* ([Tucson, AZ]: Isbell Printing Co.), 1986. 6.

CHAPTER 28 Soviet Union and Eastern Europe

1.   "Eduard Malayan Tucson Visit Notes, 1985," Belk, *Papers*, Box 44.

2.   Steve Woods and Hans Magnus, "Visit to Moscow November 23-28, 1987," Ralph J. Colwell Papers.

3.   Hans Magnus, "Preliminary Report to Board of Directors, June 27, 1988," Belk, *Papers*, Box 63.

4.   "Soviet Tour Overview, June 7-21, 1988," *Up with People Reports*, [summer 1988], 2.

5.   "Report on Russia, June 22, 1988," Belk, *Papers*, Box 73.

6.   "Itineraries/Trips 1989," Belk, *Papers*, Box 7.

7.   Ibid.

8.   *Up with People Reports*, May 1990, [1].

9.   *Up with People Reports*, [summer 1988], [3].

10. "Soviet Students Join Up with People," *Up with People Reports*, May 1990, [3].

11. "Tallinn, Estonia, USSR," *Up with People Reports*, May 1990, [3].

12. "Poland," *Up with People European Bulletin*, June 1990, 3.

13. "Czechoslovakia: March 26 to April 17," *Up with People Reports*, [fall 1991], 4.

14. "Russia: June 23 to July 10," *Up with People Reports*, [fall 1991], 4.

CHAPTER 29 Up with People's 25th Silver Anniversary Celebration

1. *Silver Celebration Report: Denver 1990* (Tucson, AZ: Up with People, 1990). 6.

2. Ibid., 3.

3. "Speeches, 1969-1992." Belk, *Papers*, Box 17.

4. "Relocation, 1991-1993." Belk, *Papers*, Box 14.

5. "Roy Romer, 1988-1995." Belk, *Papers*, Box 51.

6. Up with People. *1992 Annual Report* (Broomfield, CO: Up with People, [1993]), 8.

7. Up with People. *1993 Annual Report* (Broomfield, CO: Up with People, [1994]), 5.

CHAPTER 31 Friendships

1. Jim Michaels and Jackie Rothenburg, "Hodel Approves Sasabe Land Buy for Quail Refuge," *Arizona Daily Star*, February 21, 1985, 2A, 2B.

CHAPTER 33 The Next Frontier

1. "The Arab World Meets Up with People," *Up with People News*, April 1975, [5].

2. Meg Abu Hamdan, "Festival Audiences Respond with Enthusiasm to 'the Arab Touch From Up with People,'" *Jordan Times*, August 19, 1984, [3].

3. Rajean Shepherd, ["Cast Director's Report: Jordan, 1984"], Belk, *Papers*, Box 71.

4. Kent MacLennan, Email to archivist, February 20, 2020.

5. Up with People. *2014 Annual Report*. (Broomfield, CO: Up with People, [2014]), 9.

6. Up with People. *2015 Annual Report*. (Broomfield, CO: Up with People, 2016), 4.

7. "Up with People in Cuba," *UpBeat*, winter 2014, 3.

BIBLIOGRAPHY

The main source of information about J. Blanton Belk and his life are the J. Blanton and Elizabeth (Betty) Belk Jr. Papers at the University of Arizona Libraries, Special Collections. This collection is cited as Belk, Papers in the endnotes. It is restricted access until 2029.

The Up with People Archive, also housed at Special Collections consisting of 160 linear feet are the principal source of material by and about Up with People and J. Blanton Belk. This is an open access collection.

Archival materials from the Dwight D. Eisenhower Presidential Library and the Albert Heman Ely Jr. Family Papers at Yale University Library Manuscripts and Archives were unavailable at time of publication due to the COVID-19 pandemic.

OTHER SOURCES INCLUDE

Albert Heman Ely Jr. Family Papers, MS 1843. Yale University Library Manuscripts and Archives

Cowles Library, Drake University, Des Moines, IA. The correspondence of Charles Preston Howard

Dwight D. Eisenhower Presidential Library, Abilene, Kansas. Post-Presidential Paper's Appointment Book files for 1966-1967-1968

Louis Round Wilson Special Collections Library. University of North Carolina, Chapel Hill. The report of the Navy V-12 program

Manuscript Division, Library of Congress, Washington, DC. Moral Re-armament records, 1812-1991, including the papers of J. Blanton Belk Sr. and Jr.; the speeches and writings of Peter Howard; letters of Roland Wilson and papers and reports of Up with People. A. Philip Randolph papers, 1909-1979; The report of the Prayer Pilgrimage March

Musselman Library, Gettysburg College, Gettysburg, Pennsylvania. Dwight David Eisenhower Appointment Books, 1961-1967. Entries for 1961 begin on April 17

Paley Center for Media, New York. Super Bowl halftime performances featuring Up with People

Ralph J. Colwell Papers (privately held). Super Bowl X report, Russia and Ukraine tour notes

Richard Nixon Presidential Library and Museum, Yorba Linda, CA. Rose Mary Woods White House central files

BOOKS

Activities Report, Ezio Pinza Theatre July 1, 1965 to June 30, 1966. Stamford, CT: Stamford Museum and Nature Center, 1965.

Allen, David B. and Robin Hoar. *How to Create Your Own Sing-Out*. Los Angeles: Pace Publications, 1965.

Asia Center Odawara. *Post War Japan and the Work of Moral Re-Armament: 40th Anniversary Publication*. Tokyo: MRA House, 2008.

Bartholomew, Charles A. and William I. Milwee Jr. *Mud, Muscle, and Miracles: Marine Salvage in the United States Navy* (2nd ed.). Washington, DC: Naval History & Heritage Command, Naval Sea Systems Command, Dept. of the Navy, 2009.

Belk, J. B. *A Faith to Move Nations*. [n.p.]: Moral Re-Armament, Inc., 1969.

Connaughton, Richard M, John Pimlott, and Duncan Anderson. *The Battle for Manila*. London: Bloomsbury, 1995.

Connors, Ken. *Cast E '89 Up with People World Tour*. Edited by Ken Connor and Scott Sughrue. Indianapolis, IN: Herff Jones, 1990.

Entwistle, Basil. *Japan's Decisive Decade: How a Determined Minority Changed the Nation's Course in the 1950s*. London: Grosvenor Books, 1985.

Gentleman About Town. *Immortalia: An Anthology of American Ballads, Sailors' Songs, Cowboy Songs, College Songs, Parodies, Limericks, and Other Humorous Verses and Doggerel Now for the First Time Brought Together in Book Form*. Printed by the author, 1927.

James, Vere. *Up with People in China: December 1985*. [Tucson, AZ]: Isbell Printing Co., 1986.

Moncure, James A., ed. *The Poems of George Washington Belk*. Printed by the author, 1988.

Moore, Charles. *Daniel H. Burnham, Architect, Planner of Cities*. Boston: Houghton Mifflin, 1921.

Moral Re-Armament, Inc. *Annual Report 1965*. New York: Moral Re-Armament, 1966.

Moral Re-Armament, Inc. *Annual Report 1967*. New York: Moral Re-Armament, 1968.

Newton, James. "Amazing Grace." In *The Presbyterian Hymn: Complete Concordance and Indexes, edited by David Eicher*. Louisville, KY: Westminster John Knox Press, 2013. 649.

Pendergraph, William L. *Training programs of the University of North Carolina for the US Navy during World War II*. [Chapel Hill, NC?]: n.p., 1993.

Plato, Alexander von. *The End of the Cold War?: Bush, Kohl, Gorbachev, and the Reunification of Germany*. Translated by Edith Burley. New York: Palgrave Macmillian, 2015.

Reeve, Simon. *One Day in September*. New York: Arcade Publishing, 2011.

Silver Celebration Report: Denver 1990. Tucson, AZ: Up with People, 1990.

Skidmore, Louis A. and Chloris B. Lohl. *A History of St. Giles' Presbyterian Church*. [Richmond, VA?]: n.p., 1987.

Sturges, Jan, comp. *Special Report to Staff and Cast Members, Up with People 1975-76*. [Tucson, AZ]: Up with People,[1976].

Up with People. *1992 Annual Report*. Broomfield, CO: Up with People, [1993].

Up with People. *1993 Annual Report*. Broomfield, CO: Up with People, [1994].

Up with People. *2014 Annual Report*. Broomfield, CO: Up with People, [2014].

Up with People. *2015 Annual Report*. Broomfield, CO: Up with People, 2016.

Up with People in the People's Republic of China 1978. [Tucson, AZ]: Up with People, [1978].

Williams, Charles. *Adenauer: the Father of the New Germany*. London: Little, Brown, 2000.

ARTICLES

"100 German Youth Join Sing-Out Cast," *Tomorrow's American New*s, June 6, 1966.

"130 Fly to Japan," *Tomorrow's American News*, September 27, 1965.

Abu Hamdan, Meg. "Festival Audiences Respond with Enthusiasm to 'the Arab Touch From Up with People,'" *Jordan Times*, August 19, 1984.

"Black-Tie Audience Packs L.A. Music Center," *Tomorrow's American News*, December 16, 1968.

Boyer, Horace Clarence. "Charles Albert Tindley: Progenitor of Black-American Gospel Music." *The Black Perspective in Music* 11, no. 2 (1983): 103-132.

"China." *Up with People News*, spring 1978.

"The Crowning Experience," *Arizona Sun*, January 9, 1958. https://azmemory.azlibrary.gov/digital/collection/arizonasun/id/5520/

"Czechoslovakia: March 26 to April 17," *Up with People Reports*, [fall 1991].

Daugherty, Ellen. "Negotiating the Veil: Tuskegee's Booker T. Washington Monument." *American Art* 24, no. 3 (fall 2010): 52-77.

"Eager Beaver All Dolled Up To Barge Into Harbor Springs," *Tomorrow's American News*, July 18, 1964.

"Eisenhower Pay Tribute to Up with People," *Tomorrow's American News*, February 20, 1967.

"Giving the Right Idea to Germany," *Tomorrow's American News*, November 28, 1966.

Hall, Clarence W. "Sing Out, America!" *Reader's Digest*, May 1967.

Hicks, James L. "King Emerges as Top Negro Leader," *New York Amsterdam News*, June 1, 1957.

"Indians Open Mackinac Demonstration," *Tomorrow's American News*, June 14, 1965,

"Leadership, Press and Youth in the Thousands Spark to Sing-Out." *Tomorrow's American News*, May 16, 1966.

Lewis, David L. and Clayborne Carson. "Martin Luther King Jr." In *Encyclopaedia Britannica*, January 11, 2020. https://www.britannica.com/biography/Martin-Luther-King-Jr.

Los Angeles Times. "Japanese Apologize to Eisenhower for Rioting." March 30, 1961.

"Mackinac College Opens." *Tomorrow's American News*, October 10, 1966.

McMillan, George. "Promised Land in North Carolina," *New York Times*, May 31, 1987.

"México." *Up with People Perspective*, November 11, 1969.

Michaels, Jim and Jackie Rothenburg, "Hodel Approves Sasabe Land Buy for Quail Refuge," *Arizona Daily Star*, February 21, 1985.

New York Times. "Frank Buchman of M.R.A. is Dead." August 9, 1961.

New York Times. "Peter D. Howard Dies in Peru, Leader of Moral Re-Armament." February 26, 1965.

"Poland." *Up with People European Bulletin*, June 1990.

Public Opinion (Chambersburg, Pennsylvania). "Two Brazilian Political Foes Unite: Give Nation MRA." January 15, 1962.

"Reader's Digest Donates $1,000,000 to Scholarship Fund," *Silver Celebration Report: Denver 1990*, Tucson, AZ: Up with People, 1990.

"Reader's Digest Show," *Tomorrow's American News*, August 28, 1967.

"Resounding Rapport with Germany," *Tomorrow's American News*, May 16, 1966.

San Francisco Examiner. "How to Build." June 30, 1964.

San Francisco Examiner. "L.A. Plea for MRA Musical." September 7, 1965.

"Showboat Sets Sail July Fourth." *Tomorrow's American News*, July 3, 1965.

"Sing-Out '65 in Washington Hailed by Diplomats, Senators," *Tomorrow's American News*, August 27, 1965.

"Soviet Students Join Up with People." *Up with People Reports*, May 1990.

"Soviet Tour Overview, June 7-21, 1988. *Up with People Reports*, [summer 1988].

"Student Heads Plan Mackinac," *Tomorrow's American News*, April 19, 1965.

Sturges, Jan. "Laguna and San Juan Homeland of the Pueblo Indians," *Up with People News*, October 1975.

"Tallinn, Estonia, USSR." *Up with People Reports*, May 1990.

"Up with People!" *TV Guide*, August 17-23, 1968.

"Up with People at the White House." *Up with People Perspective*, March 2, 1971.

"Up with People in Cuba," *UpBeat*, winter 2014, 3.

Valley News (Van Nuys, California). "Sing-Out '65 Scheduled at Bowl Tonight." September 19, 1965.

Watson, Tom. "Up with People Smash Hit," *Desert Sun*, February 13, 1967.

"Watts Hails Sing-Out," *Tomorrow's American News*, September 20, 1965.

ARCHIVAL MATERIALS

Albert Heman Ely Jr. Family Papers, MS 1843. Yale University Library Manuscripts and Archives, Box 24.

Dwight D. Eisenhower Presidential Library, Abilene, Kansas. Post-Presidential Paper's Appointment Book files for 1967, Box 2.

J. Blanton and Elizabeth (Betty) Belk Jr. Papers at the University of Arizona Libraries, Special Collections, Mackinac Island Program, 1964, Box 9.

Dwight and Mamie Eisenhower, 1962-1990: Correspondence and reports. Belk, *Papers*, Box 32.

"Itineraries/Trips 1989." Belk, *Papers*, Box 7.

"Mackinac Island Speakers, 1964," Belk *Papers*, Box 10.

Magnus, Hans. "1988 Tour of the Soviet Union: Preliminary Report to Board of Directors, June 27, 1988." Belk, *Papers*, Box 64.

"Relocation, 1991-1993." Belk, *Papers*, Box 14.

"Report on Russia, June 22, 1988." Belk, *Papers*, Box 73.

"Roy Romer, 1988-1995." Belk, *Papers*, Box 51.

Shepherd, Rajean. ["Cast Director's Report: Jordan, 1984"]. Belk, *Papers*, Box 71.

"Speeches, 1969-1992." Belk, *Papers*, Box 17.

Voevodsky, Peter. "Finance Committee Meeting Notes, 1976." Belk, *Papers*, Box 57.

UNPUBLISHED SOURCES

Colwell, Ralph J. "Super Bowl X Report 2018" and "Russia and Ukraine tour notes," Ralph J. Colwell Papers.

Jean Weathersby Wysocki Journal, 1972.

Woods, Steve and Hans Magnus, "Visit to Moscow November 23-28, 1987," Ralph J. Colwell Papers.

WEBSITES

De Marbelle, Daniel, "When They Ring the Golden Bells." https://hymnary.org/media/fetch/127007

History, Art & Archives, US House of Representatives, "Timeline of 1954 Shooting Events," https://history.house.gov/Exhibitions-and-Publications/1954-Shooting/Essays/Timeline/

"Jesse Owens," *Wikipedia*, last modified July 27, 2019. https://de.wikipedia.org/wiki/Jesse_Owens

"Superbowl 10: Anthem with Tom Sullivan." Filmed January 18, 1976. YouTube video, 2:52. Posted January 25, 2015. https://www.youtube.com/watch?v=zd8OPb-s-Q4

"Tom Sullivan: Blind Entertainer, Author, Athlete, Actor & Producer." YouTube video, 5:07. Posted July 31, 2012. https://www.youtube.com/watch?v=DQ8JRWcbhQc

"We Shall Overcome." https://en.wikipedia.org/wiki/We_Shall_Overcome

INDEX

Bush, George H. W., 239, 244

Cabo Blanco, Peru, 109
Calderón, Margarita Zavala de, 291–92
Calhoun County, South Carolina, 6
California
    Jordan High School, Watts, 128, 129
    Los Angeles, 127–29, 144
    Palm Desert, 103
    Palm Springs, 138
Californian Yachts, San Diego, California, 219
Calloway, Cab, 76
"Can We Sing a Song of Peace?" (song), 238
Canada, 49–50, 116, 138, 143
Canal du Midi barge trip, south of France, 277–78
Cannon, Ray, 275–76
Canton, PRC, 231–32
Cape Canaveral, Florida, 12–13
Cárdenas, Amalia S. de, 223–24
Carnegie Hall, New York City, New York, 102, 103, 151
Carson, Johnny, 205–6
Carter, Jimmy, 165–66
Cass, Henry, 124–25
Caux, Switzerland, 52–53, 78, 87
CBS and Esquire magazine, 160
Central Conservatory of Music, Peking, PRC, 227–29
Central Institute for National Minorities, Beijing, PRC, 230–31, 233
Central Presbyterian Church, Summit, New Jersey, 70
Cernan, Barbara, 191–92, 193
Cernan, Eugene "Gene," viii, 12–13, 157, 172, 191–201, 211, 215, 220–21, 244, 245
Ceylon, 58, 59, 66, 83
Chaimovski, Roni, 288–89

Channer, Dave, 50, 58, 62
Channer, Dick, 50, 58, 62
Chapel Hill, North Carolina, 5, 7, 36–38, 46, 47
Chateaubriand, Assis, 105
Chatham, Virginia, 9
Cherokee Nation, 187
Chiba, Emiko, 141
Chicago, Illinois, 69–70, 73, 74–75, 78, 93, 173, 239, 241, 274, 280–81
China. See People's Republic of China (PRC)
Chinese People's Association for Friendship with Foreign Countries, 226, 234
Christopherson, Wes, viii, 219–20
civil rights
    JBB and Charlie Howard travel together promoting civil rights, 70, 93
    protests in the US, 113
Clark, Margaret "Peg" Wilkes, 70
Clark, Maurice "Maury," 70, 79–80
Clay, Lucius, 52, 134–35
Close, Bettine, 143
Close, William "Bill" T., 87–88, 143
Cochise County, Arizona, 270, 298, 301–4
Cochrane, Sir Edward, 100–101
Cold War, 117, 158, 287–88
colleges. See universities and colleges
Cologne, West Germany, 134, 135
Colorado
    Estes Park, 138
    Fuller's 60th birthday celebration, 244
    Up with People 25th Silver Anniversary celebration in Denver, 156, 158, 173, 239, 244–49
    Up with People moves to Denver, 249–54
Colwell, Catalina Quinn, 196

in Los Angeles, 127–29
in Massachusetts, 125
on NBC TV, 130
planning for, 124
in South Korea, 130
in Washington, DC, 125–26
Sing-Out '66, 131–34, 135, 148, 222
Sing-Out Deutschland '66, 133, 135, 142
Sing-Out Express, 127, 187–88
Sing-Out High School, 142
Sing-Out/Up with People
    "Conference for Modernizing America,"
      116, 123–25
    exciting, uncontrollable growth, 137–38
    Reader's Digest articles on, 150
    World Sing-Out Festival, 1967, 142
    World Up with People Festival, 1968,
      143
Sing-Out/Up with People performances
    at American Newspaper Publishers
      Association meetings, 159
    Carnegie Hall, New York City, New
      York, 102, 103, 151
    Constitution Hall, Washington DC,
      141
    for Eisenhower, 138–39
    in North America, 138
    in Palm Springs, California, 138–39
Smolny, Eduard, 239
de Sobrino, Father José, 180, 181
Sohma, Tokiko, 256
Sohma, Toyotane "Toyo," 106, 109, 127,
    256–59
Sophia University, Tokyo, Japan, 130
South Carolina, 1, 5–6, 11, 15–19, 20–23,
    29, 71, 74
South Korea, 130
Soviet Union, 2, 74, 214, 223, 235–43
    average age of population, 114
    Barron Hilton funds first Up with
      People tour, 158

Bykov on the young people in, 242
first cast performing in, 238–39
fulfilling the dream of linking up with,
    235–38
glasnost and perestroika, 235
and Gorbachev, 214, 235, 237
Magnus's support for Up with People
    tours in, 238–39
Ulyanov on the young people in, 239
Up with People six casts toured,
    1990–1991, 241–43
spacewalk of Gene Cernan, 193–94
Spain, 133, 144–45, 180–82
Spelman College, Atlanta, Georgia, 77
Spitz, Mark, 169
Springbok Stampede, 142
SPUTNIK (Soviet travel/exchange
    bureau), 238, 239, 240
Sri Lanka, 83. See also Ceylon
St. Christopher's School, Richmond,
    Virginia, 24, 32, 34–35, 37
St. Giles' Presbyterian Church, Richmond,
    Virginia, 32–33
St. Matthews, South Carolina, 5–6,
    15–19, 20–23
Stamford, Connecticut, 125
Stanton, Frank, 160
Starr, Frederick "Fred" S., 236
Statesman's Mission
    about, 78
    in Burma, 81–83
    in Ceylon, 83
    in Egypt, 87
    in Iran, 83–84, 86
    in Iraq, 86–87
    in Kenya, 84–86
    in Philippines, 80–81
    in Turkey, 81
Steeg, Jim, 203
Stuttgart, Germany, 56, 212–13
Sullivan, Tom, 205–6

Sulzberger Sr., Arthur Ochs "Punch"
159–61, 162–63, 225
Summit, New Jersey, 47–48, 70–71
Super Bowl X, 203–6
Super Bowl XIV, 155, 161, 203
Super Bowl XVI, 203
Super Bowl XX, 203, 233, 279
Sweden, 89–90
"Swing Those Propellers, Fellows" (song)
for US Air Force pilots and crews, 87

"Take Me There" (song), 165–66
Tallinn, Estonia, 242
Tamazawa, Tokuichiro, 109–10
Tankersley, Bazy, 207
Távora, Marshal Juárez, 107–8, 111
Tel Aviv, Israel, 288–91
Televisa, 219–20
Tennessee A&I State College, 77, 93
Terry, Anthony, 179
Terry, Fernando de, 179, 181–82
Terry, Miguel de, 270–71, 273–74
Thompson, Reed, 201, 226
Tiananmen Square, PRC, 226
The Tiger (play), 102–4, 105–8, 109–10,
112, 127
Tillman, Gina Hemphill, 246
Tinsley, Barbara Belk, 29, 32, 35, 210, 266
Tinsley, Clark "Little," 23–25, 28, 35
Tinsley, James "Jim," 32, 35, 210, 266
Tokyo, Japan, 101–3, 129–30, 192–93,
225, 232
Towers, Tom "Tubby," 43
Toyoda, Hiroko, 246–47
Toyoda, Shoichiro, 211, 213–14, 246–47,
249, 253
Toyota Motor Company, 211, 246, 283
Truman, Harry S., 51
Tuba City High School, Navajo Nation,
189
Tucson, Arizona

Benetton store, 279
as home to JBB and Betty, 117, 255,
266
host families in, 249–50
Jenny born in, 127
Jenny's wedding in, 281–82
Jesse Owens dies in, 172–73
Katie's wedding in, 284–85
University of Arizona, 194, 212,
224–25, 283, 291, 293
Up with People Archive, 215, 291, 293
Turkey, 87, 288
Tuskegee Institute, Tuskegee, Alabama,
77–78, 93
Twitchell, H. Kenaston, Jr., 146

Ukraine, 239, 240, 241
Ukrainian dance troupe, 246
Ukrainian youth, 242
Ulm, West Germany, 53–55
Ulyanov, Mikhail, 239, 241
"Unfinished World" (song), 137
Union Club, New York City, New York,
161
United States
Bicentennial Year Celebration, 60,
188–89, 202–4, 206
patriotism in WWII, 37
post-WWII rebuilding in Europe and
Japan, 51
Security Treaty with Japan, 101, 102,
110
universities and colleges
Central Institute for National
Minorities, Beijing, PRC, 230–31,
233
Duke University, Durham, North
Carolina, 6, 122
Fisk University, Nashville, Tennessee,
77, 93
Hollins College, Virginia, 26–27